BARRON'S

HOW TO PREPARE FOR THE VIRGINIA SOL

EOC ENGLISH: WRITING & READING/LITERATURE AND RESEARCH

Nina Pebworth Huff, Ed.D.
Research Instructor
Piedmont Governor's School for Mathematics, Science, & Technology
Martinsville, VA

BARRON'S

This book is dedicated to my grandmother, Nina Culpepper Pebworth, from whom I inherited both my name and my love of learning.

Acknowledgments

I would like to thank the following people without whose help I could never have accomplished this task:

- Lynn Robertson, Jennifer Dodson, and Megan Ezelle for letting me use their essays, poetry, and creative writings in the practice sections of this preparation guide;
- My husband, Lynn, and my children, Joseph and Bailey, for their constant support and understanding as I spent hours preparing this manuscript;
- My mother, Mary J. Pinch, for proofreading the text (many times);
- Gail S. Oakes, my mentor, who knows more about English than anyone I've ever met;
- Anna Damaskos, my editor at Barron's, for her help and encouragement throughout the process.

All inquiries should be addressed to:
Barron's Educational Series, Inc.
250 Wireless Boulevard
Hauppauge, New York 11788
http://www.barronseduc.com

International Standard Book No. 0-7641-2715-2

Library of Congress Catalog Card No. 2004043775

Library of Congress Cataloging-in-Publication Data

Huff, Nina P.
How to prepare for Virginia SOL in ELA / Nina P. Huff.
p. cm.
ISBN 0-7641-2715-2
1. Virginia Standards of Learning Tests—Study guides. 2. Language arts (Secondary)—Virginia—Examinations—Study guides. 3. Eleventh grade (Education)—Virginia. I. Title.

LB3060.33.V57H84 2004
428'.0071'2—dc22

2004043775

PRINTED IN THE UNITED STATES OF AMERICA

9 8 7 6 5 4 3 2 1

Contents

Introduction

As a high school student, you are on a journey to earn a high school diploma. To do so, you must earn a required number of credits, both standard and verified:

- **A standard unit of credit is earned through completion of instructional hours of a course and receipt of a passing grade.**
- **A verified unit of credit is earned through receipt of a passing grade in both the course and on its related Standards of Learning test.**

To find out the specific number of credits of both types that you must earn for specific diplomas, such as Standard or Advanced, you should consult your guidance counselor. However, passing the grade 11 English Writing SOL test and the grade 11 English Reading/Literature and Research SOL test is a requirement for each student wishing to earn a regular high school diploma. Further, public schools in Virginia will be awarded full accreditation based on whether the required seventy percent of their students pass the SOL tests in the four core areas: English, mathematics, social studies, and science.

The purpose of the English 11 SOL tests is to assess your knowledge of the skills you have been taught in your English 9, 10, and 11 courses. Although most of the SOL courses you take require only one test, given at the end of the course, the English 11 course requires two separate tests:

1. **EOC English: Reading/Literature and Research test** (EOC stands for "end of course")
2. **EOC English: Writing test,** which is given in two sections—Direct Writing and Multiple Choice.

Your English 11 class, therefore, will actually involve three days of testing in which two tests will be given. Each test, the Reading/Literature and Research *and* the Writing, is a separate assessment, so you must pass both to receive the two verified credits required for graduation. In other words, the scores are not averaged for one final score. Though the questions for each test change each term, the characteristics of the tests remain consistent. The EOC English: Reading/Literature and Research test and the EOC English: Writing Multiple Choice component—

- both contain only multiple choice questions
- both contain between 35 and 45 questions
- list four possible answers for each question
- do not use "all of the above" or "none of the above" choices
- connect all questions to reading selections of varying lengths and subject matter
- include questions relating to the Virginia Standards of Learning

The EOC English: Direct Writing component—

- has only one question, which provides the required essay topic and includes suggestions to initiate brainstorming
- permits use of a dictionary
- includes a checklist reminding the student to check format, style, and mechanics

You should try to do your very best on these tests, and there are several reasons for you to take them seriously:

- Your final score on the tests will help you to assess your own strengths and weaknesses in the subject area. The tested skills are those you will need throughout your life as you move through your education and career. Knowing how well you perform at your best will help you to identify those areas in which you may need additional practice.

- Your score, along with the scores of your peers, will help teachers and administrators evaluate and strengthen current curricula so that students will have the best opportunities for success in English.
- You can take pride in doing your best and helping your individual school to reach and maintain full accreditation.

The purpose of this guide is to present you with a focused review of the information that you will be expected to know. Perhaps you have a strong writing style, but you require some assistance in the area of mechanics or punctuation. Perhaps you need to review the writing process or the elements in a research paper. This guide contains the basic skills, along with practice exercises, that you will need to know for all three of the tests that you will be expected to pass: (1) EOC English: Writing (Multiple Choice Component); (2) EOC English: Writing (Direct Writing Component); and (3) EOC English: Reading/Literature and Research. This guide has been organized to allow for the greatest connection of skills, and the practice exercises have been designed to mirror those you will see on the actual tests. It is my sincere hope that this guide will assist you as you prepare for these examinations.

Before you actually dive into the specifics of the guide, it is important for you to be aware of some general test-taking strategies that can help you in your testing situation:

- Get plenty of rest the evening before each test. Being well rested will provide you the best opportunity to concentrate and perform well.
- Eat a good breakfast the morning of the test. You will have more difficulty staying focused on the testing task if you become hungry during its administration.
- Remember that the tests are not timed. You do not need to feel pressured to finish within any particular time frame. Do not let the fact that others may complete the test before you make you feel the urge to "hurry up and finish." Take your time, and do your very best work.
- Always read directions carefully. They will help you focus directly on the task at hand.
- Always thoroughly read any reading passages. Avoid the temptation to "skim" or to read the questions and then go search for answers. Some reading passages develop a theme from beginning to end, a theme you may not be able to comprehend by simply passing briefly over the information.
- For reading comprehension sections, you may want to look over the questions first to get an idea of the types of information you will be asked. Then, read the selection carefully, and feel free to go back to the reading passage as often as necessary.
- If you are reading sentences to look for grammatical errors, focus on one type of error at a time. For example, first look for punctuation errors, then capitalization errors, and then usage errors, and so on. This strategy will help you to focus on one problem at a time.
- When taking the multiple choice components, remember the following:

    1. Read all answers before making a decision. Sometimes, one answer seems correct until you read another that makes more sense.
    2. Cross out the answers that you know are incorrect. Then, you are left with fewer choices. It is fine to write in the test booklet, but remember that the answers "bubbled in" on the answer sheet are the only answers that will be graded.
    3. Restate (in your own words) any questions that are confusing to you. For example, suppose a question were written as follows:
       All of the following lines from the poem show metaphors *except*—
       This statement may seem confusing to you. It is saying that three of the lines show something, but one does not. In your own mind, you could say to yourself, "I am looking for the one line that does *not* show a metaphor." In this way, you will understand your goal more clearly.
    4. You should answer all of the questions. You will get credit for the total number answered correctly out of all possible answers. You will not lose points for wrong answers, so it is acceptable to guess if you are not positive of a particular answer. Of course, you should still try to narrow the choices down and then make a careful, educated guess.

Standards of Learning Tested on Virginia SOL EOC Exams

The standards of learning (SOLs) are the specific, identified goals that form the basis for the curriculum of a particular course in a public school in Virginia. The SOLs provide the basis for the construction of the tests you will take in classes for which SOL tests are given. Following are the grade 9, 10, and 11 SOLs for English courses in Virginia's public schools. You may notice that several of the standards seem to be repeated at different grade levels. That is true because some standards, or goals for student learning, need to continue to be addressed at each level of English.

Grade 9 Standards of Learning (SOLs)

9.1 The student will present and critique dramatic readings of literary selections.
9.2 The student will make planned oral presentations.
9.3 The student will read and analyze a variety of literature.
9.4 The student will read and analyze a variety of print materials.
9.5 The student will read dramatic selections.
9.6 The student will develop narrative, literary, expository, and technical writings to inform, explain, analyze, or entertain.
9.7 The student will credit the sources of both quoted and paraphrased ideas.
9.8 The student will use electronic databases to access information.

Grade 10 Standards of Learning (SOLs)

10.1 The student will participate in and report small-group learning activities.
10.2 The student will critique oral reports of small-group learning activities.
10.3 The student will read and critique literary works from a variety of eras in a variety of cultures.
10.4 The student will read and interpret printed consumer materials.
10.5 The student will read and critique a variety of poetry.
10.6 The student will read and critique dramatic selections.
10.7 The student will develop a variety of writings with an emphasis on exposition.
10.8 The student will critique professional and peer writing.
10.9 The student will use writing to interpret, analyze, and evaluate ideas.
10.10 The student will collect, evaluate, and organize information.

Grade 11 Standards of Learning (SOLs)

11.1 The student will make persuasive presentations.
11.2 The student will analyze and evaluate persuasive presentations.
11.3 The student will read and analyze relationships among American literature, history, and culture.
11.4 The student will read a variety of print material.
11.5 The student will read and critique a variety of poetry.
11.6 The student will read a variety of dramatic selections.
11.7 The student will write in a variety of forms with an emphasis on persuasion.

11.8 The student will write, revise, and edit personal and business correspondence to a standard acceptable in the work place and higher education.

11.9 The student will analyze, evaluate, synthesize, and organize information from a variety of sources into a documented paper dealing with a question, problem, or issue.

Each standard has several subcategories, but not all standards and subcategories are tested on the English SOL tests because some SOLs focus on concepts, such as oral speaking, that cannot be assessed using the multiple choice format of the written examination. This preparation manual is centered on the tested standards, so it will serve as a focused study guide.

PART ONE

TEST PREPARATION FOR EOC ENGLISH: WRITING

The purpose of the EOC English: Writing test is to assess your knowledge of the written communication skills outlined in the Virginia Standards of Learning in English. These particular SOLs provide the focus for chapters 1–3 of this preparation manual.

Chapter 1
Parts of Speech and Mechanics

1.1 Eight Parts of Speech

The eight parts of speech form the foundation for the structure of sentences and rules of grammar. That is why you began studying them as soon as you started school. Each part of speech has unique characteristics, and, once you learn them, you can use them to strengthen your understanding of the more difficult grammar concepts.

1. A ***noun*** names a person, place, thing, or idea.

> The ***girl*** in the red ***coat*** is named ***Lisa.*** (*Person, thing, specific person*)
> The ***principal*** works at ***Smithfield Elementary School.*** (*Person, specific place*)
> I believe in ***freedom*** for all ***people.*** (*Idea naming a "thing" in which I believe, plural person*)

2. A ***pronoun*** takes the place of a person, place, thing, or idea. The word to which the pronoun refers is called the *referent* or *antecedent.*

> Tammy left ***her*** book bag on the bus, but ***I*** found ***it*** for ***her.*** (*References to a girl, the person speaking, and a thing*)
> ***They*** left for the camping trip an hour before ***we*** did. (*References to two groups of people*)

Be sure that when you use a pronoun, you clearly indicate its relationship to a noun. In other words, be sure the reader knows to what or whom the pronoun is referring. The word to which a pronoun refers is called its *antecedent* or *referent.* For example, you should not begin a sentence with "it" unless the pronoun refers directly to a noun previously stated.

> *Poor pronoun usage*: ***It*** usually takes about an hour to drive to Minnesota. (*The pronoun has no clear referent.*)
> *Acceptable pronoun usage*: The drive may be long, but ***it*** is enjoyable. (*The pronoun now refers clearly to the drive, its antecedent.*)

Another point to remember in pronoun usage is this: You should not use second person (you) in formal writing unless you are directly addressing a particular reader. You may use first person (I, me) if you are speaking of personal experience, or you may use third person (they, he, she).

> *Poor pronoun usage*: I love the way that summertime makes you feel.
> *Acceptable pronoun usage*: I love the way that summertime makes me feel.
> *Acceptable pronoun usage*: People love the way summertime makes them feel.

3. An ***adjective*** describes a noun or pronoun.

> The ***beautiful*** princess found her family again, and she was very ***happy.*** (***Beautiful*** *describes the noun* ***princess; happy*** *also describes the princess.* ***Very*** *is not an adjective because it is describing happy, which is not a noun or pronoun.*)

He was ***worried*** because he could not find his ***new*** shoes or his ***silver*** tie. (***Worried*** *describes the person represented by the pronoun* ***he;*** ***new*** *and* ***silver*** *describe articles of clothing, which are nouns.*)

A ***poetry*** book can be very ***inspiring.*** (***Poetry*** *and* ***inspiring*** *both describe the book. This is a great example of why you must look at the function of a word within a sentence to determine its part of speech. In general, you might think of poetry as a noun, something you read. However, in this sentence, it is being used as a descriptor to identify the type of book.*)

Note: The words ***a, an,*** and ***the*** are called *articles*, which are types of adjectives.

4. A ***verb*** expresses action or links the subject to the rest of the sentence. (Note: the subject in a sentence is the noun or pronoun *performing* the action of the verb or being *linked* to descriptive words in the predicate.)

Mary ***walked*** home every day after piano practice. (*Mary is performing the action of walking.*)
I ***baked*** a pie and ***roasted*** the potatoes for dinner. (*I am performing two actions here. Connecting two actions to the subject creates a compound verb.*)
She ***is*** nice. (*The pronoun subject* ***she*** *is being linked to the adjective* ***nice****. There is no action being performed in this sentence. However, a sentence must always contain a verb, so if no direct action is apparent, you probably have a linking verb.*)

A linking verb connects the subject with a word that identifies or describes it. The forms of the verb ***be*** are the most common linking verbs. The verbs that have more than one word are called ***verb phrases***. They consist of a ***helping verb*** and a ***main verb***. The helping verbs add tense (present, past, future) forms to the base verb. Here are the forms of the verb *to be*:

am	be	will be	had been
is	can be	could be	shall have been
are	may be	should be	will have been
was	might be	would be	could have been
were	must be	has been	should have been
being	shall be	have been	would have been

Note: Correct use of verb tense and irregular verbs will be covered in chapter 2.

5. An ***adverb*** describes a verb, an adjective, or another adverb by telling how, why, when, or in what way or to what extent something exists or is done.

I ***carefully*** walked down the hallway so I could find the spider. (*This word describes* ***how I*** *walked. The adverb describes a verb.*)
The ***very*** noisy boy ran ***quite loudly*** through the new store. (***Very*** *describes how noisy the boy is. Because* ***noisy*** *describes the boy—a noun—it is an adjective, so the adverb* ***very*** *describes an adjective.* ***Loudly*** *describes how the boy ran, so it is an adverb describing a verb.* ***Quite*** *describes how loudly the boy ran. You already know* ***loudly*** *is an adverb, so* ***quite*** *is an adverb describing another adverb.*)

6. A ***conjunction*** joins words, phrases, or sentences together. (There are several types of conjunctions, each with its own rules of punctuation. Specifics for the different forms of this part of speech will be discussed later in this chapter and in the direct writing section dealing with sentence combining.)

I would love to go shopping, ***but*** I have no money. (*A word joining two complete sentences*)
For my birthday, I would love a new coat ***and*** a new pair of leather gloves. (*A word joining two phrases*)
I would like to go on vacation; ***however,*** I have no vacation days left at work. (*A word joining two complete thoughts separated with a semicolon*)

7. A ***preposition*** is used to form a ***prepositional phrase,*** which consists of a preposition and a noun or a pronoun. Prepositional phrases show a relationship between items in a sentence.

A prepositional phrase contains a preposition (first word), possibly an adjective or adverb combination, and then a noun or pronoun (required, last word). The noun or pronoun at the end of a prepositional phrase is called the *object of the preposition.* A prepositional phrase may contain as few as two words, or it may contain several.

List of common prepositions: about, above, across, after, against, along, among, around, at, before, behind, below, beneath, beside, between, beyond, but, by, despite, down, during, except, for, from, in, inside, into, like, near, of, off, on, onto, out, outside, over, past, since, through, throughout, till, to, toward, under, underneath, until, up, upon, with, within, without.

The child is playing ***in the yard.*** (*The preposition* ***in*** *is connected to the noun* ***yard*** *with the article* ***the*** *in between.*)
My mother, who was ***at the store in Atlanta***, found a new scarf. (*Two prepositional phrases side by side:* ***at the store*** *and* ***in Atlanta***)
The shoebox is ***near the big rock,*** hidden ***under the woodpile.*** (*Two prepositional phrases separated by the word* ***hidden***)

A preposition should not be used alone to end a sentence. For example, you would be incorrect in writing *What city are you from?* Instead, you might write *Where were you born?*

8. An ***interjection*** is a word or phrase that expresses emotion (light or heavy) and is usually at the beginning of the sentence.

Wow! I just won twenty dollars in the raffle!

No way! I can't believe you won the first-place trophy.

Hey, it's getting late.

I have finished my homework. ***Yes!***

Final note regarding the eight parts of speech: Consider the following sentence:

The bus driver is early every morning.

You might look at the word *bus* and believe that it is a noun because a bus is a thing. This sentence, however, is not providing information about a bus. The word *bus* is describing the *type* of driver, so it serves as an adjective (describing a noun). You must be careful to identify the part of speech of a word based on how it is used in a given sentence. Try the practice sentence below. Look at the words in bold, and try to determine the part of speech each serves in the sentence. Then, look at the listing of answers.

Today, Tom ***and*** I bought a canoe, and ***we*** paddled ***it*** silently around ***the*** peaceful ***lake.***

Today:	**adverb** (describing when they bought the canoe)
Tom:	**noun** (person)
I:	**pronoun** (taking the place of the speaker's name)
bought:	**verb** (naming the action performed by *Tom and I*)
canoe:	**noun** (the thing purchased by *Tom and I*)
and:	**conjunction** (connecting the two complete thoughts)
paddled:	**verb** (naming another action performed by *Tom and I*)
silently:	**adverb** (describing how the two people paddled the canoe)
around:	**preposition** (forming the beginning of the prepositional phrase *around the peaceful lake*)
peaceful:	**adjective** (describing the noun *lake*)

1.2 Punctuation

End Marks

1. A statement is followed by a period.

   My mother is taking a class in nursing.

2. A question is followed by a question mark.

   Are you sure you don't need anything from the store?

3. An exclamation is followed by an exclamation point.

   I just won twenty dollars in the name-the-cereal contest!

4. An abbreviation is usually followed by a period.

   Thomas Jr. is as tall as his father.

Commas

1. Use commas to separate items in a series (up to the conjunction).

   To have a *series* of items, you must have at least three. A conjunction (coordinating conjunction) is one of seven words used to connect words, phrases, or sentences in a series: **and, but, or, nor, for (meaning because), so,** and **yet (meaning but).**

   I must mow the lawn, trim the hedges, and plant the flowers.

2. Use a comma to separate two adjectives preceding the noun they describe. (An adjective is used only to describe a noun or pronoun).

   I have always dreamed of owning a beautiful, sleek horse.

3. Use a comma before a coordinating conjunction when it separates two independent clauses. The term *independent clause* is a formal term meaning *complete thought* or *a clause that can stand alone as a sentence*. Coordinating conjunctions were covered in rule #1 above. Therefore, this rule actually means that if you connect two complete sentences and join them with a coordinating conjunction, then you must use a comma before that conjunction. If the second statement does not express a complete thought, then you do not use a comma in front of the conjunction.

   You have started research class, and you will have a wonderful experience.

   You have started research class and will have a wonderful experience. (In this example, the statement after the conjunction begins with a verb and does not express a complete thought. If you were to add a subject to the second statement, then you would include a comma before the conjunction. That is the situation illustrated in the first example.)

4. Use a comma after an interjection or other short, introductory element.
   An interjection is a word that shows emotion. If it is excessive, it will be followed by an exclamation point. If it is mild, it will be followed by a comma. Other short introductory elements, such as individual adverbs placed at the beginning, are followed by commas as well.

   Hey, what is for dinner tonight?

   Man, I forgot my cell phone.

   Usually, I watch movies on Monday evenings.

5. Use a comma after an introductory participial phrase.

   A participle is an "action adjective." In other words, it is a word that shows action but does not function as the verb in a given sentence. A participle is only one word. A participial phrase is a participle plus any accompanying thoughts. A participial phrase will begin with a participle (most often a verb form ending in *ing*). The entire phrase, led by the participle, will act as an adjective. When such a phrase introduces a sentence, it is followed by a comma.

   Participle: That is a drinking fountain. (The verb in this sentence is a linking verb, *is*. However, the word *drinking* seems to indicate action. Because the word is being used to describe the type of fountain, it is an adjective showing action: a participle.)

   Participial phrase: My friend, gathering his courage, spoke his mind. (The base sentence is this: My friend spoke his mind. The action of the friend is *speaking*. However, *gathering* also shows action, and you must determine its function. It leads a phrase that describes the friend, a phrase that comes in the middle of the actual base sentence. The term *gathering,* therefore, is a participle introducing a participial phrase.)

   Introductory participial phrase: Gathering his courage, my friend spoke his mind. (The participial phrase is the same as it was in the previous sentence; however, it now occurs at the beginning of the sentence. It describes the friend, who serves as the subject of the base sentence. This sentence illustrates rule #5: Use a comma after an introductory participial phrase.

6. Use commas to set off a nonessential participial phrase.

   Though a participial phrase may not occur at the beginning of the sentence, it may still require commas. If it is considered nonessential, it should be set off with commas. It should be considered nonessential if it contains information that is not crucial for the identification of the noun it describes or the comprehension of the base sentence.

   My niece, attending graduate school, loves chocolate sodas! (The fact that the niece is attending graduate school is not essential to the understanding that she loves sodas.)

   Dr. Huff, walking to the school building, dropped her pencils. (Again, the participial phrase is nonessential to the understanding of the base sentence.)

   The girl wearing the yellow coat is my neighbor. (In this sentence, the participial phrase *wearing the yellow coat* is essential to the identification of the noun *girl*. If you were to remove the phrase, you would not be able to identify which girl is the neighbor. You might want to think of commas in this situation as locks that can be opened to remove a phrase that is not really necessary. If you have no commas, you cannot remove the phrase, an indication that it is necessary.)

7. Use a comma after two or more introductory prepositional phrases.

   In the country one can see beautiful trees. (In this sentence, there is only one prepositional phrase in the introductory position. Some English books consider this an introductory element and suggest usage of a comma. Other texts do not.)

   At my home in the country, the trees are tall. (Here, you see two phrases connected in the introductory position.)

8. Use a comma after an introductory adverb clause.
   Clauses are either independent or dependent. Independent clauses are complete sentences that stand alone. Dependent clauses cannot stand alone. An adverb clause is dependent. Clauses, by definition, also contain a subject and verb. That is why some people punctuate them as sentences. An adverb clause begins with a subordinating conjunction, a word that, in itself, carries meaning. That conjunction is followed by a subject, verb, etc., and the entire clause functions as an adverb does, telling how, when, or under what conditions something is done. If an adverb clause begins your sentence, you follow it with a comma.

   List of common subordinating conjunctions: as, after, although, as if, as long as, as soon as, as though, because, before, being that, considering that, if, in case, in order that, inasmuch as, insofar as, just so, lest, since, though, unless, until, when, whenever, whereas, wherever, whether, while.

   Because you are so curious, I will buy you a book.

   If Thomas practices every day, he will become a terrific golfer.

   As long as you are going to the store, will you pick up some bread for me?

9. Do not use a comma before an adverb clause that follows an independent clause.

   This rule is actually the reverse of rule #8.

   I will buy you a book because you are so curious.

10. Use a comma to set off an appositive of more than one word.

    An appositive is a noun that renames a nearby noun (usually directly before it). The only parts of speech that can come between the first noun and the appositive are adjectives and adverbs.

    My best friend, a cashier at the grocery store, is always positive and happy. (*Cashier* is the appositive renaming the noun *friend.*)

    I just finished one of my favorite novels, *The Giver.* (*The Giver* is the appositive renaming the noun *novels.*)

    My sister Ellen works for a dentist. (Although the noun *Ellen* renames the noun *sister*, the appositive is only one word and, therefore, requires no comma.)

11. Use commas to set off nouns used in direct address.

    To "directly address" means to speak directly "to" the noun. Rather than speaking *about* your friend Tom, you directly address him. The location of the noun being addressed does not affect the comma requirement. However, if the noun occurs in the middle of the sentence, be sure to put commas on both sides.

Tom, I like your new car.
I think, Tom, that you should study more.
I really like that house, Tom.

12. Use commas to set off parenthetical expressions.

    A parenthetical expression is a word or phrase that is inserted into the flow of thought. It does not deal directly with the topic at hand but, rather, adds a sort of pause for thought or reflection. (Use of the term *rather* in the previous sentence illustrates use of a parenthetical expression.)

    Common parenthetical expressions: actually, by the way, if possible, in fact, of course, nevertheless

    I think, in fact, that a picnic would be ideal for the celebration.

    Timothy, naturally, should be the one to carve the turkey.

13. Use a comma after a name followed by an abbreviation, such as Jr., Sr., or M.D.

    I just met Larry Edwards, Jr.

14. Use commas to set off a nonessential adjective clause.

    An adjective clause is another type of dependent clause. It cannot stand alone. Unlike an adverb clause that begins with a subordinate conjunction and describes how, why, or under what conditions, an adjective clause begins with a relative pronoun, follows a noun, and acts as an adjective describing that noun. If you believe the clause is necessary to the identification of the noun, then consider it essential, and use commas. If, however, you do not believe it to be essential to the understanding and identification of the noun it describes, then consider it nonessential, and use no commas.

    Relative pronouns: who, whom, whose, which, that

    Essential: The girl who is wearing the red jacket is in the third grade. (The adjective clause is essential because you need it to identify which girl is being discussed.)

    Nonessential: Tonia, who is wearing the red jacket, is in the third grade. (The adjective clause is not essential because the child being discussed is identified by name.)

Note: Use *who* to begin an adjective clause if it serves as the subject or predicate nominative of the clause and is performing the action of the clause's verb; use *whom* if it serves as an object and is receiving the action of the clause's verb.

The woman who bought the house is a marketing consultant. (In the adjective clause, the "who" is performing the action of buying the house; it serves as the subject of the clause.)

The woman whom I know is a marketing consultant. (In the adjective clause, the "whom" is receiving the action of being known; it serves as an object. The subject of the clause is *I* because *I* am the one who *knows*.)

Semicolons

1. Use a semicolon between complete sentences if they are *not* joined by a coordinating conjunction (and, but, or, nor, for, so, yet).

   It has been raining all day; I guess our picnic will be cancelled.

2. Use a semicolon between items in a series if the items already contain commas.

   I will visit Houston, Texas; Springfield, Missouri; and Richmond, Virginia.

3. Use a semicolon between independent clauses joined by a conjunctive adverb or a transitional expression.

   Unlike subordinate conjunctions, conjunctive adverbs do not attach themselves to a sentence. They simply connect complete and separate thoughts (just as coordinating conjunctions do).

   Common conjunctive adverbs: consequently, however, in addition, in fact, likewise, nevertheless, similarly, therefore

   The snowfall made traveling difficult; nevertheless, we arrived safely. (The semicolon serves as the divider between sentences, and the comma is used after *nevertheless* because it serves as an introductory element in the second statement.)

Colons

1. Use a colon between a complete introductory statement and a following list of items.

   Please bring the following items to class: pen, pencil, paper, and books.

   Please bring pens, pencils, paper, and books to class. (This sentence requires no colon because there is not a complete statement before the list. You should never place a colon between the verb in a sentence and a list that follows that verb.)

2. Use a colon between independent clauses when the second clause explains or restates the idea of the first.

   I have finally realized my lifelong dream: I have become a ballerina!

3. Use a colon between a title and a subtitle.

   Living in Today's World: A Guide for Students

Underlining/italicizing

1. Underline (italicize) the titles of books, dramatic presentations, films, magazines and journals, works of art, CDs, television series, aircraft, and ships. (When you are writing, you underline these titles. When you are typing, you italicize them.)

   In class, we are reading *The Fishermen of the Eastern Shore.*

2. Use italics for words, letters, and symbols referred to as such and for foreign words.

   Should the use of *their* for *there* be considered a spelling error or a usage error?

   Is *burrito* a Spanish word for a type of food?

Quotation marks

1. Use quotation marks to enclose a direct quotation—a person's exact words.

   Bob said, "We will go on a field trip next week."

2. A direct quotation (complete thought) begins with a capital letter even if it begins within the sentence.

   The shopper said, "The bargains this week are incredible!"

3. When the quoted sentence is divided into two parts by an interrupting expression such as *they said*, the second part begins with a lowercase letter.

   "I will be gone," mother said, "for only two hours."

4. A direct quotation is set off from the rest of the sentence by a comma, a question mark, or an exclamation point, not by a period.

   Mrs. Smith announced, "Remember your books tomorrow!"

5. Commas and periods always go inside closing quotation marks.

   "Leave your homework on the table," I said.

   Mary said, "I really hope to go to the concert."

6. Semicolons and colons are always placed outside the closing quotation marks.

   My neighbor said, "Of course I'll buy a magazine subscription"; it was lucky that I asked her on payday.

   I knew exactly what my mother meant when she said, "Excuse me": I was in trouble.

7. Question marks and exclamation points are placed inside the closing quotation marks if the quotation itself is a question or an exclamation. Otherwise, they are placed outside.

   "Dad, will you please call the doctor tomorrow morning?" I asked.
   Did your poetry instructor write the line, "The leaves fall gently on the breeze"?
   When he saw the snake, Tom yelled, "Watch out!"
   Hey! I just won an award in the poetry contest with my poem "Michigan"!

8. Use single quotation marks to enclose a quotation within a quotation.

   The teacher requested, "Jorge, please explain what Emerson meant when he said, 'To be great is to be misunderstood.'"

9. Use quotation marks to enclose the titles of articles in magazines, short stories, songs, poems, chapters and parts of books, and essays.

   My mom just read me a poem called "Springtime."

10. Use quotation marks to enclose slang words, nicknames, and other unusual uses of words.

    The basketball player is William "Stilts" Smith.

11. Use ellipsis points (. . .) to mark omissions from quoted material and pauses in written text.

    In his autobiography, *The Way I See Life,* Edward Stiller reflects, "This day . . . this hour . . . I know myself truly."

Apostrophes

1. To form the possessive of a singular noun, add an apostrophe and an *s* to the end of the word. (To form a possessive, you are indicating ownership by the noun to which you add an apostrophe.)

   The table's leg has been scratched.

2. To form the possessive of a plural noun ending in *s*, add only an apostrophe to the end of the word.

   The books' covers have been taped many times.

3. To form the possessive of a plural noun that does not end with an *s*, add both an apostrophe and an *s* to the end of the word. (Words in this category form their plurals without an ending *s*.)

   The children's names have been put onto the bulletin board.

4. Possessive personal pronouns do not require an apostrophe. They are already formatted in the possessive.

   This book is hers, not ours.

5. In compound words and words showing joint possession, only the last word uses the apostrophe.

   Tom and Janet's home is around the corner. (Tom and Janet both own the home, so the apostrophe is needed only on the second noun.)

6. When two or more persons possess something individually, each of their names is possessive in form and requires an apostrophe.

   Michael's and Lila's books need to be repaired. (Both Michael and Lila own separate books; therefore, each must take a possessive form.)

7. Use an apostrophe to show where letters, numbers, or words have been omitted in a contraction.

   I can't believe they're '99 graduates! (*can't* = can not; *they're* = they are; *'99* = 1999)

Hyphens

1. Use a hyphen to divide a word at the end of a line. You may divide a word only between syllables. Never split a one-syllable word, and never leave one letter standing alone on either line.

   This is a fascinating book, and I would love to talk about some of the interest-
   ing facts of the plot.

2. Use a hyphen with compound numbers from twenty-one to ninety-nine.

   I need to make thirty-five copies.

3. Hyphenate a compound adjective when it precedes the noun it describes.

   The well-written paper received an A. (The term *well-written* is not considered two separate adjectives because both do not directly describe paper. Instead, they work together as a team to describe paper. If a compound adjective *does not precede* the noun it describes, then you *do not* hyphenate the word. Example: The paper was well written.)

Dashes

Use a dash to indicate an abrupt break in thought or speech.

The party—I forgot to tell you about it—will begin at 3:30.

Parentheses

Use parentheses to enclose material of minor importance in a sentence.

The new school (built in 1998) is ready to open.

Brackets

Use brackets to enclose an explanation within quoted or parenthetical material.

> **The newspaper article stated that "At the time of that Democratic National Convention [in Chicago, 1968] there were many political viewpoints."**

1.3 Agreement

In the dictionary, the word *agreement* is defined as "harmony." In music, harmony refers to sounds that blend well and work together. In English, certain words must work in harmony. This is called agreement. Certain words must agree in number so that they can effectively support the rest of the sentence.

To say that words must agree in number means that they must both be singular (meaning one) or plural (meaning more than one). This section will cover two types of agreement: subject/verb and pronoun/antecedent.

Subject/Verb Agreement

Every sentence must have a subject and a verb. The subject is the noun or pronoun that identifies who or what is being discussed. The verb identifies the action of the subject. When you are identifying the subject and verb of a sentence, remember that the subject will be the person or thing performing the action of the verb, and the action of the verb will be performed by the subject. Look at the following examples.

> **Monica ate the sandwich.**
> **The children play in the yard.**

In the first sentence, *Monica* is the subject because she is the one performing the action of eating, and *ate* is the verb because it shows what Monica did.

In the second sentence, *children* is the subject because they are the ones doing the action of playing, and *play* is the verb because it tells what the children are doing. Consider one more example:

> **In the water floated a small boat.**

This sentence begins with a prepositional phrase, and you will never find your subject in a prepositional phrase. It's important to remember that a subject does not have to come at the beginning of the sentence. To find the subject, first locate the action: *floated*. Then, ask yourself, "What floated?" It was the boat. To be sure you are correct, ask yourself what the boat did. It floated. This is a good way to locate the subject and verb of a sentence.

Remember from the discussion of punctuation that clauses have their own subjects and verbs, so you must be careful not to try and connect the subject of the base sentence to the verb of a clause. Here is an example:

> **The man who whistled walked toward us.** (The base sentence is *The man walked toward us*. In that sentence, *man* is the subject and *walked* is the verb. The adjective clause is *who whistled*. In that clause, *who* is the subject and *whistled* is the verb.)

Note: In some cases, a sentence may be written in passive voice, which means that the action is done *to* the subject. Passive voice is not recommended in formal writing, but because you might encounter an example, it is important to remember to check for the subject by asking *who* or *what* after you find the verb. Here is an example:

The sandwich was eaten by the man. (The action is *eaten*. If you ask what was eaten, you will still find the correct subject: sandwich. Remember, also, that your subject will NEVER be inside a prepositional phrase.)

Once you locate the subject, you must determine whether it is singular or plural. Singular is one, and plural is more than one. That should be easy to determine. Some students, however, have difficulty telling whether a verb is singular or plural. Because you must have a singular subject with a singular verb and a plural subject with a plural verb, you must recognize the difference between singular and plural verbs. One of the simplest ways to do this is to say, "One person ______________; two people ____________. In the blank, you would substitute the verb you are analyzing. Take, for example, the word *walk*. To try the formula, you would say, *"One person walk; two people walk."* The second is correct, so you know that the verb *walk* is plural.

Another way to determine whether a verb is singular or plural is to note that the singular form of a verb is the one that ends in an *s*; the plural form does not end with an *s*. For example, *dances* is singular, and *dance* is plural; *writes* is singular, and *write* is plural. Ironically, this concept is opposite of what occurs when you form the singular and plural of almost all nouns. For example, the word *note* is singular, but when you add an *s*, the result is the plural form *notes*. *Dog* is singular, but *dogs* is plural. When you consider verb forms, think about how you form singular and plural nouns, and do the opposite!

There is one important point to remember here. For almost all verbs, you will only have to worry about focusing on subject/verb agreement when the verb occurs in the present tense rather than in the past or future tenses. For example, *dance* is present tense, *danced* is past tense, and *will dance* is future tense. The past and future tenses of most verbs will be the same for one or more people: One person *danced*; three people *danced*; one person *will dance*; three people *will dance*. However, when you look at the present tense of the same verb, you see a difference: One person *dances*; three people *dance*. The forms of *Be*, however, will have different past tense forms for singular and plural. (These verbs were discussed in section 1.1.)

Remember, in the present tense, singular verbs end with an *s*, and the plural forms of the same verbs do not end with an *s*. Here are some examples:

Tom is here. (One person *is* here; the singular subject *Tom* matches the singular verb.)

The boys are here. (Two people *are* here; the plural subject *boys* matches the plural verb.)

Andrew always listens to his mother. (One person, Andrew, *listens*.)

Andrew and Allison always listen to their mother. (Two people, Andrew and Allison, *listen*.)

The number of a subject is not changed by a phrase or clause between the subject and the verb. That is why it is so important to be sure you locate the subject and match it directly to the verb.

One of the girls in the room was drawing a picture. (The subject is *one*, a singular term. The two phrases *of the girls* and *in the room* do not affect the singular nature of the subject. So, the verb is correct. One person *was drawing.)*

The number of a subject is also not affected when the subject is followed by a phrase that begins with an expression such as *along with, as well as, in addition to*, and *together with*. This concept can get confusing because it almost looks as if you are viewing a compound subject. However, a compound subject will have two or more nouns or pronouns connected with a conjunction such as *and* or *or*.

The history teacher, along with her students, was fascinated by the artifacts. (The subject is *teacher*, a singular term. The phrase *along with her students* does not change the subject's number to plural. A compound subject would look like this: **The history teacher and her students were fascinated by the artifacts.**

Finally, here are a few rules to help you determine the number of your verb when you have true compound subjects.

1. Subjects joined by *and* take a plural verb.

   Basil and thyme are plants of the mint family.

2. Singular subjects joined by *or* or *nor* take a singular verb.

   Neither Juan nor Timothy wants to see a movie.

3. When a singular subject and a plural subject are joined by *or* or *nor*, the verb should be made to agree with the subject nearer to it.

   Neither the performers nor the director was happy with the scene.

   Neither the director nor the performers were happy with the scene.

Pronoun/Antecedent Agreement

A noun is a person, place, or thing; a pronoun is a word that takes the place of a noun so that the noun will not have to be repeated. Pronouns are words such as *he, she, it, we, our, my, you, they, us, her*, and *them.* If you are using a singular noun in your sentence and you want to use a pronoun to replace it, then you must use a singular pronoun. If you are using a plural noun in your sentence and you want to replace that noun with a pronoun, then you must use a plural pronoun.

> **One boy lost his tooth in school.** (*His* refers back to the word *boy.*)
>
> **The people forgot their appointments.** (*Their* refers back to *people.*)

It is important here to consider one special group of pronouns, called *indefinite pronouns*, that might cause you difficulty with the concept of agreement. Consider the following example:

> **Everyone in the pep club left (his/her, their) jacket on the bench**. You might think that the correct answer is *their* because the word *everyone* sounds like a lot of people. However, the word *everyone,* which is called indefinite because the person or people being discussed are not specific, is actually considered a *singular* pronoun. Therefore, every verb and pronoun matched with it must also be singular. The correct choice for the example, then, would be *his/her*: **Everyone in the pep club left his/her jacket on the bench.**

Following is a list of rules to help you:

The following indefinite pronouns are singular: anybody, anyone, each, either, everybody, everyone, neither, nobody, no one, one, somebody, someone

The following indefinite pronouns are plural: both, few, many, others, several

The following indefinite pronouns may be either singular or plural: all, any, most, none, some (You use the rest of the sentence to determine whether the focus is on *one* subject or *more than one.)*

*Always remember that when you have a subject/verb or pronoun/antecedent agreement problem, you always change the verb to match the subject or the pronoun to match the antecedent because those have already been determined.

1.4 Parallel Structure

To use parallel construction in a sentence means to present parallel ideas in coordinate form. For example, when you are creating items in a series or compound sentences, be sure to use the same pattern for all elements involved. Consider these examples:

The diagnosis showed that the man needed to lower his cholesterol level and his blood pressure needed to be monitored by him. (The parallelism is broken because the first part of the sentence takes on the "man needed to" form in active voice, but the second part shifts to passive voice with "blood pressure needed to be watched. . . .") The parallelism problem can be corrected in the following way:

The diagnosis was that the man needed to lower his cholesterol level and monitor his blood pressure. This sentence is much more clear, focused, and *active*.

Poor parallel structure: **I love fishing, hiking, and to swim!**

Good parallel structure: **I love fishing, hiking, and swimming!**

1.5 Sentence Fragments and Run-on Sentences

A ***sentence fragment*** is an incomplete thought punctuated as a complete thought. Here are some examples:

In the garden spraying the rosebushes.

When we went to the new museum.

Even though my mother is a wonderful cook.

Because I am always so sick during the asthma season.

You must have a complete thought in order to punctuate it as a sentence. Some sentence fragments are created when periods are inserted too quickly in a sentence. For example,

It turned out to be a lovely painting. After she added the fall leaves.

The fragment occurs in the second part. This sentence can be easily corrected by deleting the period and allowing the sentence to flow.

A ***run-on sentence*** occurs when you connect two sentences either without punctuation (***fused sentence***) or with simply a comma (***comma splice***). Here are two examples of run-on sentences:

The boys had a challenging day the obstacle course was very difficult.

The boys had a challenging day, the obstacle course was very difficult.

You can correct run-on sentences by ending the first sentence with a period, placing a semicolon between the sentences, or using a comma and a coordinating conjunction between the sentences. There are various ways to correct the problem, but it must be corrected if you want your writing to be effective.

1.6 Misplaced and Dangling Modifiers

A modifier is an adjective or adverb (whether a single word or in the form of a phrase). Every modifier should clearly refer to a specific word in your sentence.

A ***misplaced modifier*** causes confusion because its referent is not clear. In other words, it's modifying someone or something, but it is out of place and, therefore, causes confusion. Here is an example:

> **The teacher helped the children using a ruler.** (The confusion occurs because the reader is not sure whether the teacher used the ruler to help the children or whether she helped the children who were using rulers. It is not the job of the reader to try and figure out the writer's intention. It is the responsibility of a good writer to make his ideas clear.) The sentence could be corrected in several ways:
>
> **Using a ruler, the teacher helped the children.**
>
> **The teacher, who was using a ruler, helped the children.**
>
> **The teacher helped the children who were using rulers.**

A ***dangling modifier*** causes confusion because the referent is simply missing. In other words, a modifier is attempting to describe something or someone that is missing. Look at the following example:

> **After making dinner, the dishes were washed.** This sentence seems to indicate that the dishes made the dinner. Whoever made the dinner is missing from the sentence. Consider this revision:
>
> **After making dinner, Mom and Dad washed the dishes.**

Chapter 1 Exercises

Read the following letter, and use it to answer questions 1–10.

April 1, 2003

University of Iowa
Admissions Board
2265 Allington Highway
Ames, Iowa 29967

Dear Admissions Board:

(1) I would like to recommend Eleanor Bergman for admission to your university for the fall term, I believe she would be a wonderful addition to your program.

I have known Eleanor for about five years. **(2)** I have been her history instructor, her soccer coach and her program of studies advisor. **(3)** She has always been in my opinion a focused, dedicated student who respects the value of a strong education.

(4) In history class, Eleanor always worked very diligently. **(5)** She was prompt and always prepared for class. **(6)** Not every concept came easy to her, but she was not afraid to ask questions or request extra help after school. **(7)** In fact, she was instrumental in creating an SOL preparation group that met to study and discuss major historical concepts.

(8) Although Eleanor was very ambitious in her academic endeavors, she was also committed to her extracurricular interests. **(9)** She served as a member of both her junior and senior advisory boards, participated in girls soccer for three years, played trombone in the school band, and helped sell wrapping paper for a major school fundraising event. **(10)** Through excellent time management skills, she was able to balance her schoolwork and her club activities quite effectively.

(11) Finally Eleanor sees the importance of giving of herself to her community. **(12)** She has worked with programs to assist the elderly, Saturday play camps for children, and emergency relief efforts for tornado and hurricane victims. **(13)** She have a wonderful ability to keep her own life in order while remaining cognizant of the needs of others. **(14)** I have often heard her say, "Giving to others actually increases my worth".

(15) I believe Eleanor value education and service to others. I know she will work hard to attain success in all her endeavors, and I recommend her to you without hesitation.

Sincerely,

Simon L. Lakeland
Middletown High School

1. In sentence 1, how is <u>for the fall term, I believe</u> correctly written?
A for the fall term I believe
B for the fall term, because I believe
C for the fall term. I believe
D As it is

2. In sentence 2, how is <u>her soccer coach and her</u> correctly written?
A her soccer coach, and her
B her soccer coach; and her
C her soccer coach. And her
D As it is

3. In sentence 3, how is <u>has always been in my opinion</u> correctly written?
A has always been; in my opinion;
B has always been, in my opinion,
C has always been, in my opinion
D As it is

4. In sentence 6, how is <u>concept came easy to her, but</u> correctly written?
A concept came easily to her but
B concept came easily to her, but
C concept came easy to her but
D As it is

5. In sentence 8, how is <u>academic endeavors, she was also</u> correctly written?
A academic endeavors she was also
B academic endeavors; she was also
C academic endeavors: she was also
D As it is

6. In sentence 9, how is <u>participated in girls soccer</u> correctly written?
A participated in girls' soccer
B participated in girl's soccer
C participated in girls's soccer
D As it is

7. In sentence 11, how is <u>Finally Eleanor</u> correctly written?
A Finally! Eleanor
B Finally; Eleanor
C Finally, Eleanor
D As it is

8. In sentence 13, how is <u>She have a wonderful ability</u> correctly written?

A She had a wonderful ability
B She has a wonderful ability
C She's has a wonderful ability
D As it is

9. In sentence 14, how is <u>increases my worth".</u> correctly written?

A increases my worth,".
B increases my worth."
C increases my worth'."
D As it is

10. Sentence 15 contains which error?

A Subject/verb agreement
B Pronoun/antecedent agreement
C Punctuation
D Parallel structure

Read the following announcement, and use it to answer questions 11–17.

Announcement of Auditions

(1) Auditions for the play "People and Dreams" will be held on Wednesday, August 23, at 2:00 P.M. in the conference room of the Whitaker Library. **(2)** This production revolves around the story of a man who wishes to be a poet but doesn't want to abandon his current career as a veterinarian, which he also finds most fulfilling. **(3)** The cast, in addition to this main character, includes his wife, his two grown children, various friends, employees, and neighbors, and a sporadically appearing "conscience" that helps the main character face his conflict.

(4) Those who are interested in auditioning for parts should bring: a folding chair, a list of prior theatrical experience, and an 8 × 10 color photograph. **(5)** Anyone interested in working with lighting, costume design, or musical accompaniment may also apply. **(6)** The selected cast and crew will practice every evening (6–9 P.M.) from August 26 through September 27. **(7)** The final production will run for three consecutive nights; September 28–30.

(8) For more information, call Tina Bravinder at (223) 555-6361 or stop by the library to pick a flyer up. **(9)** When calling for information, a message may be left.

11. Which sentence requires the use of one or more semicolons?

A 2
B 3
C 5
D 8

12. In sentence 1, how is <u>the play "People and Dreams"</u> correctly written?

A the play People and Dreams
B the play *People and Dreams*
C the play (People and Dreams)
D As it is

13. In sentence 3, how is <u>character, includes his wife</u> correctly written?

A character, including his wife
B character, include his wife
C character, included his wife
D As it is

14. In sentence 4, how is <u>should bring: a folding chair,</u> correctly written?
- A should bring a folding chair,
- B should bring, a folding chair,
- C should bring; a folding chair
- D As it is

15. In sentence 7, how is <u>three consecutive nights;</u> correctly written?
- A three consecutive nights
- B three consecutive nights:
- C three consecutive nights—
- D As it is

16. In sentence 8, how is <u>pick a flyer up</u> correctly written?
- A pick a flyer up,
- B pick up a flyer.
- C pick, a flyer up.
- D As it is

17. Sentence 9 contains which error?
- A Subject/verb agreement problem
- B Misplaced modifier
- C Comma error
- D Dangling modifier

Read the following information regarding portfolios, and then use it to answer questions 18–22.

> **(1)** A portfolio is a compilation of one's accomplishments, experiences, projects, goals, and plans for the future. **(2)** By developing a portfolio, you can assess your personal, academic, and career development. **(3)** They document ones preparedness to go to college, technical training, or work. **(4)** Portfolios documents a progression of experiences, activities, and courses that help one develop their future career options.
>
> **(5)** Through career exploration and with the cooperation of his parents, teacher's, and guidance counselors, one may elect to enter a specific program of study focusing on a career area that combines his interests and abilities.

18. In sentence 2, how is <u>you can assess your personal, academic, and career development.</u> correctly written?
- A one can assess your personal, academic, and career development.
- B one can assess his/her personal, academic, and career development.
- C one can assess their personal, academic, and career development.
- D As it is

19. In sentence 3, how is <u>They document ones preparedness to go to college, technical training, or work.</u> correctly written?
- A They document one's preparedness to go to college, technical training, or work.
- B It documents ones preparedness to go to college, technical training, or work.
- C It documents one's preparedness to go to college, technical training, or work.
- D As it is

20. In sentence 4, how is <u>Portfolios documents a progression of experiences, activities, and courses</u> correctly written?
- A Portfolios document a progression of experiences, activities, and courses
- B Portfolio's document a progression of experiences, activities, and courses
- C Portfolios' document a progression of experiences, activities, and courses
- D As it is

21. In sentence 4, how is <u>that help one develop their future career options</u> correctly written?

A that helps one develop their future career options
B that helps one develop his/her future career options
C that help one develop his/her future career options
D As it is

22. In sentence 5, how is <u>and with the cooperation of his parents, teacher's, and guidance counselors,</u> correctly written?

A and with the cooperation of his parent's, teacher's, and guidance counselor's,
B and with the cooperation of his parents, teachers, and guidance counselors,
C and with the cooperation of his parents, teachers, and guidance counselors
D As it is

Read the following note, and then use it to answer questions 23–25.

Dear Mom,

(1) I have gone over to Tanya's house so that we can study for our science and math exam's. **(2)** I should be home around 8:00 P.M. **(3)** If you need me before then, you can call me at her house. **(4)** Her number is 555-3451. **(5)** Tanya and I plan to order a pizza for dinner, so you don't have to worry about fixing me anything when I get home. **(6)** I also want to thank you for the terrific lunch you packed for me today, it was absolutely delicious! **(7)** Say hi to dad for me; I'll see you later this evening. **(8)** Working late, you might be asleep, so I won't wake you.

(9) Love, Emily

23. In line 1, how is <u>so that we can study for our science and math exam's.</u> correctly written?

A so that we can study for our science and math exams.
B so that we can study for our science and math exams'.
C so that we can study for our science and math exams's.
D As it is

24. In line 6, how is <u>lunch you packed for me today, it was absolutely delicious!</u> correctly written?

A lunch you packed for me today, It was absolutely delicious!
B lunch you packed for me today; it was absolutely delicious!
C lunch you packed for me today; It was absolutely delicious!
D As it is

25. Sentence 8 contains which type of error?

A Subject/verb agreement error
B Misplaced modifier
C Comma usage error
D Error in parallel structure

Answers to Chapter 1 Exercises

1. **(C)** The sentence contains a comma splice; you must end the first thought before beginning the second. Answer *A* creates a fused sentence, and answer *B* contains a comma error (comma before an adverb clause).

2. **(A)** The commas in a series of items should continue up to the conjunction. Answer *B* incorrectly uses a semicolon in a series, and answer *C* creates a fragment.

3. **(B)** Always use commas around a parenthetical expression. You would not use semicolons around such a phrase, and you must place a comma on both sides unless the parenthetical expression ends the sentence.

4. **(B)** The term *easy* must be changed to *easily* because it is used as an adverb telling how the concept came to her. Answer *A* uses *easily* but neglects to show the comma necessary when you use a coordinating conjunction between two complete thoughts.

5. **(D)** This is correctly written. A comma, no other mark of punctuation, follows an introductory adverb clause.

6. **(A)** The word *girls* needs to show ownership. Because the soccer belongs to all the girls, the apostrophe is placed after the *s* in the plural words *girls*. Answer *B* indicates ownership by one girl, and answer *C* contains a word that is not an acceptable usage.

7. **(C)** The word *finally* is being used as an introductory element to introduce the last topic in the letter. A semicolon would not be used after one word, and the use of an exclamation point makes the reader wonder if Eleanor has only now gotten around to being ambitious.

8. **(B)** The subject *she* is singular; therefore, its verb must be singular. The tense cannot be changed to past (*A*), and choice *C* actually says, "She has has. . . ."

9. **(B)** Periods and commas always go inside closing quote marks. Further, answer *A* uses more than one punctuation mark where only one is required, and answer *C* indicates the use of single quote marks, which are not needed in the sentence.

10. **(A)** *Eleanor* is singular, so she *values* education.

11. **(B)** You are to use semicolons to separate items in a series when they already contain commas. There should be semicolons after *wife*, *children*, and *neighbors*.

12. **(B)** The titles of plays are italicized, not quoted.

13. **(D)** The wording should not be changed. Answers *A* and *C* indicate the need for a tense shift. Answer *B* indicates a shift from singular to plural, and the subject *cast* is singular—one group.

14. **(A)** Remember that you use a colon before a list of items only when it follows a complete thought. You do not insert a colon between a verb and a list of items following it. The sentence flows without needing punctuation before the list.

15. **(B)** This is similar to the answer for number 14. The first statement is a complete thought introducing a kind of list, a statement that explains the point just addressed.

16. **(B)** You should not end a sentence with a preposition alone.

17. **(D)** The person being described by the statement, "When calling for information," is not in the sentence. The descriptor has no referent, so one must be added. If the

referent were elsewhere in the sentence, this would be a misplaced modifier. There is no subject/verb agreement problem, nor is there a need for a comma.

18. **(B)** Second person should not be used in formal writing. Therefore, the third-person pronoun *one* is appropriate as the subject. Because the subject is singular, the pronoun used later to refer to it must also be singular (his/her).

19. **(C)** Because sentence #2 uses the singular term *portfolio*, sentence #3 should begin with a singular reference pronoun (*it*). Also, the possessive term *ones* requires an apostrophe (*one's*).

20. **(A)** *Portfolios* is plural, not possessive, so it should not contain an apostrophe. Also, the singular verb *documents* must be changed to the plural form *document* to agree with the plural subject *portfolios*.

21. **(C)** The plural verb *help* must remain because it must agree with the compound subject (*experiences*, *activities*, and *courses*). Also, because the pronoun *one* is used as an antecedent, the singular pronoun *his/her* must be chosen.

22. **(B)** No apostrophes are needed in the names because they are all simply plural, not possessive. Further, the comma after *counselors* is needed because it follows two prepositional phrases serving as the introduction to the second half of the compound sentence.

23. **(A)** The word *exams* is plural, not possessive. Answer *B* shows a plural possessive form of the word *exams*, and answer *C* contains a format that would never be used.

24. **(B)** The sentence contains a run-on error that needs to be corrected. Answer *A* is still a run on, and although answer *B* has the run-on corrected, it shows a capital letter in the word after the semicolon. You would only capitalize the word after a semicolon if that word were normally capitalized.

25. **(B)** Sentence 8 begins with a participial phrase, *working late*. That phrase should be modifying Emily (*I* in the note), but it appears to be modifying the mother. There is no error is subject/verb agreement, and the commas are correctly used: one after the introductory participial phrase and one in front of the conjunction that connects the two independent thoughts.

Chapter 2
Usage

This chapter still deals with grammar, but it focuses on various individual writing concerns rather than one major section, such as punctuation. The purpose of this chapter is to make you aware of some potential usage errors that can occur in your writing.

2.1 Words Often Confused/Misspelled

There are several sets of words that are often used incorrectly, one from a pair being substituted for another. If you become familiar with the definitions, parts of speech, and usage of the following terms, you will avoid these errors and be a better writer.

it's	a contraction for *it is* **(It's time for us to leave for work.)**
its	possessive form of the pronoun *it* **(The dog lost its new bone.)**
they're	a contraction for *they are* **(I wonder if they're ready yet?)**
their	possessive form of the pronoun *they* **(I just love their new living room furniture!)**
you're	a contraction for *you are* **(Did you say you're visiting Montana this summer?)**
your	possessive form of the pronoun *you* **(I really enjoyed your club's presentation.)**
who's	a contraction for *who is* **(Who's opening at the concert next week?)**
whose	possessive form of the pronoun *who* **(I need to know whose boots were left in the gymnasium.)**
desert	a verb meaning *to abandon*; a noun meaning *a dry region* **(I hope the main character does not desert the dog in the desert!)**
dessert	a noun meaning a confectionery treat **(If you eat all of your supper, you may have dessert.)**
to	a preposition used to begin a prepositional phrase **(I went to the picnic yesterday.)**
too	an adverb meaning *also, more than enough*, or *more than necessary* **(I love piano lessons, and Edna does too.)** **(I believe you have put too much sugar in this coffee.)**
two	the written form of the number *2* **(Thomas owns two cats.)**
a	an article (adjective) used before a word beginning with a *consonant sound* **(John lifted a heavy crate for the elderly woman.)**
an	an article (adjective) used before a word beginning with a *vowel sound.* **(Students will have an essay due next week.)** **(Dawn has an hour to complete the exam.)**

affect	a verb meaning *to influence* or *change* **(How will the storm affect your plans for the outdoor celebration?)**
effect	a noun meaning the *result* of some change or influence **(What was the effect of the storm on your plans?)**
between	a preposition used to refer to only two people, places, or things **(Keep this secret between the two of you!)**
among	a preposition used to refer to more than two people, places, or things **(This secret will be kept among the members of the group.)**
fewer	an adjective used to describe individual items that can be counted **(There are fewer students here today than there were yesterday.)**
less	an adjective used to describe a total sum or portion that tells *how much.* **(We have less time than we had yesterday to do our work.)**
number	a noun used to refer to individual items that can be counted **(The number of students in the contest has increased since yesterday.)**
amount	a noun used to refer to a total sum or portion that tells *how much.* **(The amount of sugar in the cookies is listed on the recipe.)**
good	an adjective used to describe a noun or pronoun **(This pizza is really good.)**
well	an adverb describing how something is done **(This pizza was prepared well.)**

Note: *Well* may also be used as an adjective meaning *healthy*: **I don't feel well.**

lie	a verb meaning to recline or sleep **(I want to lie down; I usually lie down in the afternoon.)**
lay	a verb meaning to put something somewhere **(Just lay the book on the table.)**
sit	a verb meaning to rest in a seat, such as a chair **(I sit on the left side of the classroom at school.)**
set	a verb meaning to put something somewhere **(Just set the dishes on the shelf, and set the glasses on the counter.)**
rise	a verb meaning to move upward **(I have seen the sun rise in the sky.)**
raise	a verb meaning to move something upward **(I will raise my hand to show the teacher I have an answer.)**

Notice that the verbs *lay, set*, and *raise* all involve an action toward an object, called the *direct object.* The direct object receives the action of the verb. I *lay something* down, *set something* down, and *raise something* upward. The verbs *lie, sit*, and *rise* do not take direct objects. In other words, they are simply performed; they are not performed *on* an object. I lie down; I do not lie something down.

2.2 Verb Tense/Irregular Verbs

In Chapter 1, you reviewed the role of verbs. Action verbs show the action of the subject, and linking verbs express a state of being or link the subject to a descriptor in the predicate. Because action or state of being (associated with linking verbs) can take place at different times, verbs have the characteristic of *tense.* If an action is occurring now, the verb is said to be in present tense. If the action occurred yesterday or last year, the action is said to be in past tense. The form of a verb changes based on its tense, and it is important to remember that tense must remain consistent in writing. Consider the following sentence:

We watched the circus, and then we walk to the snack stand for popcorn.

The first verb, *watched*, occurred in the past. If people *watched* the circus, then they performed that action previous to the present. Look at the second verb, *walk.* This verb is in the present tense format. If it were in the past, it would have been written in a different format, *walked.* When writing an essay, you must be sure to use the same verb tense. Of course, there are instances where a verb change is appropriate. Look at the following sentence:

This morning, I saw a bird in the tree, but now, I only see a nest.

Notice that the first verb, *saw,* is in the past tense, but the second verb, *see*, is in the present tense. This is appropriate because the first sentence occurred earlier in the day. The second sentence is occurring now. The point is that when you are writing, you should monitor your verb usage to be sure that you do not switch unnecessarily between present and past, that is, unless the sentence indicates the need to do so.

Another problem that students have with verbs is their tendency to use irregular verbs incorrectly when tenses change. To understand this, you need to know the difference between *regular* and *irregular* verbs.

Regular verbs form their past and past participles by adding –d or –ed to the base, or present, form. The past participle form of a verb is that form that is used after one of three helping verbs: *have, has*, or *had.*

For example, the base form of the verb *dancing* is *dance*. The past tense form is *danced,* and the past participle form is also (have) *danced.* Most verbs are regular and follow this pattern. Have you ever heard a young child use a past participle form incorrectly? A toddler might say "I *goed* to the store" because that pattern has been evident in all the surrounding adult speech. Those few verbs that are not regular are called irregular because they do not follow the –d/–ed pattern. They change more dramatically. These verbs simply have to be learned. Most students actually know them; they just have to make a habit of using them correctly. Look at the following example:

I done the work.

The base form of the verb done is *do*. To find out what form needs to be used, first decide what tense to use. You know the action already occurred, so the tense will be past. Now, try using the following pattern, filling in the correct words from memory:

I *(present)* the work; I *(past)* the work; I *(past participle)* the work.

I *do* the work; I *did* the work; I have *done* the work.

If you try this pattern, you may recognize the correct format. Then, you can simply use the appropriate form in your writing. It does not hurt to try this with all verbs because it works with regular verbs as well. Following is a list of the most common irregular verbs. You can also check your English book for a more comprehensive list.

Base Form	Past Form	Past Participle Form
begin	began	(have) begun
blow	blew	(have) blown
break	broke	(have) broken
bring	brought	(have) brought
choose	chose	(have) chosen
do	did	(have) done

draw	drew	(have) drawn
drive	drove	(have) driven
eat	ate	(have) eaten
fall	fell	(have) fallen
fly	flew	(have) flown
freeze	froze	(have) frozen
give	gave	(have) given
go	went	(have) gone
grow	grew	(have) grown
hide	hid	(have) hidden
know	knew	(have) known
overdo	overdid	(have) overdone
ride	rode	(have) ridden
ring	rang	(have) rung
see	saw	(have) seen
shake	shook	(have) shaken
shrink	shrank	(have) shrunk
speak	spoke	(have) spoken
steal	stole	(have) stolen
swear	swore	(have) sworn
swim	swam	(have) swum
take	took	(have) taken
tear	tore	(have) torn
throw	threw	(have) thrown
wake	woke	(have) woken
wear	wore	(have) worn
write	wrote	(have) written

Most English books have a listing of common irregular verbs, so you can review them before your test. However, when you are actually writing your paper, you must pay special attention to the consistency of tense and the form of each verb.

Of course, there are additional tenses, such as *future* (action that will occur at some later date) and *progressive* (the –ing forms of verbs), but these rarely cause students the difficulty that past and past participle forms do.

For your assistance, here are the present, past, and past participle forms of the three troublesome verbs discussed earlier:

Present	**lie**	**lay**
Past	**lay**	**laid**
Past participle	**(have) lain**	**(have) laid**
Present	**sit**	**set**
Past	**sat**	**set**
Past participle	**(have) sat**	**(have) set**
Present	**rise**	**raise**
Past	**rose**	**raised**
Past participle	**(have) risen**	**(have) raised**

2.3 Pronoun Usage

One difficulty that students have with pronouns is using the correct form depending on sentence construction. Pronouns can be in the *nominative*, *objective*, or *possessive* case. Possessive pronouns don't normally cause much difficulty because their forms clearly indicate ownership. The following are possessive pronouns:

Singular possessive: my, mine, your, yours, his, her, hers, its

Plural possessive: our, ours, your, yours, their, theirs

The other two cases, however, are often confused. For example, you may not know whether to use the pronoun *I* or the pronoun *me* in a particular sentence. First, think about the difference between the nominative and objective cases. The nominative case of a pronoun is that form used when the pronoun serves as the subject in a sentence or clause. The objective case of a pronoun is that form used when the pronoun serves as the object in the sentence or clause. Here are the nominative and objective forms of personal pronouns:

Nominative singular: I, you, he, she, it

Nominative plural: we, you, they

Objective singular: me, you, him, her, it

Objective plural: us, you, them

Look at the following example:

I bought a gift for him.

In this sentence, the pronoun *him* serves as the object in the prepositional phrase *for him*. Therefore, you would choose *him* instead of *he.* You will probably not have difficulty when the pronoun is used alone; however, when the pronoun is combined with another noun, such as in a compound subject, you may not be sure which case to use. Look at the next example:

My mother and I went shopping.

In this sentence, both my *mother* and *I* are subjects. Because you are placing the pronoun *I* in the subject, you know that you must select the nominative form, not the objective form *me*.

Please save the directions for Father and me.

Now the pronoun is serving in an object position, so it must take the objective form. To help you determine quickly which pronoun is correct in a compound situation, try this hint: Say the sentence to yourself, and leave out the noun. In your mind, only include the pronoun, and try both the nominative and objective forms. The correct one will sound natural, and the incorrect one will sound very odd. Look at the example:

Jessica and me have a project due on Thursday.

Try saying the sentence to yourself without the noun *Jessica*. You will have two choices:

Me have a project due on Thursday.

I have a project due on Thursday.

I is obviously the correct choice, so you know that the correct subject phrase is *Jessica and I.*

2.4 Comparisons

When you use adjectives and adverbs to make comparisons, you must remember that they have three forms: positive (the base form of the word), comparative (used in a comparison between two), and superlative (used in a comparison involving three or more). Here are some examples:

Positive	Comparative	Superlative
nice	nicer	nicest
fresh	fresher	freshest
beautiful	more beautiful	most beautiful
careful	more careful	most careful

Notice that two of the terms form their comparative and superlative forms by adding –er and –est. The others have *more* and *most* added to their base forms. You will usually know which form to use based on the sound. For example, you would not say that one friend was "energeticer" than another; you would say that one friend was more energetic than another. In case you are unsure, however, you can rely on some basic rules:

- Most one-syllable adjectives and adverbs will add –er and –est to create their comparative and superlative forms.
- Adjectives and adverbs with more than two syllables will use *more* and *most* to create their comparative and superlative forms.
- Adjectives and adverbs with two syllables may use either method; if you have access to a dictionary, you can check the format. If not, you will have to rely on sound and prior knowledge.
- No matter which method you choose, be sure that you do only one or the other. Don't, for example, choose to use the word *more* and also add –er to a word. Look at the following example:

My hands got more dirtier than yours in the garden.

You would either say your hands were *more dirty* or that they were *dirtier*.

2.5 Double Negatives

To understand this concept, think about the field of math. If you multiply a negative number by another negative number, you get a positive number. In other words, the negatives cancel each other out. The same concept holds true in grammar. If you use two negative words where only one is needed, they will cancel each other out, and the result will be a poorly worded sentence with a meaning other than the intended one. The use of double negatives is considered poor format. Consider the following example:

I have not found no bargains today.

If you have not found something, then the point is made, and another negative word is unnecessary. To go on to use the "no" to describe *bargains* creates the double negative. Actually, this sentence means that you did find bargains. There are two ways to correct this sentence:

I have not found bargains today.

I have found no bargains today.

Each sentence contains one negative that helps the reader understand that you have not been successful in your search for bargains. Be careful to avoid the use of double negatives in your writing.

2.6 Capitalization

There are lots of rules regarding capitalization, but you already know and follow most of them. You learned many years ago that you capitalize nouns that name specific people, places, and things. For example, you would not capitalize the first letter in the word *girl*, but you would capitalize the letter M in *Mary* because the noun names a specific girl. You also learned that you capitalize the titles of books, movies, CDs, and magazines. Most rules of capitalization are easy to understand and use, and you have probably mastered them over the years. However, there are a few that continue to cause students difficulty, so those will be covered in this brief chapter review.

Geographic locations: You capitalize the first letter in geographic locations (north, south, east, west) only if you are using them as part of another proper noun, such as the name of a street, or if you are using them to denote a particular part of the country. If you are simply stating a direction, then you do not use capital letters. Look at these examples:

I live on *East* Hanover Road.

Someday, I would love to live in the *East*.

To get to Smith Road, travel *east* for 12 miles.

Notice that in the first sentence, *East* is part of the name of the road. In the second sentence, the speaker is designating the *East* as a particular part of the country. When you read that sentence, you may imagine certain states that you believe comprise the *East*. The third sentence is simply using the word *east* to denote a direction of travel.

Family relationships: Many students think that words that show a family relationship—such as *mom, dad*, and *aunt*—are always capitalized, but this is not so. You capitalize these words only when they are part of a name, such as *Aunt* Mary, or when they are not preceded by a possessive pronoun, such as *my* or *your*. Consider the examples:

My Uncle Thomas lives in New York City.

My uncle is a veterinarian.

I'm sure my dad will be here soon.

I'm sure Dad will be here soon.

In sentence one, *Uncle* is part of the name, so even though it follows a possessive pronoun, it is still capitalized. In sentence two, *uncle* is not part of a name, and it follows a possessive pronoun, so it is not capitalized. In the third sentence, *dad* is used after a possessive pronoun, so it is not capitalized. Finally, in the fourth example, *Dad* is capitalized because it is used alone, not following a possessive pronoun.

Another way to quickly determine whether to capitalize words that show a family relationship (not used as part of proper names) is to see if using an actual name in the sentence makes sense. If so, then the word should be capitalized. Look at the examples below:

Today, my *dad* installed our new dishwasher.

Today, *Dad* installed our new dishwasher.

Suppose the father's name is Tom. Try saying the sentences with this name:

Today, my *Tom* installed our new dishwasher.

Today, *Tom* installed our new dishwasher.

You can see the first one makes no sense. You can use any name to try this quick check, but be sure that you don't change any other words in the sentence. Simply replace the word that shows the family relationship with a proper name.

School subjects: Capitalize school subjects that are followed by numbers, and capitalize all school subjects that name languages. General school subjects are not proper and should not be capitalized. Here are some examples:

I take *English*, algebra, history, and *Chemistry I*.

Don't be concerned about this looking inconsistent. *English* is capitalized because it's a language, and *Chemistry I* is capitalized because it is followed by the Roman numeral I, which denotes a specific chemistry course, not a general one. The other two subjects—algebra and history—are general terms.

Brand names: You capitalize brand names, but you do not capitalize the actual type of product. Examples follow:

Angela loves to use *Campbell's soups* in her recipes.

Have you ever tried the new *Swiffer dusters*?

***York Swoops* are a new type of mint chocolate candy.**

In the third sentence, the *Swoops* is part of the name. It is capitalized because it is a specific candy name created by the York company. If the sentence had simply named a general candy, such as *mints*, then the word would not have been capitalized.

Titles: As discussed earlier, you are probably aware that you should capitalize all titles. However, you may not be aware that not every word is capitalized. The rule for titles basically says that you capitalize the first word, the last word, and all important words in between. How do you know which words are "important"? It is easier to think about which words are considered unimportant: articles, prepositions, and conjunctions of four letters or fewer. Remember, however, if one such word is the first or last, then it is still capitalized.

Have you read *The Land Before Time*?

My favorite book is *Goldilocks and the Three Bears*.

***For Whom the Bell Tolls* is a wonderful movie!**

Letter closings: When you write the closing to a business or friendly letter, you capitalize only the first word of a multiword closing. For example, if you close with the phrase "Very truly yours," only the first word is capitalized. The other words begin with lowercase letters. Here are some other examples:

Truly yours,

Sincerely yours,

With appreciation,

Very sincerely yours,

Chapter 2 Exercises

Read the following letter, and then use it to answer questions 1–8.

September 25, 2003

Matfield's Restaurant
Mr. John Sykes, Manager
226 east Fifth Street
Atlanta, Georgia 22786

Dear Mr. Sykes:

(1) On a recent visit to you're Restaurant, I was surprised to see that you no longer offer the daily lunch specials. **(2)** I have ate lunch their every Wednesday for the past ten years and have always enjoyed the value and taste of your lunches. **(3)** Now, however, the value is gone. **(4)** For example, a open-faced roast beef sandwich used to cost $1.20, but now it costs $2.50. **(5)** Its difficult for those of us on fixed incomes to afford the higher prices. **(6)** I first ate in your diner ten years ago when my Uncle took me their for lunch. **(7)** Ever since, I have gave you my business. **(8)** Please reconsider your decision. **(9)** There is a huge amount of people who will have to stop eating they're if you don't. **(10)** Thank you for your time and consideration.

Sincerely,

Mr. Daniel Etheridge
Atlanta

1. **In sentence 1, how is <u>visit to you're Restaurant,</u> correctly written?**
   A visit to you're restaurant,
   B visit to your restaurant,
   C visit to your Restaurant,
   D As it is

2. **In sentence 2, how is <u>I have ate lunch their every Wednesday</u> correctly written?**
   A I have eaten lunch there every Wednesday
   B I have eaten lunch their every Wednesday
   C I have ate lunch there every Wednesday
   D As it is

3. **In sentence 4, how is <u>a open-faced roast beef sandwich</u> correctly written?**
   A an open-faced roast beef sandwich
   B an open faced roast beef sandwich
   C a open, faced roast beef sandwich
   D As it is

4. **In sentence 5, how is <u>Its difficult for those of us on</u> correctly written?**
   A Its difficult for those, of us, on
   B It's difficult for those of us on
   C It's difficult for those, of us, on
   D As it is

5. **How is sentence 6 correctly written?**
   A I first ate in your diner ten years ago when my uncle took me their for lunch.
   B I first ate in your diner ten years ago when my uncle took me there for lunch.
   C I first ate in your diner ten years ago when my Uncle took me there for lunch.
   D As it is

6. How is sentence 7 correctly written?

A Ever since, I given you my business.
B Ever since, I gave you my business.
C Ever since, I have given you my business.
D As it is

7. In sentence 9, how is <u>There is a huge amount of people who will have to stop eating they're</u> correctly written?

A There is a huge amount of people who will have to stop eating there
B There is a huge number of people who will have to stop eating their
C There is a huge number of people who will have to stop eating there
D As it is

8. In the address, how is <u>226 east Fifth Street</u> correctly written?

A 226 east 5th Street
B 226 East Fifth street
C 226 East Fifth Street
D As it is

Eight-year-old Dana and her seven-year-old cousin Alex decided to play school. They wanted to have rules for the students, so they wrote ten class guidelines on a poster board. However, they made some usage errors. Use their play list to answer questions 9–12.

1. **Arrive on time.**
2. **Set in assigned seat.**
3. **Lie pencils on desk when not writing.**
4. **Always write in good english.**
5. **Ask Teacher before speaking.**
6. **Use pass too go to the bathroom.**
7. **Don't take no one else's things.**
8. **Always use good manners.**
9. **Share toys between all children.**
10. **Turn work in on time.**

9. Which of the following rules contains an error in capitalization?

A 2
B 5
C 8
D 9

10. Which of the following rules contains an error in verb usage?

A 3
B 6
C 9
D 10

11. Which of the following rules contains no errors in usage?

A 2
B 6
C 7
D 8

12. Which rule contains use of a double negative?

A 4
B 6
C 7
D 9

Read the following, and use it to answer questions 13–15.

Attention members of the senior class:

(1) Your votes for senior superlatives are due on Friday, May 21. **(2)** Each of you was gave a list of superlative categories last week, but one category, "Most Nice," was not included. **(3)** Please add this category and make your selections before submitting you're papers. **(4)** Votes will be tabulated before the senior assembly next week. **(5)** Turn all votes in to Mrs. Smith in room 229. Thank you.

13. In sentence 2, how is <u>Each of you was gave a list</u> correctly written?

A Each of you was gaven a list
B Each of you was given a list
C Each of you has given a list
D As it is

14. In sentence 2, how is <u>but one category, "Most Nice," was not included.</u> correctly written?

A but one category, "Most Nicest," was not included.
B but one category, "Nicest," was not included.
C but one category, "Nicest", was not included.
D As it is

15. In sentence 3, how is <u>make your selections before submitting you're papers</u> correctly written?

A make you're selections before submitting your papers
B make you're selections before submitting you're papers
C make your selections before submitting your papers
D As it is

Answers to Chapter 2 Exercises

1. **(B)** The contraction *you're* should be changed to the possessive pronoun *your*, and the noun *restaurant* should not be capitalized because it does not name a specific restaurant.
2. **(A)** The verb should be in the past participle form (have eaten), and the possessive pronoun *their* should be changed to the word *there*, meaning "place."
3. **(A)** You must change the article *a* to *an* because it precedes a vowel sound, and the compound adjective *open-faced* must be hyphenated because it precedes the noun it describes.
4. **(B)** The possessive pronoun *Its* must be changed to the contraction *It's*, which stands for *It is*; also, there is no reason to separate the prepositional phrase *of us* with commas.
5. **(B)** The word *uncle* should not be capitalized here because it is neither part of a name nor is it being used in direct address. Also, the possessive pronoun *their* should be changed to the word *there*, meaning "place."
6. **(C)** The verb form needs to be changed to the past participle form, *have given.*
7. **(C)** The noun *amount* must be changed to *number* because people can be counted, and the contraction *they're* must be changed to the word *there*, meaning "place."
8. **(C)** The entire street name should be capitalized.
9. **(B)** *Teacher* is a general noun and should not be capitalized.
10. **(A)** The verb *lie* should be changed to *lay* because the action is being performed on the pencil (direct object).
11. **(D)** Sentence 2 contains an error in verb usage (*set* should be *sit*), sentence 6 contains a word error (*too* should be *to*), and sentence 7 contains a double negative.
12. **(C)** The double negative occurs in rule 7. It should read, "Don't take anyone else's things."
13. **(B)** The verb should be in the past participle form, *was given. Gaven* is not a word, and *has given* is not correct because the students *received* the superlatives; they did not give them.
14. **(B)** The phrase "Most Nice" should be changed to "Nicest" because the base word *nice* is a one-syllable word. Answer *C* is not correct because the required comma has been placed outside the closing quote marks, not inside as required.
15. **(C)** The contraction *you're* must be changed to the possessive pronoun *your.*

Chapter 3
The Writing Process

When you are given a writing task, you may wonder where to begin, or you may feel that you don't know enough about the topic to write about it. However, you *can* write, and you can write *well*. Writing is a process, and if you follow the steps of the process, you will produce a good product. Also, as with any other activity in life, the more you practice, the better you will become. The purpose of this chapter is to review and illustrate the writing process using one particular topic, but you can follow the same procedure using any topic presented to you.

3.1 STEP I: Thinking About the Purpose of the Writing Task

When you take the SOL direct writing test, you will be given a writing *prompt,* or topic for your essay. When you look at the prompt, you need to think about the purpose for the paper you are about to write. Is it to persuade, explain or inform, describe, or narrate? Knowing *why* you are writing helps you decide *what* to write and *how* to begin planning. Suppose you are given the following prompt:

Write about your goals for the future. Think about what career you want, and think about what you want your life as an adult to involve.

This prompt includes not only the topic for writing but also some hints to start your thinking process. Be sure that you read the entire prompt and use all of the information available to you because the evaluators will be analyzing your essay for references to the information requested in the prompt. So, pay careful attention to the wording. The suggested topic makes reference to the following: (1) goals, (2) career, and (3) your life as an adult. Goals is the main topic, and career and life are subtopics within that major area. Now is the time to think about the purpose of the essay:

1. **Persuasion: Is the purpose to persuade others about your goals for yourself? Will you use logical and/or emotional examples to support your opinion?**
2. **Explanation: Is the purpose to inform the reader of your goals and explain them? Will you provide reasons to support your ideas?**
3. **Description: Is the purpose to describe (through sensory details) your goals? Will you use words that appeal to the senses of taste, touch, smell, sight, and hearing to bring a *picture* to the minds of the readers?**
4. **Narration: Is the purpose to write a story about your goals? Will you entertain the reader with a story or anecdote?**

The focus of the suggested prompt in this chapter is to explain and inform. The prompt is requesting a discussion of what you believe to be your goals for the future. The subcategories that prompt you to "think about what career you want" and "think about what you want your life as an adult to involve" imply a request for explanation. Determining the purpose of the writing is a major step because it automatically gives focus to a developing paper.

3.2 STEP II: Making a Personal Connection with the Topic

If you can connect yourself personally with the topic, you will write with more reality and conviction because the thoughts will come from within you. The topic for this practice discussion already connects to you because it asks for your personal goals, but don't treat the need for further personal connection here too lightly. If you simply write about general goals that you believe every student should have, your paper will not be as solid or thorough as it could be. In other words, the goals, career, and life you describe should be truly *yours*. When you think about the type of career you want, imagine yourself training for that career and actually performing that job or service; when you think about the life you want, imagine yourself living in a particular area of the world, having certain hobbies, or meeting the ideal mate. These are *your* goals. Can you imagine how much more interesting and informative the discussion will be if the goals come from your heart and mind?

At this point, you may be wondering how to make other possible topics personal. Well, in some situations, you may have to really use your imagination. For example, if a prompt instructs you to write about the most serious problem in the world today, how will you make a personal connection? You can think about many of the world's current problems, such as overpopulation, pollution, international relations, poverty, and crime. You can continue to list possible topics until you have a long list from which to choose. Once you have the list, you can think about which problem you might have experienced during your teenage years. Perhaps someone you know served in the military during a conflict with another country. Perhaps you know someone who was the victim of a burglary. Maybe you have worked with a group that has adopted a highway and has been involved in cleaning up litter along the roadway shoulders. The point is that if you can think about a major world problem of which you have some personal knowledge, the purpose of the paper (expository, here) becomes more realistic to you and helps you to focus on details that will add strength to the product. Perhaps the problem you write about will not be the one you absolutely consider the worst, but it will be one that you consider very serious and one that has made a lasting impression on you.

Suppose that another prompt instructs you to convince another teenager not to smoke (purpose: persuasion). Think about those in your life who are or who have been affected by smoking. That will give you some personal connection with which to begin writing. Suppose that you have never known another teenager who smoked, and no one in your family has ever smoked. From where will you get a personal connection? You have seen many advertisements and heard many speakers in school talk about the dangers of smoking. Put yourself in that place. Imagine that a friend or a family member were facing an illness due to the use of tobacco. Imagine how you would feel. What would you tell that person? Use those feelings to write this fictional paper and convince your teenage friend to stop smoking.

Consider one more example. Imagine that the prompt asks you to talk about the person you most admire. Right off the bat, you might think about a famous person, such as George Washington or Thomas Jefferson. These are wonderful and admirable people, to be sure, but do you know enough about them, without consulting an encyclopedia or other reference book, to write a solid essay at this time? Perhaps it would be more advisable to settle on a person (perhaps even fictional, if the prompt allows) that you have known personally or have studied at length. Remember that you are expected to write a solid essay with a great deal of support and detail, so you must choose your focus wisely.

For any topic given, you can either reflect on or create a personal connection. Once you have accomplished that, the details will flow more easily, and the paper will begin to take form.

3.3 STEP III: Brainstorming

This part of the paper is fun because it allows you to let your thoughts go in any direction with regard to the subject. There are formats for brainstorming, but more important than the chosen format is the commitment to this step in the process. If you simply begin writing, you will lose the opportunity to imagine and create details that will make the final product much more effective. Brainstorming simply involves thinking about the topic and writing down those thoughts. Though there are many ways to record these ideas, it is important to do so in a way that will help lead to their organization. One effective brainstorming technique is clustering. To cluster, you simply draw a circle or square in the middle of the page and insert the main topic. Then, you begin to draw "branches" out from the topic to record your subtopics. From the subtopics, you begin drawing branches to record details for those ideas, and so on. Look at the sample clustering activity on page 38 for the prompt about goals:

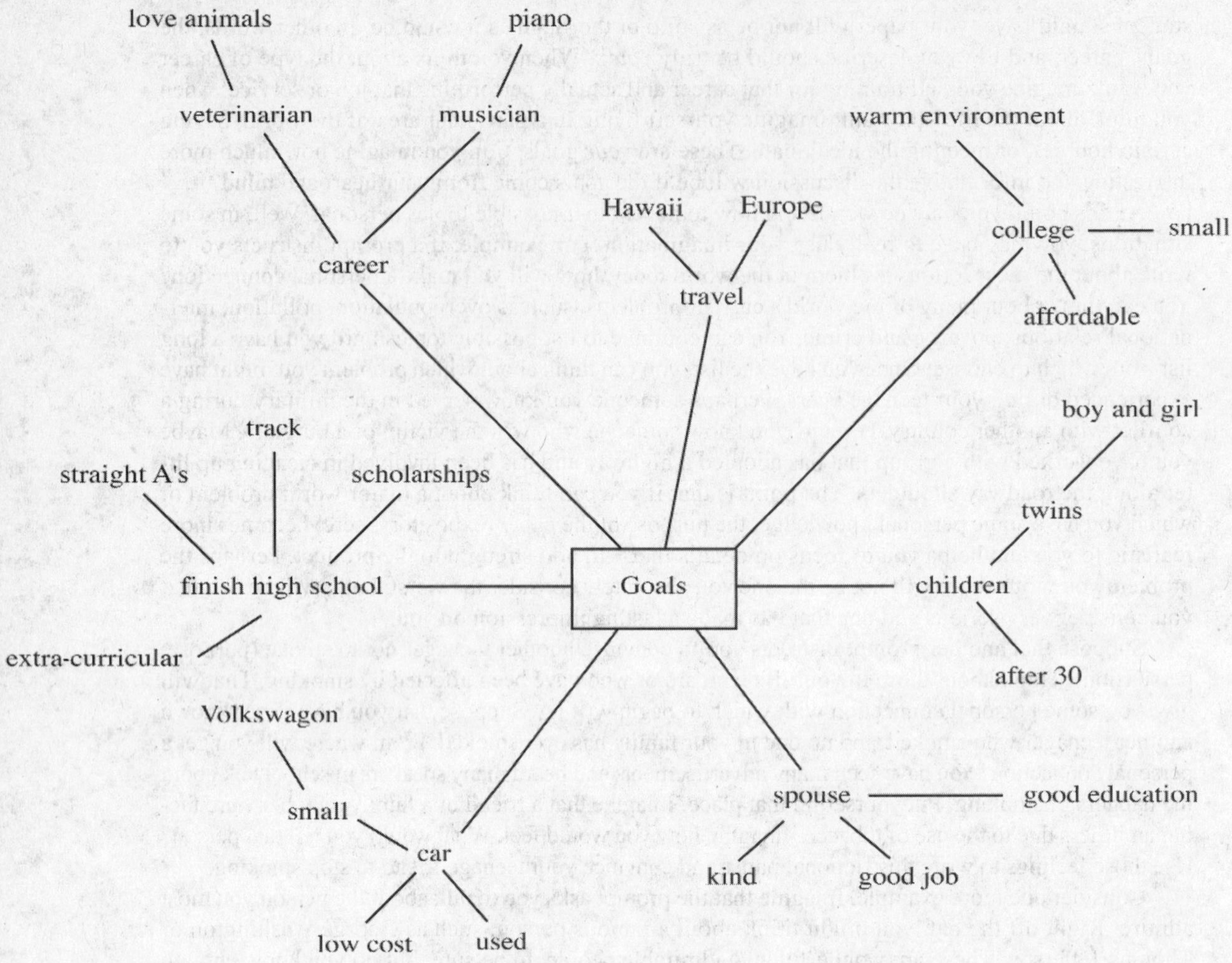

Notice that the main topic of *goals* is in the center position. The subtopics, or goals to be discussed, are connected by branches. They are *car, finish high school, career, travel, college, children*, and *spouse*. Of course, you could probably come up with several more depending on how much time you spend on the brainstorming. Then, notice that for each subtopic, certain details are listed. This step is critical because if you simply note large categories, what will you do when you get to the written portion? You have to eventually create details, and if you do it now, during the planning stage, you have the opportunity to organize them and fill in any gaps before you begin writing.

3.4 STEP IV: Outlining

Now that you have completed your brainstorming, you are ready to organize what you have written in preparation to begin the actual essay. It is important to remember that you do not have to include every aspect of the brainstorming in the outline and essay. The brainstorming stage is simply to get the ideas flowing and give you time to reflect on the subject before starting the essay itself. It is important, however, to take the time to organize what you will write before you begin. If you do not, your essay will not flow effectively. Many students do not take the time to brainstorm and outline, but if you do, then you will find that the bulk of the work is done, and the essay falls easily into place.

As you look at the sample brainstorming, begin thinking about which categories are similar and which are different. See if you can form groups of similar ideas. For example, both the *high school* and *college* categories of goals fall under a more major heading of *education.* Likewise, the *spouse* and *children* categories are more related to personal goals. Most essays contain a minimum of five paragraphs. The first is the introduction, the middle three make up the body, and the fifth is the conclusion. You must always introduce and conclude your work so that you ease the reader both into and out of the topic. As you look at the web, try to imagine three different areas of goals that can be used to form the body of the paper. Consider this: (1) educational goals, (2) personal goals, and (3) career goals. This is only one suggestion. There are many possibilities, but the main purpose is to organize the categories into groups for the body paragraphs.

Once you have analyzed your brainstorming web of ideas for categories, you may begin composing the outline. Consider the following sample outline:

I. Introduction
II. Educational goals
    A. High school
        1. Grades
        2. Extracurricular activities
        3. Track
    B. College
        1. Size
        2. Warm climate
        3. Cost
III. Career goals
    A. Music
        1. Lessons
        2. Goals
    B. Veterinarian
        1. My pets
        2. Love of animals
IV. Personal goals
    A. Spouse
        1. Kind
        2. Good education
        3. Good job
    B. Children
        1. Age 30
        2. Twins
    C. Travel
        1. Hawaii
        2. Europe
V. Conclusion

Roman numerals are used for main headings, capital letters are used for subheadings, and numbers are used for categories within the subheadings. Notice that the format of the essay is now organized for you, thanks to the time you spent preparing. All the small details that you have included will help you to explain and provide support for your major ideas.

You not only have a full body but also know the order in which you will discuss the items so the information will follow a logical pattern. These goals are organized by *education*, *career,* and *personal*, but they could be organized in other ways, depending on the order in which you hope to accomplish them. It seems logical to see education as a goal before a career and a career as a goal before marriage and children. If all of the goals you intend to discuss are personal, then you will organize them in the order that you feel makes the most sense to you. Suppose you are writing a description of a car, and you plan to discuss the interior, the body, and the stereo system. If you describe for the reader the great stereo, then move "outside" to write about the body, and then return "inside" to discuss the great leather seats, the body of your work will not follow a logical pattern. Take the reader on a smooth journey through the work. You can first discuss the leather interior and then move to a specific feature of the interior, the stereo, and then move outside to the body of the vehicle. You not only will have a logical pattern but also will leave the reader, at the end of the essay, with a mental picture of the full vehicle. Organization is a necessity for effective writing.

There are four basic organizational styles: *order of importance, logical order, chronological order,* and *spatial order*. As the writer, you must choose the style that will provide the most effective paragraph development. *Order of importance* arranges the details from most to least important or least to most important, depending on whether you want to begin or end your paragraph with the heaviest impact. This arrangement of details is very much up to the writer. *Logical order* calls for details to be arranged into logical groups in order to show relationships among details. For example, if you were writing a paper on the negative aspects of smoking and you decided to include *yellow teeth, smelly clothing, early facial wrikles,* and *cost,* you might recognize that several of the aspects relate to physical effects while one relates to finances. This grouping helps you determine how to order the details for the most fluid style. *Chronological order* lists details according to how they occur in time. Stories, historial information, and directions that involve a process all use chronological order. Finally, *spatial order* considers how details are arranged in space (left to right, etc.). You might use this type of order to describe your house or a scene in nature. If you were describing the scene outside your window, for example, you might use spatial order to talk first about the closest details near the window, then move to the yard beyond, and then, perhaps, to the mountain range in the far background. This order helps the reader to follow your "visual" description. Sometimes, more than one type of order is evidenced in writing, but the main point is that you should identify the type of order you plan to use in your own writing so that you can try to ensure a smooth, effective paper.

3.5 STEP V: Creating a Rough Draft

Now that you have prepared your work, you are ready to put it into the format of an actual essay. You should feel confident at this point because the main part of the work—the planning—is done. Now all you have to do is join all of the thoughts together, paying special attention to the format of the outline you have already prepared. Your first step is the *introduction.* The purpose of the introduction is to make the reader aware of the topic and purpose of the essay. There are several types of introductions, and the more experience you gain as a writer, the more you will branch out into this variety. For the purpose of this practice, however, you may rely on one general and common type: the funnel introduction.

The funnel introduction is given that name because its form resembles the "image" of a funnel—large at the top and small at the bottom. That means that the introduction starts with general information and "funnels" into the thesis statement—the sentence that basically states the purpose of the essay. Consider the following funnel introduction for the sample essay regarding goals:

> Setting goals is an important part of life, especially for teenagers. Making plans for their futures and thinking about what they want to do as adults will help them stay focused and, therefore, take advantage of opportunities available to help them reach success. Because I recognize the value of planning for my future, I have set clear educational, career, and personal goals.

Notice how the general information about teenagers and decisions funnels into the statement about the writer's goals for the future. The thesis statement (usually the last sentence of the introductory paragraph of an essay) states clearly the purpose of the work. You must remember, always, that the thesis statement sets the topic for the paper. If you write a paper that does not follow the thesis statement, you will have to either adjust the thesis statement or change some of the information in the body. Think of the thesis statement as a table of contents in a book. Once you read that information, you expect the book to contain those topics, in that order. Your essay should follow the same pattern. Consider, for example, the following thesis statement:

Owning a pet is extremely rewarding in many ways.

If this were the thesis statement of an essay, the writer could not include a paragraph about the costs involved in raising a pet because the thesis does not include that negative aspect. If the writer wants to include that aspect, then the thesis statement will need to be changed. For example:

Owning a pet can be costly, but it can also be extremely rewarding.

Just remember to make the thesis statement the main idea, the main "theme" of the essay. Knowledge of this purpose can also make reading others' essays and writings easier. If you know that the thesis indicates the direction and purpose of the work, then you are prepared for the topics that will be presented in the text.

The funnel introduction can be adapted to include such things as quotes or brief stories. For example:

> "Life is what you make it." I can still hear my grandmother's words ringing in my ears though she died when I was ten. She was an educator for most of her eighty-three years, and she always impressed upon me the idea that it was up to me to create a successful life for myself. Throughout my childhood, I remembered her words, and now that I am a teenager, I have set clear educational, career, and personal goals.

Just remember, the introduction should engage the reader from the beginning and should smoothly, interestingly lead to the thesis statement. The reader should know, after reading the introduction, the focus and direction of the essay.

Now that you have written the introduction, you are ready to tackle the body paragraphs. Look back at the outline. You know that you are going to introduce the topic of educational goals first. Just as the introduction has a focus—the thesis statement—each paragraph must also show direction. That is accomplished in the first sentence of each. The first sentence, called the *topic sentence*, tells the topic of that section of the essay. Because your first paragraph topic is *educational goals*, you should make that point clear to the reader. A poor writing style that many students use is writing as if they were talking directly to the reader: "In this paragraph, I will tell you about. . . ." You should never use this style. Instead, use the topic sentence to simply express the first idea. Here are some sample topic sentences for the first body paragraph. You can choose from various styles, but the purpose must be clear. Also, you must remember not to start giving specific information in this topic sentence. Its only purpose is to get the paragraph started. Here are some sample topic sentences for the paragraph on educational goals:

The first goal in my life is to complete my high school and college educations.

My first goal is educational.

First, I want to complete my education.

Education is the most important of my life's goals.

A poor example of a topic sentence would be the following:

First, I want to get a good education by earning good grades.

This is a poor example because it includes the first subcategory as well as the topic. You should keep these items separate.

Once you have introduced the topic, begin discussing the reasons to support the idea. The outline indicates that *grades, extracurricular activities*, and *track* will be discussed. Introduce each idea, and then provide a sentence or two of "discussion" for each. In other words, don't just write that you hope to earn good grades. Write about which grades you hope to earn and why good grades are an important part of your goal. For example:

> The first goal in my life is to complete my high school and college educations. To begin meeting this goal, I intend to try to earn good grades, at least all A's and B's. This is important because I want to keep a competitive grade point average so that I can be accepted into a good college. I also want to be sure that I am gaining a lot of knowledge from my courses, and I want to make my parents proud.

Notice that all of this information relates to grades. The paragraph has not gone into the next item, extracurricular activities. To move smoothly from one idea to the next both within paragraphs and between them, use *transitional phrases*, such as *another reason, in addition, also, secondly, next,* and *not only/but also.* Use of transitions helps create a smooth flow. Notice how transitions are used in the above example: "The first goal" (in the topic sentence) and "To begin" (in the first example). Notice how transitions (underlined) help move the following paragraph through all the examples.

> The first goal in my life is get a good education. To begin meeting this goal, I will try to earn good grades through the remainder of high school. This is important because I want to keep a competitive grade point average so that I can be accepted into a good college. I also want to participate in extracurricular activities. I know that involvement in clubs will help me earn the respect of my teachers, and it will also help me to gain experience in working with groups and school organizations. Furthermore, I plan to earn a place on the varsity track team. I love sports, and I believe tough physical training and competition help to instill positive values. Once I finish high school, I hope to attend a small college. I enjoy getting to know the people around me, and I don't think I would like a huge campus with classes of hundreds of students. I also would like to be in a part of the United States that is warm because I don't enjoy the cold weather. Finally, I have to consider the cost. I want to go to a well-respected college, but my family may not be able to afford a high tuition bill. Hopefully, my grades and accomplishments during high school will help me to earn scholarships that will help me meet this goal.

Another important element of style that you want to remember relates to sentence variety. Because of habit and ease of construction, most students begin sentences with the subject, follow that with the verb, and end with some combination of phrases. However, a paragraph made entirely of sentences in this format can be quite boring and choppy. You should try to vary the style of your sentences and remember that this can be an easy task. Below, you will find several strategies for varying the style. For each strategy, you will see a sentence in the usual subject/verb format and then a newer version applying the strategy introduced:

- Try starting some of the sentences with adjectives or adverbs.
  The boy ran happily toward the ice cream truck.
  Happily, the boy ran toward the ice cream truck.

- Try starting some of your sentences with phrases.
  You must work hard to achieve your goals.
  To achieve your goals, you must work hard.

- Try starting some of your sentences with subordinate clauses.
  Students must submit applications on time if they wish to get scholarships.
  If students wish to get scholarships, they must submit applications on time.

You can check for sentence variety in the revision stage of your paper (discussed later in the chapter). In other words, go ahead and let the ideas flow as you prepare your rough draft, but when you get to the final editing stages, look at your sentences to see if you can rearrange the wording to achieve sentence variety. Evaluators will be looking for this skill in your writing because sentence variety adds to the "flow" of your selection.

Another consideration with respect to sentence structure is length. If you vary the length of your sentences, they will combine within the paragraph to form a more interesting product. Below are some strategies for varying sentence length:

- Use coordinating conjunctions to combine sentences. Because coordinating conjunctions have their own meanings, they can create relationships between the sentences they combine.

  I would love to go to the circus with you, *but* I do not have any money.
  My little brother is not feeling well, *so* I need to stay home with him today.
  I would like to take an electronics course *and* then open a computer store.

- Use subordinate conjunctions to connect sentences. A subordinate conjunction, discussed in section 1.2, attaches itself to a sentence and "subordinates" it, creating a dependent clause (one that cannot stand alone as a sentence). Subordinate conjunctions also have their own meanings, so they can add a lot of power to a sentence combination.

  I have never owned a cat *even though* I think they are beautiful animals.
  ***Because* I received a gift certificate for Christmas, I think I will buy a new coat.**
  ***Unless* you are absent on Friday, you will need to submit the project.**
  Usually, Thomas gets a cold *whenever* the weather changes.

- Use a semicolon to connect two thoughts that are directly related to one another. A semicolon is more final than a comma but less final than a period. One point to remember is that the word after the semicolon is not capitalized unless it is a word that is normally capitalized, such as a proper noun or adjective.

  Edward will be home any minute; let's get ready to yell "Surprise!"
  The wedding was beautiful; I've never seen such a lovely gown.
  Let's go; I don't want to be late.

- Combine sentences by avoiding repetition and combining ideas. Below are some sentences revised to delete repetition and add variety.

  I would love to own a truck. The reason I want a truck is that I have a farm.
  ***Revised*: I would love to own a truck because I have a farm.**
  ***Revised for variety*: Because I have a farm, I would love to own a truck.**

  The book was old. The book was also torn. I bought the book from Al.
  ***Revised*: I bought the old, torn book from Al.**
  ***Revised for variety*: Though Al's book was old and torn, I bought it.**

One other strategy for making your sentences more interesting relates to word choice. As you revise your essay, look for situations where you can replace general terms with more specific ones. **This does not mean simply loading your essay with lots of adjectives and adverbs.** A well-chosen word—adjective, adverb, verb, or noun—can be extremely powerful. Look at the examples and revisions below:

The man walked through the halls.
***Revision*: The man shuffled through the halls.**

Doing her dance routine, Christina impressed the audience.
***Revision*: Performing her graceful routine, Christina impressed the audience.**

During winter, I love to watch the snowflakes fall to the ground.
***Revision*: During winter, I love to watch the snowflakes drift toward the ground.**

Just the simple change of a word can bring strength to a sentence, so when you read your rough draft, try making some simple changes to bring the sentences to life.

From this point, you are ready to move on to the next body paragraph. Don't forget the topic sentence, and don't forget to follow the outline prepared earlier.

> My next goal is to work in a wonderful career. My first choice would probably be the field of music because I have been taking lessons since I was ten years old. I enjoy music, and I would like to become better, perhaps even someday playing in an orchestra. My other major area of interest is veterinary medicine. I love animals, and I have always taken care of our family's pets. I know this career would take lot of training and education, but I think it would be worth the time and effort. Whether I decide to be a musician or a veterinarian, I know I will be happy.

Notice that each paragraph does not have to be extremely long. Each should just offer clear and thorough support for the topic sentence, and all statements should logically follow one another. You are now ready for the final body paragraph.

> In addition to my educational and career goals, I have personal goals. First, I want to meet and marry a wonderful spouse who is kind, well educated, and settled into a career. I want my mate to be a good person who has clear goals, just as I do. I also want to have children, but I plan to wait until after I am thirty because I don't want to be responsible for raising children until I have my education and career in place. When I do have children, however, I would love to have twins, a boy and a girl. Finally, it is my personal goal to travel. I have never been far from my home here in Virginia, so I would love to experience Hawaii and even Europe. I would enjoy seeing the lifestyles of others and visiting the sights of those places.

Notice the focused topic sentence stating the goal of the paragraph: personal goals. Also, notice the transitions that lead from thought to thought. Each point in the paragraph is supported by a sentence or two, and the organization is clear.

At this point, the essay is nearly complete. All it needs is a conclusion. You don't want to simply "drop off" and leave the reader hanging. When you were young, you might have ended an essay by writing something like, "This is the end of my essay." Although this ending is not appropriate at this level of writing, you also don't want to use the conclusion to simply repeat yourself. This technique is quite boring and repetitive:

> **In conclusion, I want to complete my education, have a wonderful career as a musician or veterinarian, and then marry, have children, and travel.**

Use the conclusion to make a reference back to the thesis statement and then a reflective or interesting comment. For example:

> **I have set many goals for myself, and whether I end up being a musician in Europe or a veterinarian in the United States, I know I will work hard to be successful.**

> **It is so important for one to set goals. Hopefully, I will be successful in achieving those I have set for myself.**

3.6 STEP VI: Revising and Proofreading

Following the steps of the writing process, you have completed the rough draft, so the work is almost complete. Now you are responsible for checking the essay for problems or errors, a process that is done in two stages: revision and proofreading.

Revision should be done first because it involves major structural errors. **Remember that you are not simply recopying the rough draft; you are reading with the intention of improving the**

work. At this stage, you want to reread the essay thoroughly to be sure that you have a solid introduction, specific body paragraphs, and a strong conclusion. You want to be sure you have clear topic sentences for each paragraph, and you want to check the "flow" of the paragraphs to be sure they move smoothly through the use of transitions. As you prepare to revise, try to pretend for a moment that you are the reader, not the writer, to look at the work from another point of view. Here is a basic checklist for the revision stage:

_____ Is the introduction clear and interesting?
_____ Is the thesis statement clear and focused?
_____ Does each body paragraph have a topic sentence related to the thesis?
_____ Does each body paragraph contain details to support the topic sentence?
_____ Are the details in the best order?
_____ Are there transitions to take the reader between ideas and paragraphs?
_____ Are the sentences varied in length and style?
_____ Does the conclusion leave the reader with an interesting point of closure?
_____ Has the work been checked for correct spelling?
_____ Has the work been checked for correct capitalization?
_____ Has the work been checked for correct usage and punctuation?

Proofreading should be done after revision. At the proofreading stage, you check for any mechanical errors in punctuation, capitalization, usage, and spelling. Remember that for the direct writing portion of the SOL test, you will be allowed to use a dictionary, so you can look up the spellings of words to be sure that you have them correctly written. Pay special attention to the words that can be commonly confused, verb tense, point of view, and subject/verb agreement. The evaluators want to see that you have an overall solid grasp on standard writing style, so you must check your work thoroughly and carefully. There is no time limit, so be analytical.

3.7 STEP VII: Writing the Final Draft

You have completed the revision and proofreading stages, and now you are ready to rewrite the final draft. Be sure that you use only the lined pages in the booklet, and be sure that you do not write more than the space allows because that information will not be graded. Follow your corrected rough draft carefully, correcting all errors and writing neatly and carefully. You should be proud of this final product. If you have followed the steps of the process, your work will surely be focused, organized, clear, and interesting.

Chapter 3 Exercises—Direct Writing

Choose one of the following prompts, and, following the steps of the writing process outlined in this chapter, construct a solid and well-written essay. Then, use the editing checklist to revise and proofread your work. When your essay is complete, share it with your family members, and ask them to make comments or suggestions.

Imagine that you have been selected to present a speech to eighth-grade students about the value of a high school education. What would you tell them? How would you make the speech meaningful for them?

_____ Is the introduction clear and interesting?
_____ Is the thesis statement clear and focused?
_____ Does each body paragraph have a topic sentence related to the thesis?
_____ Does each body paragraph contain details to support the topic sentence?
_____ Are the details in the best order?
_____ Are there transitions to take the reader between ideas and paragraphs?
_____ Are the sentences varied in length and style?
_____ Does the conclusion leave the reader with an interesting point of closure?
_____ Has the work been checked for correct spelling?
_____ Has the work been checked for correct capitalization?
_____ Has the work been checked for correct usage and punctuation?

Imagine that you are forty years old. Describe, in realistic terms, the life that you would like to be living when you reach this age. Include ideas about your family and where you live, your career, and your hobbies.

_____ Is the introduction clear and interesting?
_____ Is the thesis statement clear and focused?
_____ Does each body paragraph have a topic sentence related to the thesis?
_____ Does each body paragraph contain details to support the topic sentence?
_____ Are the details in the best order?
_____ Are there transitions to take the reader between ideas and paragraphs?
_____ Are the sentences varied in length and style?
_____ Does the conclusion leave the reader with an interesting point of closure?
_____ Has the work been checked for correct spelling?
_____ Has the work been checked for correct capitalization?
_____ Has the work been checked for correct usage and punctuation?

Describe your favorite childhood memory. Why was it so memorable for you? How did the experience influence your life?

_____ Is the introduction clear and interesting?
_____ Is the thesis statement clear and focused?
_____ Does each body paragraph have a topic sentence related to the thesis?
_____ Does each body paragraph contain details to support the topic sentence?
_____ Are the details in the best order?
_____ Are there transitions to take the reader between ideas and paragraphs?
_____ Are the sentences varied in length and style?
_____ Does the conclusion leave the reader with an interesting point of closure?
_____ Has the work been checked for correct spelling?
_____ Has the work been checked for correct capitalization?
_____ Has the work been checked for correct usage and punctuation?

Parenting styles and techniques have changed a great deal over the years. What do you feel are the most important characteristics of a good parent?

_____ Is the introduction clear and interesting?
_____ Is the thesis statement clear and focused?
_____ Does each body paragraph have a topic sentence related to the thesis?
_____ Does each body paragraph contain details to support the topic sentence?
_____ Are the details in the best order?
_____ Are there transitions to take the reader between ideas and paragraphs?
_____ Are the sentences varied in length and style?
_____ Does the conclusion leave the reader with an interesting point of closure?
_____ Has the work been checked for correct spelling?
_____ Has the work been checked for correct capitalization?
_____ Has the work been checked for correct usage and punctuation?

What aspect of technology do you believe is most influential in today's society? Has it brought positive or negative influences? Do you believe there are ways to use this technology effectively?

_____ Is the introduction clear and interesting?
_____ Is the thesis statement clear and focused?
_____ Does each body paragraph have a topic sentence related to the thesis?
_____ Does each body paragraph contain details to support the topic sentence?
_____ Are the details in the best order?
_____ Are there transitions to take the reader between ideas and paragraphs?
_____ Are the sentences varied in length and style?
_____ Does the conclusion leave the reader with an interesting point of closure?
_____ Has the work been checked for correct spelling?
_____ Has the work been checked for correct capitalization?
_____ Has the work been checked for correct usage and punctuation?

Part Two

TEST PREPARATION FOR EOC ENGLISH: READING/LITERATURE AND RESEARCH

The purpose of the EOC English: Reading/Literature and Research test is to assess your knowledge of the reading comprehension, literary analysis, and research skills outlined in the Virginia Standards of Learning in English. These particular SOLs provide the focus for chapters 4–7 of this preparation manual.

Chapter 4
Reading Comprehension

Reading comprehension, or the understanding of what you are reading, is an ability that is developed and strengthened over time. It is not a skill, such as how to use a lawnmower, that can be easily taught in a brief period. Your ability to read began when you were in elementary school and started learning letters and sounds. As you continued through school, you added new vocabulary and knowledge of various sentence structures to allow you to read and understand more complicated writing. Now that you are in high school, you have textbooks and novels to read, as well as items you select yourself, such as newspapers and magazines. The more you read, the more access you have to ideas, phrases, figurative language, vocabulary, and writing styles. You are learning without even realizing it. It is very important that you read as often as possible for the purpose of learning and for your enjoyment. Simply reading something every day is the most helpful step you can take toward becoming a strong, insightful reader. There are, however, several useful strategies and tactics that you can use in your journey to becoming a good, comprehensive reader of the literature presented to you both inside and outside of school. In addition, these suggestions will aid you in your goal of passing the EOC English: Reading/Literature and Research test.

4.1 General Reading Strategies

You are probably a better reader than you might believe yourself to be. Actually, much of the challenge of reading well relates to one's attitude toward the task. As you review the specific reading strategies below in preparation for the SOL test, remember one important point: If you expect to understand what you are reading, you have to want to do so. You must approach the task with a clear, focused mind. That attitude, along with the use of several tactics, will help you to become more successful.

- **Before you begin reading, look over the selection to see how it's organized**. Perhaps the work is split into labeled sections or paragraphs. Are there footnotes available for use with unfamiliar vocabulary? Are there two selections as part of one reading? Just preview the piece to become generally familiar with it. Then, go back to the beginning and start reading.
- **Be sure you read the entire passage (including the title, if one is given).** Skimming the material and picking through it for answers simply will not do. Themes and ideas are often developed throughout a writing, and if you skim, you'll miss much of the essence of the work. Students often don't feel like reading a long selection, so they are tempted to simply look over the main points and move directly to the questions. Again, this will limit your ability to successfully answer the questions related to the passage as a whole.
- **If you get confused at any time during the reading, simply stop and return to the last sentence you read before getting "lost."** Then, begin from that point, slowly, and read the next sentence carefully. Try to restate the next thought in your own words, and then watch for support, details, explanation, or development of the thought.
- **As you are reading, look for, and even underline or highlight, details that you believe support the topic sentence or thesis statement.** You learned in chapter 3 that writing, for whatever purpose, supports the ideas presented. So, as you identify the topics of discussion, look for the supporting details and examples. Further, determine the order of these details. Have they been arranged chronologically, spatially, or logically (order of importance)? Is the chosen arrangement appropriate for the selection?
- **Pause often to reflect, to ask yourself if you understand what is being stated, or to review the previous ideas.** At this point, you might ask yourself questions about what you have read or make predictions about what may occur in the rest of the selection. You might also make inferences, or educated conclusions, based on the information you are reading.

Some may describe this tactic of "reading between the lines" as most helpful for attempting to look past the words and into the heart and mind of the writer.

- **Listen for the tone of the selection.** Do you get a feeling of anger, frustration, peace, or fear as you read? Are certain vocabulary words used to help create this feeling? Refer to section 6.1 for the discussion of denotation versus connotation. A writer's choice of the word *scam* over the word *lie,* for example, can cause a definite shift in the tone of the work. The term *scam* implies the predetermined intention to cheat or deceive someone; the term *lie* refers to any form of untruth, with or without a planned deception.
- **Try to make a personal connection to the text.** Perhaps you have had an experience similar to the one being discussed or described. Thinking about your feelings may help you to understand more of what is being shared in the selection you are reading. If you are reading a selection about Native Americans, think about what you already know about their culture and traditions. This reflection may just help you to take more ownership of the information you are reading.
- **Try to figure out the meanings of any unfamiliar words.** If you encounter terms that you do not understand, check for footnotes. If there are none available, look at the word itself to see if you can determine the meaning of a prefix or root that can provide you a clue to the word's definition.

Common Prefixes		
anti-	**against**	**(antidote)**
bi-	**two**	**(biweekly)**
hemi-	**half**	**(hemisphere)**
mis-	**wrongly**	**(misspoke)**
non-	**not**	**(nonfat)**
over-	**more**	**(overload)**
post-	**after**	**(postgraduate)**
pre-	**before**	**(preliminary)**
re-	**again**	**(remind)**
trans-	**across**	**(transatlantic)**
un-	**not**	**(unclear)**

Common Roots		
-aud-	**hear**	**(auditory)**
-bene-	**good**	**(beneficial)**
-biblio-	**book**	**(bibliography)**
-chron-	**time**	**(chronology)**
-cogn-	**know**	**(cognitive)**
-dem-	**people**	**(demographics)**
-gen-	**origin**	**(generation)**
-graph-	**writing**	**(telegraph)**
-ject-	**throw**	**(trajectory)**
-magn-	**large**	**(magnificent)**
-micr-	**small**	**(micron)**
-ped-	**foot**	**(pedals)**
-phil-	**love**	**(philanthropist)**
-phon-	**sound**	**(telephone)**
-port-	**carry**	**(transport)**

Then, use *context clues,* the words before and after a particular term, to look for clues about its meaning. You may even be able to use the surrounding sentences. Look at the following example:

The research scientist was studying animals that give birth to live offspring, but I would rather study oviparous animals, such as birds and alligators.

Although you may not know the actual meaning of the word *oviparous,* you can probably use the context clues to make a good guess. If the research scientist is studying animals that give birth to live offspring, and you would rather study animals such as birds and alligators, you can make the assumption that these animals do not give birth to live offspring; they produce eggs. The dictionary defines *oviparous* animals as those that *produce eggs that hatch outside the body.*

- **Identify the purpose of the selection.** Is it to inform, persuade, narrate, or describe? If it is to inform, you should be able to identify explanations and facts. If it is to persuade, you should see logical arguments and supporting statements. If it is to narrate, you should see a clearly developed storyline with characters, events, setting, conflict, and other story elements. If it is to describe, you should be able to identify many descriptive, sensory details. Knowing the purpose of the piece will help you to determine whether the information given is both appropriate and solid.
- **Don't take any reading selection too lightly.** Some of the selections you will be asked to read may take the form of applications, warranties, or other technical documents. The main technique you must use here is careful, thoughtful reading without worrying about the time involved. If you are reading a sample job application, whether or not personal information is included, you will be expected to pay strict attention to the instructions. You should actually read the entire application to familiarize yourself with the questions asked, the order of those questions, and the various categories covered on the form. Often, though these particular sections of the SOL test appear "easy," students perform poorly on them because they feel they don't have to read them as closely as they do the selections written in full essay or prose format.
- **Upon completion of the reading, ask yourself what you have learned or what conclusions, in general, you have reached.** Simply think to yourself, "Now that I've read the selection, what do I think about . . . ?" This type of reflection will help you to assess the themes of the work. In thinking about the themes, you are trying to determine the *overall* point of the work. Each selection will have facts, ideas, and concepts that support the main idea but do not, in and of themselves, represent the *main* point of the *whole* passage. When you take your test, you may be asked to identify a theme, and you may be given possible answers that contain statements that *do* appear in the text but *do not* represent the overall point. For this reason, you must read the entire passage carefully so that you can allow the independent ideas to merge into one main idea.

Read the following selection, keeping in mind the strategies discussed above, and then follow the accompanying discussion.

ATTENTION

(1) The National Society for the Prevention of Blindness cautions against wearing contact lenses in a laboratory environment. **(2)** Delay in removing such lenses, especially when chemicals have been splashed into the eyes, can negate the recommended copious flushing of the eyes with water. **(3)** Chemical fumes may damage contact lenses and irritate the eye, causing excessive tearing, which may dislodge one or both lenses. **(4)** Accidental displacement or loss of a contact lens may occur without warning, thereby causing immediate incapacitation by sudden change of vision, excessive tearing, light sensitivity, and involuntary squeezing together of the eyelids.

1. As you look over this piece, you see that it is fairly short and can be read quickly. It is not separated into sections or categories, so you can assume that the entire piece relates to one main idea, probably stated as the topic sentence. Look at the first sentence to see if your assumption is correct: **The National Society for the Prevention of Blindness cautions against wearing contact lenses in a laboratory environment.** This is a focused topic statement indicating the direction of the paragraph, so you can now expect details about why this directive has been made.

2. Be sure that you read the entire selection carefully. Because it is so brief, you might even want to read it twice.
3. Suppose that as you are reading sentence two, you become confused by the terminology or structure of the sentence. You may not be totally sure of the intended meaning. Stop, and go back to the last sentence you read before getting confused. That was the topic sentence. You might say to yourself, "Ok, I know that this paragraph is about why one should not wear contact lenses in the laboratory, and I believe that sentence two is providing the first reason for that rule." At this point, go back to sentence two and break it down:

Delay in removing such lenses, especially when chemicals have been splashed into the eyes, can negate the recommended copious flushing of the eyes with water.

Sample comprehension process for understanding sentence #2

"Delay in removing lenses"—This means the time it would take to remove the lenses from the eyes. . . .

". . . especially when chemicals have been splashed into the eyes . . ."—This refers to a situation in which the student might be trying to remove the lenses because a chemical splashed into the eye and irritated it. . . .

". . . can negate the recommended copious flushing of the eyes with water."—This means that something could stop (because *negate* is a verb form of the word *negative*) one from doing what is recommended, which is flushing the eyes with water. . . .

The word *copious* is unclear, but because it describes how eyes would be flushed with water, and because the flushing is required to remove potentially harmful chemicals, *copious* probably means *heavily*. . . .

ANALYSIS—The sentence basically means that the wearing of contact lenses during laboratory experimentation can cause a problem with safety because, if chemicals are splashed into the eyes, the time it takes to remove the lenses would delay the usual treatment, which is to flush the eyes with lots of water.

4. You already know that sentence two provides the first supporting detail. Look at sentences three and four, and determine if they provide further support. Sentence three refers to the possible chemical damage and resulting loss of lenses, and sentence four relates to the potential of danger resulting from the sudden loss of a lens. Both sentences directly relate to the topic and provide clear support.
5. You might pause during the reading to be sure you are following the topic. You might even try to visualize a person in a laboratory situation being splashed with chemicals and trying to remove a contact lens.
6. Is there a particular feeling associated with this selection? In other words, how do you think the writer feels about the subject? It seems to be factual and written in a straightforward manner, but it does contain a sense of "warning" or "urgency," as if the writer wants the reader to take the topic quite seriously. Phrases such as *caution, without warning*, and *immediate incapacitation* help reflect this tone.
7. Try to make a personal connection. Have you ever taken a course that involved laboratory experimentation? Can you imagine what it would feel like to have a chemical splashed into your eye and then have to try to quickly remove a contact lens amid the burning and tearing involved? What if you were able to remove the lens, but it was destroyed or lost? How would you continue the experiment? If you can imagine how such an experience might feel, you can more easily understand the importance of the selection.
8. You have already identified *copious* as an unfamiliar term and have worked through an analysis of its definition. Are there other terms that are confusing? Can you use the context clues to help make the definition clear? How about *incapacitation* in sentence four? Look again at the sentence:

Accidental displacement or loss of a contact lens may occur without warning, thereby causing immediate incapacitation by sudden change of vision, excessive tearing, light sensitivity, and involuntary squeezing together of the eyelids.

The sentence indicates that immediate *incapacitation* is *caused* by the sudden loss of a contact lens. If a lens dropped out without warning, one would have no time to prepare for the inevitable blurring of the vision, tearing of the eye, or squeezing of the eyelid and would be unable to continue to focus on the experiment taking place in the laboratory. So, you know that the word *incapacitation* would have something to do with one's immediate inability to continue with the task at hand, and that situation could prove dangerous to the student or others in the room.

9. What is the purpose of the selection? Is it narrative (a story), expository (an explanation), descriptive (a selection filled with sensory details), or persuasive (an opinion backed with logical arguments)? You know that the selection explains why one should not wear contact lenses in the laboratory during experimentation, so the basic purpose is expository. However, do you note also a little persuasion? Through the use of some of the more dramatic terms, it seems the writer is really trying to convince you that the rules are not only recommended but also logical and smart.
10. Although the selection is short, you should take it seriously and read it just as carefully and thoughtfully as you would a longer piece.
11. Upon completion of the passage, ask yourself what, in general, you have learned. Perhaps after reading the warning about the use of contact lenses in the laboratory, you have learned that there are some good reasons to leave the contacts at home on laboratory experiment days. Further, you may come away with the knowledge that you cannot prevent or prepare for some of the dangers associated with the wearing of the lenses, and so it would be best not to take the chance.

4.2 Poetry

One of the most common complaints of students trying to read and interpret poetry is that they simply "don't understand it." However, you can approach poetry in a positive way by remembering a few important points:

- Many students get frustrated because the language in poetry is often figurative or seems archaic. In chapters 5 and 6 of this guide, you will read about all of the different styles of poetry and types of figurative terms that poets use to create their unique poetry. Recognizing the use of these devices can help you to understand much of what may, at first, seem incomprehensible. The language in some poetry may seem outdated simply because the poem itself is dated. Poetry from the time of Shakespeare may sound odd or "old fashioned" to you because you don't recognize many of the words or phrases used. In Shakespeare's time, however, the language he chose was quite familiar to his audience. Often, there are footnotes to provide common definitions of seemingly archaic terms.
- One misconception about the reading of poetry lies in the particular reading of stanzas. Many a student reads "line by line," regardless of punctuation. To correctly read poetry, you should read by the punctuation. If there is a period at the end of a line of poetry, stop, and then begin slowly with the next line. If there is a comma, pause briefly, and go on. If there is no punctuation, neither pause nor stop. Keep reading smoothly. If you "break" a line before the punctuation indicates that you should do so, you will lose the whole "feeling" of the line, thus leading to a comprehension problem. Look at the following excerpt from the poem "Holy Sonnet 10" by John Donne:

> Death, be not proud, though some have callèd thee
> Mighty and dreadful, for thou art not so;
> For those whom thou think'st thou dost overthrow
> Die not, poor death, nor yet canst thou kill me.

Try reading this section using the "line by line" format, stopping at *thee, so, overthrow*, and *me*. As you read it aloud, listen carefully to how the lines sound, and try to determine what they might mean. The phrase *mighty and dreadful* seems to be the introduction to the second line. The last line almost seems to be saying to death, "Die not," almost as an instruction or a request.

Now, try reading the section out loud again, but this time read according to the punctuation, even though it may seem strange. This time, you should have heard a difference. Now, you see that the phrase *mighty and dreadful* is being used as part of the first line to make the point that some people have called death *mighty and dreadful*. It should be more clear now that the first two words of the last line refer to those whom death *thought* he overthrew; they "died not."

- Poets are allowed what is known as "poetic license," meaning that their poetry is not bound by the formal rules of standard writing. That is why some poets use dashes in odd places or end complete thoughts with commas. Don't let the various styles concern you; just read according to your basic knowledge of the meaning carried by each punctuation mark. Actually, many poets use punctuation to create a more intense relationship between the reader and the poem or to help create a desired mood in a particular selection.
- Pay particular attention to the speaker in a poem. In poetry, the author is not necessarily the speaker. If you, a high school junior, write a poem in which a doll is expressing feelings of fear about being given away to a charity, the doll is the speaker. You are the poet, the creator of the doll's character, but the doll itself is the speaker. Recognizing the speaker's relationship to the events or feelings expressed in the poem can help you to understand the poem's meaning more easily. As you read a poem, identify the speaker—whether it is a character, a narrator, an animal, or an object—and let that knowledge help guide you through the poem. Look back at the excerpt from "Holy Sonnet 10" above. The speaker is a human who is telling death that he is not as terrible as many might think him to be. Perhaps this speaker has heard many tales of death or lost loved ones. When you read about poets' backgrounds, you often understand why they write certain types of poetry, and you imagine that they themselves are the actual speakers. On the SOL test, however, you won't have the opportunity to study biographies, so it is important that you try to determine what you can about the speaker and his/her reasons for revealing certain feelings and ideas.

Chapter 4 Exercises—Reading Comprehension

Read the following information about American poet Robert Frost, and then use it to answer questions 1–5.

Mini-biography of Robert Frost

American poet Robert Frost was born in California, but after the death of his father, he and his family moved to Massachusetts, where he received the bulk of his secondary education. After finishing high school, Frost entered Dartmouth College, but he left after only a few months and returned to Massachusetts to work in the mills. He already felt his calling as a poet, but writing, at this point, would earn him no living. After his marriage to Elinor in 1895, Frost enrolled in Harvard University, but he left before earning a formal degree. He tried various other jobs, including farming, but he became frustrated because his true desire was to write poetry. In 1912, the couple moved to England, and it was here that Frost made the acquaintance of some noted British poets who both inspired and assisted him. Three years later, in 1915, Frost and his wife returned to the United States, and by this time, he had published two collections of poetry entitled *A Boy's Will* and *North of Boston*. His reputation was established, and he became one of the most respected poets in America. He published many more poems and was honored with many awards, including several Pulitzer Prizes and a Congressional Medal. He was even asked to recite "The Gift Outright" at the inauguration of President John F. Kennedy in 1961. Most of Frost's poetry was inspired by scenes and life in New England, and he remained true to many of the traditional forms of poetry even as new literary movements shook the poetic community. However, his works were complex, meaningful, and full of life. His death in 1963 brought an end to the creation of new works, but those he left behind remain a cornerstone of American poetry.

1. The general purpose of the selection is—

A to inform
B to persuade
C to describe
D to narrate

2. Which of the following methods has the author chosen for the order of details?

A Order of importance
B Chronological
C Spatial
D Funnel

3. According to the selection, Frost experienced all of the following *except*—

A a meaningful career
B a college degree
C admiration from others for his poetry
D opportunity to travel abroad

4. Which of the following can you infer about Robert Frost after reading the selection?

A Frost did not enjoy life in New England.
B Frost preferred living in England to living in the United States.
C Frost sought a change of scenery in Europe, but his heart was still in the United States.
D Frost did not have much respect for the style of poetry of the British writers he met.

5. What is the tone of this selection?

A Respectful
B Arrogant
C Sympathetic
D Satirical

Read the following sets of guidelines, and use them to answer questions 6–10.

Parent-Student Laboratory Safety Verification

The following is to inform both students and parents of the safe conduct that is expected of the students during laboratory activities and consequences resulting from failure to comply. Because proper behavior is an essential part of laboratory safety, these rules, designed for the protection of the students and their classmates, must be observed.

The students agree to do the following:

1. Follow instructions explicitly;
2. Perform only authorized experiments;
3. Protect eyes, face, hands, body, and long hair;
4. Practice good housekeeping within the work area;
5. Get help, as needed, from predetermined sources;
6. Know the location of the first-aid and firefighting equipment;
7. Report at once all accidents and unusual occurrences;
8. Never “horse around”;
9. Ask questions if they do not understand instructions.

Students will be removed from the science activity area by the teacher for any of the following reasons:

1. Their personal appearance or dress is such that they can cause injury to themselves or to other students.
2. They are behaving in such a manner that they can cause injury to themselves or to other students.
3. They are not following the prescribed safety rules for the laboratory or the particular science activity being conducted.
4. They are going beyond the limits of the science activity into areas that may lead to an unsafe situation.
5. They have not completed the preexperiment activities that will allow them to work safely in the laboratory situation.

LABORATORY ACTIVITIES MAY BE DANGEROUS, AND INJURIES ARE POSSIBLE IF PROPER PRECAUTIONS ARE NOT TAKEN.

6. What is the general purpose of the form?
A To explain the dangers of the laboratory setting
B To ask parents for their help in creating a safe environment
C To make students and parents aware of laboratory safety rules
D To convince students not to take a laboratory course

7. Which of the following would not provide a reason for a teacher to remove a student from the science activity area during an experiment?
A Performing unscheduled experiments
B Failing to complete the preliminary work leading to the experiment
C Wearing a tank top
D Arriving tardy to class

8. What can you infer about the term *predetermined sources* in item #5 in the first numbered section?
A The students must always work individually.
B This item will be discussed by the instructor before laboratory experiments begin.
C Students should consult their science textbooks for a definition of the term.
D All questions must be written and saved until the end of class.

9. The majority of the responsibility for safe laboratory experiences lies with whom?
A The parents
B The students
C The instructor
D The laboratory supply company

10. The laboratory safety form implies all of the following *except*—
A Students must wear goggles during laboratory experiments.
B Students must wear long-sleeved shirts during laboratory experiments.
C Students must tie up long hair during laboratory experiments.
D Students must not wear jewelry of any kind during experiments.

Read the following poem, and then use it to answer questions 11–15.

The Road Not Taken

Two roads diverged in a yellow wood,
And sorry I could not travel both
And be one traveler, long I stood
And looked down one as far as I could
To where it bent in the undergrowth;

Then took the other, as just as fair
And having perhaps the better claim,
Because it was grassy and wanted wear;
Though as for that, the passing there
Had worn them really about the same,

And both that morning equally lay
In leaves no step had trodden black
Oh, I kept the first for another day!
Yet knowing how way leads on to way,
I doubted if I should ever come back.

I shall be telling this with a sigh
Somewhere ages and ages hence:
Two roads diverged in a wood, and I —
I took the one less traveled by,
And that has made all the difference.

—Robert Frost

11. In line 1, the meaning of the word *diverged* is—

A lay
B disappeared
C split
D bent

12. The speaker experiences all of the following emotions *except*—

A sadness
B peace
C determination
D fear

13. Which of the following *best* states the poem's theme?

A It is important for humans to love nature.
B Unknown aspects of life can be frightening.
C Taking an unknown "path" can be rewarding.
D People often regret decisions made in haste.

14. What is ironic about the title of the poem?

A It is short, but the poem is lengthy.
B It focuses on the road that did *not* make a difference in the author's life.
C It focuses on the road that *did* make a difference in the author's life.
D It is not the original title.

15. What is the overall tone of the poem?

A Reflective
B Confused
C Apprehensive
D Bitter

Answers to Chapter 4 Exercises

1. **(A)** The main purpose of the selection is to inform the reader about the life of Robert Frost.

2. **(B)** The writer tells about the events of Frost's life in the order in which they occurred. Also, "funnel" is a type of introduction, not a type of order used for details.

3. **(B)** Although Frost attended college, he never earned a degree.

4. **(C)** Frost left the United States for England after several failed attempts at college and a career, so you can infer that he wanted a change, but the fact that he returned three years later and remained in the United States indicates that his heart was in America. There is no information to indicate that he did not enjoy life in the United States or that he preferred England. Also, the selection indicates that British poets supported and encouraged him, so he probably did have respect for them.

5. **(A)** The writer provides a professional and respectful mini-biography of Frost. The writer does not exhibit arrogance (conceit), sympathy, or satire (sarcastic humor).

6. **(C)** The form is for students and their parents so they will be aware of the rules. The form contains reference to potential dangers and mentions the responsibility of parents, but those do not constitute the overall purpose of the selection.

7. **(D)** There is no discussion of attendance on the form.

8. **(B)** The term *predetermined* indicates that if students need help, they will already know whom they should ask. Obviously, if the teacher is conscientious enough to provide such specific rules, the process for requesting assistance will most likely be thoroughly discussed as well.

9. **(B)** Because the students are the ones in the room participating in the laboratory experiment, they are most responsible for knowing and following the rules.

10. **(D)** Jewelry is the only item not mentioned. The others—goggles, long-sleeved shirts, and ties for long hair—are implied in item #3 regarding the protection of the body.

11. **(C)** Because the speaker had to make a decision between two roads, you can assume that the main road on which he traveled split into two, thus causing his dilemma.

12. **(D)** The speaker does not indicate any feelings of fear. He is *sad* because he can't take both roads, *determined* to try and return to the other road, and at *peace* with himself because the choice he made turned out to make a difference in his life.

13. **(C)** The events in the poem and the speaker's "sigh" and tone indicate that the road not taken led him to some measure of success or reward. There was nothing in the poem about the speaker being frightened or regretting his decision. Nature was a part of the poem's setting, but a specific love for nature was not a developed theme.

14. **(B)** The title relates to the road *not* taken, but the speaker indicates that the road that *was* taken was the one that made the difference. Perhaps the road *not* taken is symbolic of the "easy" choice that the speaker refused to take.

15. **(A)** The author is reflecting on the past decisions of life. There is no expression of confusion, apprehension (fear), or bitterness (hatred).

Chapter 5
Poetic Forms and Sound Devices

5.1 Poetic Forms

Sometimes students have difficulty with poetry because they have a preconceived idea that they won't be able to understand it. However, if you understand some basic forms, terms, and poetic devices, you can approach poetry in a much more effective way. Whether poetry originates from the era of Shakespeare or from modern times, you can become familiar with its interesting forms and characteristics. The more comfortable you feel with what you're reading, the more prepared you will be to investigate themes, ideas, and specific poetic elements. This section will introduce various general poetic forms.

Lyric poetry – poetry that shares the thoughts and feelings of the speaker about a particular subject. If a poem is termed a *lyric,* it deals with feelings. It does not tell a story. If, for example, a poet wants to talk about the beauty of a rose or a sunset or about the love a parent feels for a child, the resulting poem will be a lyric. Perhaps you remember being in elementary school and writing a poem. Maybe you wrote about your friends, parents, or even your favorite toy. If you were talking about how you felt, then you were writing lyric poetry. One point to remember is that the speaker in a poem is the one sharing ideas, and he or she *may* or *may not be* the author. For example, you could write a lyric poem from the viewpoint of a flower sharing its feelings about the sky. You would be the poet, but not the speaker. Look at the following excerpt from Robert Frost's lyric poem "The Sound of the Trees":

I WONDER about the trees.
Why do we wish to bear
Forever the noise of these
More than another noise
So close to our dwelling place?
We suffer them by the day
Till we lose all measure of pace,
And fixity in our joys,
And acquire a listening air.

Sonnet – a lyric poem that is fourteen lines in length. You have learned that a lyric poem shares thoughts and feelings, so you know that a sonnet achieves the same goal. The difference between lyric poetry in general and a sonnet is that a sonnet is exactly fourteen lines long. The individual lines are similar in length because they generally follow a metered pattern, iambic pentameter. This concept will be discussed in section 5.2 (Sound Devices). A sonnet will never consist of more or fewer than fourteen individual lines. The following example shows the first four lines of a sonnet:

I see the beauty of the dazzling eve,
The stars as messengers of hope unseen;
Oh, as I gaze into their knowing eyes,
My heart partakes of secrets and of lies.

There are different types of sonnets, such as Petrarchan or Shakespearean. These terms relate to the ryhthm and rhyme schemes used by great poets of the past. The **Petrarchan (Italian) sonnet** is named after the Italian poet Petrarch, who lived during the fourteenth century. It has fourteen lines, like all sonnets. However, its first eight lines (octave) ask a question or suggest a situation that needs to be solved. The last six lines (sestet) respond to the *problem* suggested in the first eight lines. The

Shakespearean (Elizabethan) sonnet was made famous by William Shakespeare, a famous English playwright and poet. Instead of using an octave to present a problem and a sestet to respond, this type of sonnet uses three quatrains (four lines each) and a couplet. Usually, the first twelve lines (three quatrains) discuss a particular concept, and the final two lines (couplet) make some concluding statement or observation.

Ode – a dignified lyric poem written about a serious subject. An ode is basically a poem of praise because it usually pays tribute or honor to a person, group, event, or concept. For example, suppose you write a poem entitled "Ode to a Battlefield" to bring about an awareness of the bravery shown by a group of soldiers. By focusing your poem on the battlefield, you bring meaning to the event, the setting, *and* the people involved. Such a poem does not tell a story; it shares thoughts and feelings of honor. Your lyric poem of praise is called an *ode.* Here is an excerpt from "Ode to the West Wind" by Percy Bysshe Shelley:

O Wild West Wind, thou breath of Autumn's being,
Thou, from whose unseen presence the leaves dead
Are driven, like ghosts from an enchanter fleeing,

Yellow, and black, and pale, and hectic red,
Pestilence-stricken multitudes: O thou
Who chariotest to their dark wintry bed

The winge'd seeds, where they lie cold and low,
Each like a corpse within its grave, until
Thine azure sister of the spring shall blow

Her clarion o'er the dreaming earth, and fill
(Driving sweet buds like flocks to feed in air)
With living hues and odours plain and hill:

Wild Spirit, which art moving everywhere;
Destroyer and Preserver; hear, O hear!

Narrative poem – a poem that tells a story. Unlike lyric poems and sonnets, which share feelings, narrative poems tell a story. Of course, if you are going to write a "story poem," then you must include story elements, such as characters, plot, theme, and conflict. A narrative poem is, actually, a story written in the format of a poem with stanzas and, perhaps, rhyme. Do you remember reading or hearing the story of *Cinderella*? Imagine rewriting this story in a poetic format to create a narrative poem. It is important to note that a narrative poem may also contain lyric elements. For example, there can be some discussion of feelings on the part of the character or even the narrator; however, because a narrative poem definitely tells a story, it is placed into the major category of narrative poetry. Usually, narrative poems are a great deal longer than lyric poems because the poet must develop the story's plot and characterization. Consider the following examples:

1. I see the lovely roses,
Their brilliance a testimony to my
Loving attention;
Yellow, red, pink, and even white,
The colors of a natural palette.

2. The skies outside were a beautiful blue,
A journey begun for a lonely traveler;
His whirling thoughts took a ghastly form,
And he whistled as he rode.

The first poem involves a speaker sharing feelings about roses, and the second involves a narrator discussing a character who is taking a journey of some sort. Selection 2 seems to be introducing a story.

Epic poem – a long, narrative poem that tells the adventures of a hero and sometimes contains graphic or gory language. An epic is a type of narrative poem, but it has the added characteristics of length and a heroic character. Many epics, such as *The Odyssey,* tell stories of great warriors fighting mythological beasts or huge monsters. Many epics can be traced back to the time when stories were shared orally, rather than in written form. Traveling storytellers tried to make the tales interesting and, thus, sometimes included many gory details of war or battle. They also included many of the literary devices discussed in section 5.2. The term *epic* is still used today to describe stories of great adventures. Sometimes, advertisers refer to movies as *epic adventures*. Although current movie heroes may be depicted differently than those from history, their stories still include challenges and exciting experiences. The term *hero* can bring about different ideas, depending on the period of history and the values of a particular society. For example, the qualities of a hero in the time period of great warriors might focus on physical strength and ability in battle, but to those experiencing westward expansion during the early years of America, a hero may have been characterized as one who had extensive education, great intellect, or the drive to explore new lands.

Ballad – a narrative poem that is meant to be sung. A ballad is also a story poem that often involves a relationship between two people who love one another, someone perhaps searching for love or happiness, or some variation of this idea. There are, however, ballads that focus on other concepts. A major characteristic of a ballad's construction is that it lends itself to the rhythm of a song. When you recite a ballad out loud, you hear a specific rhythm for which you can easily create a musical "beat." Also, it might have certain repeated sections (refrains), similar to the "chorus" of a song. Look at the following excerpt from Edgar Allen Poe's famous ballad "Annabel Lee."

It was many and many a year ago,
  In a kingdom by the sea
That a maiden there lived whom you may know
  By the name of ANNABEL LEE;
And this maiden she lived with no other thought
  Than to love and be loved by me.

I was a child and she was a child,
  In this kingdom by the sea,
But we loved with a love that was more than love—
  I and my ANNABEL LEE;
With a love that the winge'd seraphs of heaven
  Coveted her and me.

Dramatic poem – a poem in which the situation, setting, characters, and actions are revealed through the dialogue of two or more characters. When you look at the term *dramatic,* you might think of the word *drama,* which relates to acting and the stage. When you see a performance taking place on stage, you, as a member of the audience, know what's going on because you hear the words of the characters. In a dramatic poem, the characters "speak" through the written word. The dialogues in dramatic poetry provide the key to understanding the poem's events. Consider the following example:

> "What color are the skies today, my love?" the maiden whispered.
> "The skies are of a beautiful blue, the color of your eyes."

Through this short example, you can see that there are two characters speaking to one another, and, through their dialogue, you learn that they may have a romantic relationship, that one has blue eyes, and that the setting involves beautiful weather. So, rather that being *told,* you may *discover.* A dramatic poem does not have to be written entirely in dialogue, but the poet will add it as an intentional means of sharing information.

Dramatic monologue – a poem in which one speaker talks to one or more silent listeners. Because a dramatic poem involves the element of *drama,* you know there will be direct speaking. However, the term *monologue* must also be considered. The prefix *mono-* means "one." Therefore, a dramatic monologue involves one person speaking, instead of two or more persons having a dialogue. It is important to note that this one person who is speaking is still having a form of discussion with one or more *silent listeners* who do not actually speak. Often in this type of poetry, the speaker, through the monologue, reveals specific and sometimes personal aspects of his or her personality. Here is an example:

> "So, my love, you wonder about the color of the skies?
> Then I shall tell you; they are of a beautiful blue."

You know that the listener has asked about the skies, but you do not actually hear the question as we did in the previous example of dramatic poetry. If this poem went on, it would continue in the same way with the speaker talking to one or more listeners. From the monologue, you learn about the other characters, but you create your own knowledge of them based on the ideas presented by the speaker. You have to infer information about their reactions, personalities, and feelings. Following is an excerpt from "My Last Duchess," which is a dramatic monologue written by Robert Browning:

> That's my last Duchess painted on the wall,
> Looking as if she were alive. I call
> That piece a wonder, now: Frà Pandolf's hands
> Worked busily a day, and there she stands.
> Will 't please you sit and look at her? I said
> "Frà Pandolf" by design, for never read
> Strangers like you that pictured countenance,
> The depth and passion of its earnest glance,
> But to myself they turned (since none puts by
> The curtain I have drawn for you, but I)
> And seemed as they would ask me, if they durst,
> How such a glance came there; so, not the first
> Are you to turn and ask thus. Sir, 'twas not
> Her husband's presence only, called that spot
> Of joy into the Duchess' cheek: perhaps
> Frà Pandolf chanced to say "Her mantle laps
> Over my lady's wrist too much," or "Paint
> Must never hope to reproduce the faint
> Half-flush that dies along her throat": such stuff
> Was courtesy, she thought, and cause enough
> For calling up that spot of joy. She had
> A heart—how shall I say?—too soon made glad,
> Too easily impressed; she liked whate'er
> She looked on, and her looks went everywhere.

Elegy – a sad poem about death. An elegy is a poem that is focused on death or mourning (grief felt over death). An elegy could focus on the passing of a certain person, such as a loved one, or it could focus on a broader concept, such as the death of a certain aspect of society or a time in history. For example, you might write an elegy expressing sadness over the passing of the age of a certain type of music. Following are four stanzas from Thomas Gray's "Elegy Written in a Country Churchyard":

> Here rests his head upon the lap of Earth
>   A youth to Fortune and to Fame unknown;
> Fair Science frown'd not on his humble birth
>   And Melancholy mark'd him for her own.

Large was his bounty, and his soul sincere;
  Heaven did a recompense as largely send:
He gave to Mis'ry all he had, a tear,
  He gain'd from Heav'n ('twas all he wish'd) a friend.

No farther seek his merits to disclose,
  Or draw his frailties from their dread abode,
(There they alike in trembling hope repose)
  The bosom of his Father and his God.

Concrete poem – a poem written in the shape of some object, person, place, or idea. The shape of the poem represents or relates to the topic, the theme, or both. For example, if you write a poem about love and form the lines into the shape of a heart, you have created a concrete poem. A concrete noun names a specific person, place, thing, or idea; likewise, a concrete poems "shows" a specific person, place, thing, or idea.

Haiku – a poem of Japanese origin that uses syllable patterns to form the poetic lines. Haiku has various formats, but the most common is the following three-line format:

Line 1 – five syllables
Line 2 – seven syllables
Line 3 – five syllables

The lines depend on the number of syllables, not words. Therefore, line 1 can consist of one five-syllable word or five one-syllable words (or any other combination leading to five total syllables). Because the Japanese culture has a great deal of respect for nature, haiku usually depict a scene or vision in nature. Here is an example:

The autumn calls me	(five syllables: the au-tumn calls me)
Many shades of red and gold	(seven syllables: ma-ny shades of red and gold)
Fill my soul with peace	(five syllables: fill my soul with peace)

Couplet – two consecutive rhyming lines of poetry. A couplet consists of two lines, one right after the other (consecutive) that rhyme. A couplet can be within a poem or may stand alone. The following lines form a couplet:

The skies outside are of a beautiful blue,
But the clouds are aflame with a reddish hue.

A couplet may be the first two lines of a sonnet or the last two lines of a lyric poem. As long as there are two together, they form a couplet.

Quatrain – a four-line poem or a four-line stanza (individual unit) in a poem. A quatrain consists of four lines. It does not have to include two couplets, but it can. For example, if you have two rhyming lines followed by two more rhyming lines, you have a quatrain consisting of two couplets. However, if you have a poem of four lines in which the first and third lines rhyme and the second and fourth lines rhyme, you have a quatrain but not two couplets. A ballad (story poem meant to be sung) often consists of a series of quatrains because that style lends itself to the rhythm of song. There are also six-line and eight-line sections of poetry, usually discussed with reference to sonnet forms. A six-line group is called a sestet, and an eight-line group is called an octave.

Conclusion: Poetic Forms

Knowing the many forms of poetry will be helpful to you on the SOL test for various reasons. First, you may encounter a direct question about the format. Second, because you will be familiar with the format of the poems themselves, you will be more confident as you analyze the elements within them. For example, if you recognize a particular poem as a sonnet, then you may feel confident that it will have a particular meter and pattern of rhyme (discussed in section 5.2 of this chapter), and that may help you answer a question about rhyme scheme. Your ability to read poetry critically will be strengthened as you learn to recognize its form and elements.

5.2 Sound Devices

Now that you know the major forms of poetry, you need to practice analyzing poems for some of the specific elements that poets use to achieve their chosen patterns of rhythm and rhyme. Most people do associate poetry with rhyme, so this section will begin with a discussion of rhyming patterns.

End rhyme – rhyming words at the ends of two or more lines. Simply put, end rhyme occurs when words rhyme at the *ends* of lines of poetry. Here is an example:

The children traveled into town
To see the very famous clown.

The words that form the end rhyme in the previous example are *town* and *clown.* This example also forms a couplet because the rhyming lines are consecutive. Here is another example:

The children traveled into town
One bright December morning,
To see the very famous clown
They'd heard about from friends.

In this example, end rhyme still occurs, but it is not in the form of a couplet. The words *town* and *clown* are separated by another line. Therefore, end rhyme occurs in the first and third lines, and there are no couplets because no rhyming lines are consecutive.

Internal rhyme – rhyme that occurs within the same line of poetry. For internal rhyme to occur, the rhyming words occur within one line rather than at the ends of two or more lines. For the clown poem to have internal rhyme, the line has to be rewritten in the following way:

The children traveled into town to see the very famous clown.

The words *town* and *clown* still form a rhyme pattern, but because they are inside the same line, they form internal rhyme.

Approximate rhyme – rhyming that is close but not exact. Approximate rhyme is also known as *slant rhyme.* In approximate rhyme, the focus words are close in form but do not create an exact rhyme (the repetition of vowel sounds in accented syllables and all succeeding syllables). The following example shows approximate rhyme:

The child was truly happy
When she saw the darling puppy.

The words *happy* and *puppy* form a close rhyme. It isn't exact, but it is closer than, say, *happy* and *clown*. An exact rhyme for *happy* would be a word such as *snappy*.

Rhyme scheme – the pattern of rhyme in a poem. When you look at rhyme in a poem, you can attach a pattern to it using the letters of the alphabet. To do so, select a poem. Look at the last word in line one, and label it with an *a.* Then, look at the last word in line two. If it rhymes with the word labeled *a,* then it will also be labeled *a.* If not, it will be labeled *b.* You then continue with the last word in line three, and so on. Look at the simple poem below, and determine its rhyme scheme:

The men on board the ship held tight
As wind and waves rushed by;
The sea was angry, white with foam,
Glistening in the captain's eye.

The rhyme scheme is *a, b, c, b.* The sonnets discussed earlier in this chapter have very particular rhyme schemes. In the Petrarchan sonnet, the octave has an *abba abba* scheme, and the concluding sestet has a rhyme scheme of *cde cde.* The three quatrains in a Shakespearean sonnet have the following rhyme scheme: *abab cdcd efef.* The final couplet has a *gg* scheme.

Alliteration – the repetition of consonant sounds at the beginnings of three or more words in lines of poetry placed closely together. The tongue twisters that you may remember from your childhood provide a wonderful example of alliteration. An example would be "Peter Piper picked a peck of pickled peppers." A poem may not have such obvious examples, but the idea is the same. If you are searching for alliteration in a poem, you are looking for several words near one another that all begin with the same consonant sound. It is important to remember that this definition refers to consonant *sounds*, not consonants *themselves.* You know that the letter *s* and the letter *c* are different consonants, but they can make the same sound, such as in the words *sit* and *center.* Likewise, the words *center* and *cake* begin with the same consonant, but they do not form a pattern of alliteration because one *c* is soft (center) and one is hard (cake). The following lines contain an example of alliteration:

My mother worked miracles in the kitchen,
A gentle manager of our daily meals.

Alliteration is achieved through use of the words *mother, miracles, manager,* and *meals*. These words all begin with the same consonant sound. A poet may use alliteration to create a rhythm (beat) or mood. For example, a repeating of the *c* sound, such as you hear in the word *crush*, creates a harsh, sharp sort of feeling. However, the repetition of the soft *g* sound, such as you hear in the word *gentle*, creates a more soothing atmosphere. Alliteration does not occur by chance. Poets know why they select every word.

Consonance – repetition of a final consonant sound on accented syllables. Whereas alliteration occurs at the beginnings of several words, consonance occurs within words. For example, in the word *ticktock,* you can see the repetition of the hard *c* sound at the end of the word and at the end of the accented syllable (first syllable). This technique is sometimes used in place of rhyme to form a pattern within poetic lines.

Assonance – the repetition of similar vowel sounds. The repetition of vowel sounds is another technique used by poets to create mood and rhythm. For example, if you see a repeated *oo* sound in a poem, such as in the words *mood* and *soon*, you may sense, perhaps, an eerie mood.

Onomatopoeia – the use of words that imitate their meaning. The use of onomatopoeia involves words that seem to create sound when they are spoken. Further, the sound you hear when you say the word is basically the sound that the word itself is attempting to describe. For example, suppose you want to use the word *whoosh* to describe the sound of a plane taking off. When you say the word aloud, it sounds just like the word you want to use to explain the plane's sound. That is the point of onomatopoeia. Poets use this device to help create an image in the ears and minds of the reader. The following lines contain an example of onomatopoeia:

"Clang!" sounded the captain's bell
As mother called us home again.

The word *clang,* which describes the sound of the bell, actually sounds like the bell itself. When you read the word in a poem, you *hear* it in your mind, and so the poem seems to come to life.

Metered poetry – poetry that has structured patterns of rhyme and rhythm. Although this information may seem a bit confusing at first, it will, through a series of steps, become clear. The discussion of meter begins with the term *syllable*. The number of syllables in a word refers to the number of sections into which it can be divided when spoken. In grade school, you may have been taught to find syllables by clapping your hands, tapping your feet, or snapping your fingers. For example, the word *blue* has only one syllable. The word *happen* has two syllables, and the word *attitude* has three. If you want to know how many syllables are in a word or where the syllables are split, you can consult a dictionary. When you say the word *attitude* out loud, you can listen for the syllable that you seem to say the loudest. It's the first syllable. You say *AT-ti-tude*. You have a heavy accent on syllable one and a light accent on syllables two and three. Suppose that you pronounced the last syllable the most heavily. It would now sound this way: *at-ti-TUDE*. That would change the entire rhythm and feeling of the word.

When you put several words together, you heavily accent some syllables and lightly accent others. This pattern of heavy and light accents creates the ***rhythm.*** Try this example out loud. Say the following line from a nursery rhyme:

"Humpty Dumpty sat on a wall . . ."

There are eight syllables in the entire line. Which did you most heavily accent? How about one, three, five, six, and seven (HUMP-ty DUMP-ty SAT ON A wall)? Try saying the line again, and this time, heavily accent syllables one, three, and five only (HUMP-ty DUMP-ty SAT on a wall). The rhythm in the second part of the phrase completely changes; thus, if you make the same changes throughout the rhyme, the rhythm of the entire poem changes.

In poetry, a *foot* is a general term for a combination of lightly and heavily accented syllables. There are many specific types of feet, each with its own combination. For example, a *trochee* is a foot made up of two syllables—one heavy accent followed by one light accent—such as can be found in the word *fancy.* When you say this word, you more heavily pronounce the first syllable (FAN-cy). Another type of foot is called the *iamb.* An iamb also consists of two syllables, but it involves one light accent followed by one heavy accent, which you hear in the word *below* (be-LOW).

First and foremost, metered poetry has a regulated rhythm. In other words, the arrangement of accented and unaccented syllables forms a particular pattern. Consider the following quatrain:

The flowers are pretty,
They brighten my heart;
They lift up my spirit,
Of me, they're a part.

You can feel the regulation of the poem. It follows a particular beat from beginning to end. Now, consider this selection:

The flowers are pretty,
I love the way they brighten my heart;
And, they surely lift my spirit,
They are a part of me.

This example sounds less formal and regulated, more *free*. If a poem has a regulated, structured rhythm, it is called a *metered poem*. If not, it is called *free verse*, a concept discussed later in this section.

Scansion – the analysis of a poem to determine its meter. When you mark the heavy and light stresses throughout the syllables in a line of poetry, you are analyzing its meter and rhythmic pattern.

Iambic pentameter – a line of metered poetry that contains five iambs. This term is commonly used in the discussion of poetry, especially sonnets. This is a type of meter used in poetry. First, consider the term *iamb,* which is a foot consisting of one lightly stressed syllable followed by one heavily stressed syllable. Now, think about the prefix *penta-*. It refers to the number five. Finally, think about the word *meter.* You know that this refers to the poem's rhythm and that it will be formal and regulated. Iambic pentameter, therefore, is poetic style involving five iambs per line, creating a regulated rhythm. Many famous works by Shakespeare, Milton, and others were written in iambic pentameter. The iamb was the most commonly used metric foot because it is the most reflective of English speech. If a poem is written in iambic pentameter but is unrhymed, it is called *blank verse.*

Free verse – poetry without regular rhyme or rhythm. Free verse has no *regular* rhyme or rhythm. A poem written in free verse can have some rhyme; it just will not have a *regular* pattern throughout the selection. Further, all poetry has rhythm. Because rhythm is formed from the combination of lightly and heavily stressed syllables, all word formations create rhythm. However, a *regulated* rhythm is not found in free verse. When you write free verse, you simply share your ideas without forcing the lines into specific patterns or formats. Free verse may also contain some or all of the sound devices discussed in this chapter. The main difference between free verse and metered poetry is the presence of a regimented pattern of rhythm and rhyme.

You have reviewed both poetry's major forms and a large selection of the sound devices used by poets to enhance their individual styles. Remember that poetry is not created haphazardly. Just as painters consider every stroke of their brushes, so do poets carefully plan each word, line, and element of their poetry. Specific devices are used to achieve certain results and to give poetry its style and magic.

Chapter 5 Exercises—Poetic Forms and Sound Devices

Directions: Read the following poem. Then, use the information to answer questions 1–4.

Sonnet 130

My mistress' eyes are nothing like the sun;
Coral is far more red than her lips' red;
If snow be white, why then her breasts are dun;
If hairs be wires, black wires grow on her head.
I have seen roses damask'd, red and white,
But no such roses see I in her cheeks;
And in some perfumes is there more delight
Than in the breath that from my mistress reeks.
I love to hear her speak, yet well I know
That music hath a far more pleasing sound;
I grant I never saw a goddess go;
My mistress, when she walks, treads on the ground.
And yet, by heaven, I think my love as rare
As any she belied with false compare.

—William Shakespeare

1. Describe the rhyme scheme used by Shakespeare in "Sonnet 130."
- A abab cdcd efef gg
- B aabb ccdd eeff gg
- C abba cddc effe gg
- D abbb cddd efff gg

2. Which lines form a couplet?
- A 1 and 3
- B 6 and 7
- C 11 and 12
- D 13 and 14

3. Which line from the poem contains an example of alliteration?
A 7 – “And in some perfumes is there more delight”
B 10 – “That music hath a far more pleasing sound.”
C 11 – “I grant I never saw a goddess go;”
D 14 – “As any she belied with false compare.”

4. This sonnet is written in which of the following forms?
A Blank verse
B Free verse
C Iambic pentameter
D Paired couplets

Directions: Read the following poem. Then, use the information to answer questions 5–9.

Concord Hymn

By the rude bridge that arched the flood,
Their flag to April’s breeze unfurled,
Here once the embattled farmers stood
And fired the shot heard round the world.

That foe long since in silence slept;
Alike the conqueror silent sleeps;
And Time the ruined bridge has swept
Down the dark stream which seaward creeps.

On this green bank, by this soft stream,
We set to-day a votive stone;
That memory may their deed redeem,
When, like our sires, our sons are gone.

Spirit, that made those heroes dare
To die, and leave their children free,
Bid Time and Nature gently spare
The shaft we raise to them and thee.

—Ralph Waldo Emerson

5. Which of the following terms describes the format of the poem’s stanzas?
A Sonnets
B Quatrains
C Couplets
D Octaves

6. Lines 10 and 12 form an example of which sound device?
A Onomatopoeia
B End rhyme
C Approximate rhyme
D Internal rhyme

7. Which of the following devices is not used in this poem?
A Alliteration
B Couplet
C End rhyme
D Meter

8. Which of the following best describes the rhyme scheme of this poem?

A abab cdcd efef ghgh
B abcd abcd abcd abcd
C aabb ccdd eeff gghh
D abba cddc effe ghhg

9. Which of the following poetic forms *best* characterizes this poem?

A Sonnet
B Epic
C Dramatic monologue
D Lyric

Read the following excerpt, and then use it to answer questions 10–15.

from **"The Raven"**

Once upon a midnight dreary, while I pondered, weak and weary,
Over many a quaint and curious volume of forgotten lore—
While I nodded, nearly napping, suddenly there came a tapping,
As of some one gently rapping, rapping at my chamber door.
"'Tis some visitor," I muttered, "tapping at my chamber door—
Only this and nothing more."

Ah, distinctly I remember it was in the bleak December,
And each separate dying ember wrought its ghost upon the floor.
Eagerly I wished the morrow;—vainly I had sought to borrow
From my books surcease of sorrow—sorrow for the lost Lenore—
For the rare and radiant maiden whom the angels name Lenore—
Nameless *here* for evermore.

And the silken, sad, uncertain rustling of each purple curtain
Thrilled me—filled me with fantastic terrors never felt before;
So that now, to still the beating of my heart, I stood repeating:
"'Tis some visitor entreating entrance at my chamber door—
Some late visitor entreating entrance at my chamber door;—
This it is and nothing more."

Presently my soul grew stronger; hesitating then no longer,
"Sir," said I, "or Madam, truly your forgiveness I implore;
But the fact is I was napping, and so gently you came rapping,
And so faintly you came tapping, tapping at my chamber door,
That I scarce was sure I heard you"—here I opened wide the door;—
Darkness there and nothing more.

—Edgar Allan Poe

10. Which of the following statements about "The Raven" is *not* true?

A Each stanza contains internal rhyme.
B This excerpt contains no alliteration.
C This excerpt is written in blank verse.
D This excerpt consists of four quatrains.

11. The literary device *most* evident in the last line of each stanza (6, 12, 18, 24) is—
A assonance
B onomatopoeia
C alliteration
D consonance

12. Which of the following lines contains an example of alliteration?
A 3
B 7
C 17
D 21

13. This excerpt represents what type of poem?
A Ode
B Narrative
C Sonnet
D Lyric

14. Which of the following statements about "The Raven" is true?
A Lines 1 and 2 create a couplet.
B Line 9 contains an example of onomatopoeia.
C Line 12 is written in iambic pentameter.
D Lines 20 and 22 create end rhyme.

15. The rhyme scheme of stanza 3 is—
A abcbbb
B dbebbb
C fbgbbb
D hbibbb

Answers to Chapter 5 Exercises

1. **(A)** There are four quatrains, each with an alternating rhyme. The final couplet completes the sonnet's rhyme scheme.
2. **(D)** The final two lines form a consecutive two-line rhyming pattern.
3. **(C)** The words *grant*, *goddess*, and *go* begin with the same initial consonant sound.
4. **(C)** This sonnet is written in the iambic pentameter version, which was very popular with Shakespeare; because it rhymes, it cannot be blank verse, and because it is metered, it cannot be free verse.
5. **(B)** Each of the four stanzas forms a quatrain (a four-line stanza or four-line unit). A sonnet would be a complete fourteen-line poem, a couplet would be a two-line rhyming unit, and an octave would be an eight-line unit.
6. **(C)** The words *stone* and *gone* form approximate rhyme. When pronounced, they sound close but not exactly alike (exact rhyme). Because there are no rhyming pairs within either of these lines, there is no internal rhyme. Further, there are no *sound* words, such as *whoosh*, so there is no evidence of onomatopoeia.
7. **(B)** There is no evidence of a couplet. All of the rhymes (or approximate rhymes) occur in every other line, such as 1 and 3 or 2 and 4. A couplet must involve consecutive rhyming lines. Alliteration occurs throughout the poem, such as with the *s* sound in lines 5 through 8. End rhyme occurs several times, such as in lines 5 and 7 (slept and swept). This poem is metered. It has a consistent rhythm and pattern of rhyme.
8. **(A)** The rhyme pattern is formed by the rhyming of every other line, hence *abab,* etc.
9. **(D)** Lyric would provide the best characterization of this poem's form. It cannot be a sonnet because it is sixteen lines in length. It neither tells a story nor involves a hero, so epic is not correct. It does have a speaker who appears to be talking, but his words are directed toward the reader. In a dramatic monologue, it is apparent that some other person or group is involved in a discussion with the speaker but is simply not adding to the conversation at that point. Therefore, lyric is the only choice left. This poem does have a speaker sharing his thoughts and feelings regarding the contributions of those who fought for liberty. Lyric is the best choice. You might consider this an ode, and if ode had been a choice, you might have considered it because the poem seems to praise and honor the fighters and is written in lyric form. However, an ode will normally be much longer and more developed than this short selection.
10. **(D)** Four quatrains consist of sixteen lines. This poem has twenty-four, so each stanza consists of a sestet.
11. **(A)** The repetition of the "o" sound constitutes assonance. There is no alliteration (patterns of repeated initial consonant sounds) or consonance (repetition of word patterns within words). Also, there are no individual words that represent sounds (onomatopoeia) although overall end rhyme is apparent.
12. **(A)** Alliteration occurs in the sequence of *n* words—*nodded, nearly, napping.*
13. **(B)** The excerpt tells part of a story. It is not a poem of praise (ode), it is not fourteen lines in length (sonnet), and it does not share only the thoughts and feelings of the speaker (lyric).
14. **(D)** The words *implore* and *door* create an end rhyme pattern. Lines 1 and 2 do not rhyme, line 9 does not contain any words that represent sound, and line 12 contains seven syllables, not the ten required for iambic pentameter.
15. **(C)**

Chapter 6
Literary Terms

6.1 Literary Elements

- **Symbol** – Authors and poets often use symbols in their writing. A symbol is a noun that has a literal meaning but also stands for some greater meaning. For example, in the story of *Cinderella*, the glass slipper is a piece of footwear the girl wears to the beautiful ball, but it also represents the prince's search for happiness and love. When he looks at the glass slipper, he is reminded of the beautiful night he spent with Cinderella. The fact that it is glass can also be a symbol of the fragile nature of Cinderella herself. She is delicate and easily hurt. You may sometimes see symbolism in a story because of some experience you have had personally. Perhaps a story about a rose holds special meaning for you because you were given a rose by someone special in your life. You can even see many symbols in the world today: the American flag (a symbol of our country), a golden ring (a symbol of the commitment of marriage), and the Statue of Liberty (a symbol of freedom).

- **Irony** – Irony is defined as the difference between appearance and reality. This definition is not extremely helpful, but irony itself is quite easy to recognize. In fact, you have probably witnessed it many times, saying to yourself things such as, "Oh my gosh, that was so weird!" Have you ever picked up the phone to call someone only to find a caller already on the line? Have you ever thought about an old friend only to suddenly see that friend in a store? Perhaps you have wondered how you would afford a birthday gift for a friend and then found twenty dollars in an old jeans pocket. These kinds of situations are ironic. What you expected to happen was different from what actually happened. If you read a story that had a surprise ending, you experienced an ironic twist. All the examples of irony above are *situational irony* because what happens is different from what you expect. There is also *verbal irony*, which occurs when you say one thing but actually mean something else. For example, when actors tell one another to "break a leg," they don't actually wish harm to one another. They are actually wishing one another luck in a production. Finally, there is *dramatic irony*, which occurs when the reader, or "audience," knows something that the characters do not know. If you know that the main character's best friend is actually the criminal and is deceiving the main character, then you know more than the character does, and the suspense of the story is increased.

- **Tone** – The tone of a story or poem refers to the author's attitude toward the topic and is shown through the choice of vocabulary and style of the writing. Suppose that you are angry with a friend and sit down to write a letter expressing your feelings. You will most likely choose words that express your present mood, and the reader will feel that mood when reading the story. As you read literature, try to *listen* to the words and *feel* the mood of the writer as he puts the words to paper.

- **Mood/atmosphere** – The mood, or atmosphere, of a story or poem is the overall feeling that you get as you read. Perhaps a story's events make you feel sad, or maybe they make you feel angry. Any emotion that you, as the reader, feel comes from the connection of elements in the work.

- **Oxymoron** – An oxymoron is a two-word phrase in which the two words are opposites, but they work together to form one meaning without confusing the reader. For example, if you say that you ate *jumbo shrimp* for supper, you are using an oxymoron. The words *jumbo* and *shrimp*, when used alone, have opposite meanings. However, the words, when used together, describe a type of food. Oxymorons are common in our language. There are even websites dedicated to them.

- **Paradox** – A paradox is similar to an oxymoron in that it involves seemingly contradictory ideas. However, upon further examination, you will find that a paradox actually expresses a truth of some sort. For example, you might hear someone say that the funeral was a happy occasion for all. These two concepts—*funeral* and *happy occasion*—seem contradictory, as if both cannot occur at the same time. However, perhaps the person who passed away was very sick and in a great deal of pain. Those who attended the funeral feel "happy" that their beloved family member no longer has to endure such suffering. What seems a contradiction at first actually expresses a truth.

- **Rhetorical question** – A rhetorical question is one to which you do not actually expect an answer. It is stated to emphasize or stress a point. For example, have you ever heard anyone say, "Do you think money grows on trees"? If someone were to ask you this, you would not feel that you had to answer, "No, money is made by machines." In fact, such an answer would probably annoy the one who asked the question.

- **Euphemism** – A euphemism is a "delicate" term or phrase that is substituted for one that could be considered offensive or harsh. For example, if I visit a friend in the hospital and I want to inquire about upcoming surgery, I might say, "When will the procedure be performed?" rather than "When will they take out your heart?" Rather than excusing yourself from the dinner table to go to the "toilet," you might say that you need to visit the restroom or, simply, that you need to be excused.

- **Denotation versus connotation** – The denotation of a word is its actual dictionary definition. The connotation of a word is the feeling associated with it. For example, the words *mother* and *mommy* have similar definitions. They both identify a woman who has a child or children. However, they inspire different feelings when spoken. The word *mother* seems more formal than the word *mommy*.

- **Imagery** – Imagery is the use of words that create "pictures" in the mind of the reader. These images are usually created through the use of descriptive terms that relate to the reader's senses of sight, hearing, touch, taste, and smell. Imagery is used to help the reader experience the scene. If you want to describe the color of your new car, you can say that it is red. If you want to actually create a picture of the new car, you can say that it is shiny, candy-apple red, glistening with the sheen of a new coat of wax. Imagery is a wonderful technique used by writers and poets to help the reader imagine a part of the story or scene.

- **Allusion** – When one work of literature includes a reference to another well-known work of literature, event, person, or place, you know that the author has used allusion. For example, if a story describes a character as being another "Ebeneezer Scrooge," then the reader gets an immediate picture of the character in the story. The use of allusion allows the writer to give a lot of information without actually stating it. Examples of allusion are not always so explicitly stated, but they are usually effective in helping to create a visual for the reader.

- **Aphorism** – An aphorism is a short, wise saying that expresses a truth of some sort. For example, "No pain, no gain" is an aphorism that indicates that to achieve success, one may have to endure challenge or difficulty. Other aphorisms could be "One rotten apple spoils the barrel" or "Here today, gone tomorrow."

- **Anecdote** – An anecdote is a short, usually funny account of an event in someone's life. When you tell someone about a situation that happened to you, you are relating an anecdote. An anecdote is an interesting way to begin the introduction of an essay.

6.2 Literary Terms

The term *figurative language* is a general term that includes language that is not meant to be taken literally. Earlier, when you read about verbal irony, you were given an example of figurative language because actors don't actually mean for cast members to "break their legs." All of the following terms are considered forms of figurative language.

- **Simile** – A simile is a comparison between two things, using the words "like" or "as" to make the comparison. For example, if you say "Tom is as tall as a tree," you are using a simile because it compares Tom to a tree by using the word *as*. It is also considered figurative because you do not actually mean he is as tall as a tree; you are just indicating that he is very tall.

- **Metaphor** – A metaphor is similar to a simile, the only difference being that it does not use the words *like* or *as* to make the comparison. A metaphor is considered an unstated comparison. For example, if you want to make the previous example of a simile into a metaphor, you simply say, "Tom is a tree." Suppose you write the following line of a poem: "Life's waves sometimes dash me against the hardened and crusty shores of despair." You are making an unstated comparison between life and the ocean. You never actually say that life is like an ocean (which would be a simile), but the reader infers that connection by reading and analyzing the poem's lines. Metaphors are another device that helps writers create meaning and visions for their readers.

- **Analogy** – An analogy, like a simile or metaphor, makes a comparison between two things; however, an analogy is usually presented as a situation rather than simply as a phrase. For example, if you write a paragraph comparing the growth of a child to the growth of a flower, you might compare *blooming* to maturing and the *root system* to one's choice of home. The developed comparison would be an analogy.

- **Idiom** – An idiom is an expression that has an overall meaning that is different from the literal meaning of each of its words. For example, if you say that there is a "fork in the road," the literal interpretation means that a silver utensil is in the middle of a roadway. However, the phrase figuratively means that a road splits into two separate paths. Idioms are common, so you are usually not confused about their intended meanings.

- **Hyperbole** – Hyperbole is an intentional exaggeration used for emphasis. If you have been waiting at the doctor's office for forty-five minutes, and you tell someone that you've been waiting for three days, you have used a hyperbole. Have you ever said you're hungry enough to eat a horse? You used a hyperbole, a major form of figurative language.

- **Understatement** – Just the opposite of a hyperbole, an understatement states less than is true to emphasize a point. It, ironically, is a form of exaggeration. Suppose that on a given night, you have twenty pages of math homework, ten pages of history, and an English essay to write. When your mother or father asks you if you have much homework, you reply, "Yes, I'm going to be a *little* busy tonight." You have understated what is actually true. You are probably going to be *very* busy. If you, instead, reply, "Yes, I have five million hours of homework to do," you will have used a hyperbole.

- **Jargon** – The use of jargon involves the use of highly technical terms or of terms associated only with particular sports, careers, or hobbies. For example, if a sportscaster reports that "John drove the ball hard," he is using jargon (drove). Those who play that sport in question will understand the term, but others may not. It is important to be aware that writers may use jargon as a figurative tool.

- **Personification** – Personification involves giving human characteristics to nonhumans. For example, a poet may write that the "waves hear him crying." Waves cannot hear.

Books that involve animals going to work and living in houses also make use of personification. You may even use this in your everyday language when you say something like this: "That phone just loves to ring whenever I'm watching television." Your indication that the phone has the ability to feel emotion or ring intentionally involves the use of personification.

- **Apostrophe** – Apostrophe is similar to personification; however, instead of speaking about inanimate objects as if they were human, the speaker in a literary work may speak directly to the object. Have you ever spoken to your car or your pet? If so, then you have used apostrophe to speak to something that is unable to use human speech to answer you. The use of apostrophe also involves speaking to abstract concepts or absent people. Suppose you are disappointed to find that a close relative is not going to be able to join your family during a holiday season. You might, in a moment alone, say, "I wish you could be here." You are using apostrophe. Most examples, however, are more directly stated toward inanimate objects.

6.3 Drama Terms

- **Soliloquy** – A soliloquy is a long speech given by a character alone on stage, pouring out his or her feelings. If you have read *Romeo and Juliet*, you may remember Juliet's speech just before she takes the poison. She is sharing her fears about waking early in the tomb and her concern that perhaps the friar is not trustworthy. This is an example of a soliloquy, and it helps the reader to learn a lot about Juliet's state of mind.

- **Aside** – An aside is like a secret told on stage. If two actors are standing on the stage, surrounded by other characters, and one wants to tell the other something private, the secret will have to be loud enough for the audience to hear, but the other characters will seem to take no notice of the comment. In a play, the word *aside* will be written in parentheses before the comment to let the reader know it is meant only for certain characters and the audience to hear.

- **Dramatic irony** – Dramatic irony occurs when the audience knows something that the characters don't know. For example, if you are watching a mystery show, and you know that the person who robbed the bank is the same person who is pretending to help the police officers, then you are aware of something the characters are not. This is dramatic irony. Use of such a technique adds a great deal of emotion and suspense on the part of the reader or audience.

6.4 Literary Influences

- **Rationalism** – This was a belief that the world's problems could be solved through reason, rather than through emotion, intuition, faith, or tradition. This seventeenth-century philosophy occurred during the Age of Reason, also known as the Enlightenment. Although this rationalist concept originated in Europe, its effects were seen in the colonies in the thoughts of such writers and thinkers as Benjamin Franklin, the journalist and inventor, and Patrick Henry, who delivered the famous "Speech in the Virginia Convention." Rationalists did believe in God, but they believed that he gave human beings the gift of reason and expected them to improve their lives and solve their problems through science and logic.

- **Romanticism** – This influential movement was a reaction against the logical ideas of rationalism as people began to see limits to the success of a "reason only" philosophy. Romanticism began in the eighteenth century and included several specific characteristics: love of imagination and intuition over reason; search for truth through reflection and contemplation of nature; a true love for nature, poetry, and the "self" or individual; and fascination with the supernatural. Romantics placed a great value on poetry as most symbolic of imagination. Two basic ways in which the Romantics sought to look past the "negativity" of the world were through nature and through exotic, gothic settings. Some of the writers during the period of Romanticism were Edgar Allen Poe, whose psychological themes were characteristic of the Romantic ideas; Henry Wadsworth Longfellow, whose poetry incorporated many of the lessons found in nature; and Washington Irving, author of the famous "Legend of Sleepy Hollow."

- **Renaissance** – This time during the nineteenth century involved an explosion of American literary production. The term *renaissance* means "rebirth," so it was an appropriate word to use for the great increase in literary works. The Renaissance period also saw a great deal of social change in New England, improvements occurring in areas such as public education and women's rights. The period also saw the emergence of "utopian" groups that desired a better society.

- **Transcendentalism** – This was also a nineteenth century movement that suggested individuals could obtain "truth" by moving, figuratively, past the physical world and reflecting on spiritual and sensory experiences. Transcendentalists believed that humans could reach perfection by searching for the true, "real" world of ideas. This idea, supported by such noted writers as Ralph Waldo Emerson and Henry David Thoreau, was a "rosy" view—too rosy, in fact, for some. Herman Melville, author of *Moby Dick*, and Nathaniel Hawthorne, author of *The Scarlet Letter*, saw evil in humans and the world. They did not believe that perfection and truth could be achieved, or even pursued, because of the natural sin existing in men's hearts. It is interesting, for example, to compare Emerson's ideas about one's ability to commune with nature or believe in himself with Hawthorne's story of hidden sin and psychological manipulation.

- **Realism** – This nineteenth-century literary movement suggested that life should be portrayed as exactly as possible without idealizing it or making it sound better than it actually was. Because the Civil War occurred during this time, much of the writing surrounded the theme of war. Some selections, such as those by Melville, focused on the dark side of war, the suffering; other selections, such as those by Walt Whitman, celebrated the drive, heroism, and endurance of the American people during what was basically a horrible period. Much of the literature of this period, however, took the form of journals, letters, and personal diaries from those directly involved in the war. Other famous Realists include Jack London, a writer intrigued by themes of survival; Stephen Crane, author of *The Red Badge of Courage*; John Steinbeck, whose Southern novels often contained a humorous twist, and Bret Harte.

- **Naturalism** – This nineteenth-century movement was an extension of realism; it suggested that humans were shaped and influenced by their environments, over which they have no control. Naturalist writers saw humans as living in a world where they had little choice or control over their own lives; they existed according to their natural instincts, tendencies created in them by the environments in which they were raised.

- **Regionalism** – A subcategory of realism, regionalism involves stories set in specific geographic locations. To make the stories realistic, the author uses story elements—such as dialect—to mirror the actual people who live in that area. Regional writers included William Faulkner, John Steinbeck, and Mark Twain (Samuel H. Clemens), author of the famous *Adventures of Huckleberry Finn.*

- **Modernism** – This was a period in the early twentieth century during which writers began to take bold, new approaches to writing literature and poetry. Topics, styles, and attitudes all changed to reflect a desire to shed the "romantic" past. Some modernists were Carl Sandburg, Ezra Pound, Edgar Lee Masters, e.e.cummings, and William Carlos Williams. They turned from traditional poetic forms and subjects to new, imaginative styles. For example, one modernist poem describes the jump of a grasshopper by mixing all of the poem's words around on the page. Another poem focuses on the death of a child's pet hen by describing the swollen, purple knot left by the sting of a bee.

6.5 Story Styles

- **Stream of consciousness** – This is a technique that attempts to imitate the natural flow of thoughts in a character's mind. You know how when you are sitting and thinking, your thoughts sometimes drift from one subject to another? If you write down your thoughts exactly as they occur, they will probably be a little confusing for someone else to read. That is why this technique is difficult to use effectively, but it can add a great deal of reality to stories. A great example can be found in one particular story entitled "The Jilting of Granny Weatherall," written by Eudora Welty. In this story, Granny is quite old, and her thoughts are often confused. She sometimes thinks she is young again, with young children. Her thoughts move back and forth between the present and the past. Welty effectively uses stream of consciousness to help present the state of mind of the elderly Granny. This is much more effective than having a narrator say that Granny is often confused about the past and the present.

- **Fantasy** – A fantasy is a story that cannot happen. *Cinderella*, with the changing of pumpkins into coaches and fairy godmothers, is a type of fantasy.

- **Fable** – A fable is a story that usually has animals as characters, and it usually teaches a lesson or moral. The story of *The Country Mouse and the City Mouse* is an example of a fable. Each mouse thinks the other has a better life until they switch lives. They learn that they were already quite blessed with their own environments.

- **Allegory** – An allegory is a story in which the characters, events, and even the setting serve both a literal and a symbolic purpose. In other words, main story elements can represent other events, people, or even abstract concepts. Suppose a story is written about a girl named Hope. In the story, she encounters Richie, a boy who loves money above all else, and Jewel, a girl who loves material possessions. Hope's friendship with these characters helps them to appreciate the true joys of life. This story is an allegory because Hope, Richie, and Jewel all represent not only people but also major concepts in life. Allegories often end with the revelation of a wonderful lesson or vision.

- **Parable** – A parable is a short story in which a simple situation from life can teach a valuable lesson or moral. Suppose you read a story about two students, one who studies diligently for two weeks before taking a test and one who wastes time and has to cram all night before the big examination. In the end, the student who diligently works receives an A and learns a lot about the subject, but the student who procrastinates receives a D and forgets all the material quickly. The story is teaching you that it is always better to work hard and prepare, no matter what the task.

- **Legend** – A legend is a blend of fact and fiction, meaning that the story might be true, false, or anywhere in between. Sometimes a legend is created from an event that was originally true but that gained a great number of fictional details over time and numerous retellings. People enjoy both sharing and hearing these stories, and that is why they are widely believed, but they are not verifiable. For example, the story of Robin Hood is a legend. Was there actually a Robin Hood who stole from the rich and gave money to the poor? Is this legend the result of an exaggerated tale that began with the robbery of one rich man? Other legends include those surrounding King Arthur and his famous knights and the story of the infamous Loch Ness monster in Scotland.

- **Myth** – A myth is an anonymous story that usually attempts to explain a belief or ritual of a particular culture. Myths are traditional tales passed through generations of families and usually involve some sort of god or superhuman.

- **Tall tale** – A tall tale is a funny, exaggerated story that is not completely believable. These wild stories are part of the heritage of folk literature both in the United States and in other countries. The characters in tall tales commit outlandish and impossible acts, and although the stories are unbelievable, they are definitely humorous!

- **Science fiction** – A science fiction story usually takes place far into the future or in space. Stories about computers taking over the world or life in the year 2098 would be science fiction selections.

- **Fiction versus nonfiction** – A fiction selection is not true; a nonfiction selection is true. Cinderella is fiction, but a biography about George Washington is nonfiction. Some stories may contain some elements of each. For example, a story about George Washington meeting President Bush will contain some nonfictional elements (the existence of both people), but it will also contain fictional elements because George Washington lived long ago and would not be able to meet the current president.

- **Autobiography versus biography** – An autobiography is a story about someone's life written by that person. You can write your own autobiography. A biography is a story about someone's life written by someone else. You can write someone else's biography.

- **Novel** – A novel is a long work of fiction. Many of the stories you read for English class are novels. If they are true stories, they are nonfiction, a different type of literature.

- **Parody** – A parody is a funny interpretation of a serious subject. If you watch the show *Saturday Night Live,* you are watching parodies. A skit designed to parody a television show, for instance, involves characters who look like those on the show and a humorous, though related, storyline.

- **Short story** – A short story is a brief work of fiction. A short story can usually be read in one sitting. If you are reading a short "story" that is true, then you are reading nonfiction.

- **Satire** – Satire is writing that pokes fun at people, politics, society, or life in general to show weaknesses and, possibly, bring about change. One of the greatest examples of satire is *Gulliver's Travels*, written by English author Jonathan Swift. In one chapter of this book, Gulliver visits an island inhabited by tiny humans who are fighting with another island of similar humans over whether one should crack an egg on the rounded end or the pointed end. In the story, this argument actually results in war between the islands' inhabitants. Of course, this argument seems silly to the reader, just the point Swift wanted to make. He was attempting to show the futility of the religious wars that were occurring in England, dividing neighbor against neighbor.

6.6 Story Terms

- **Plot** – The plot of a story is the series of events that happen. If you tell a friend that you saw a movie about a man who finds a stray dog and then raises it to be a great hunter, you are telling the plot of the story.

- **Setting** – The setting of a story indicates where and when it takes place. The setting can be either general or specific. You might say that a story takes place in a school, or you might find that it takes place in room twenty-five of a small elementary school in the mountains of North Dakota. When a story takes place is also important. You might be told the year, the time of day, or perhaps only the century.

- **Theme** – The theme of a story is the main idea, lesson, or point it conveys. In other words, what do you learn from the story after you have finished reading it? Perhaps the story leaves you with a lesson or a realization about life. The writer uses the characters, plot, and setting to help create and illustrate the theme. Using the *Cinderella* example again, you can say the theme is that if people remain hopeful, they can always achieve their dreams. It is important to remember that different readers may see different types of themes in stories, but they are usually quite related. Also, you must remember that the theme is not the same as the plot. Themes are general ideas that can relate to many different stories.

- **Characters** – The characters in a story are those that perform the action of the plot. Characters are usually people, but they can be bugs or even trees, depending on the type of story. The **protagonist** is the main character of the story, and the **antagonist** is the character (or characters) who opposes the main character. In *Cinderella*, Cinderella is the main character, and the step-sisters and step-mother are antagonists.

- **Point of view** – The point of view relates to who is telling the story. If one of the characters in the story is the speaker, then the point of view is said to be *first person*. If a story is written in first person, you see a character using terms such as *I* and *me*. If the speaker in the story is not a character but, rather, a narrator, then the story is written in *third person*. A person not involved in the plot of the story is telling what happened to the characters. If the story is written in third person, you see a character using terms such as *he, she, they,* and actual names to refer to the characters. Look at the following opening story lines:

  As I opened the window, I could hear the faint, yet distinct, chirping of a nest full of baby birds.

  As John opened the window, he could hear the faint, yet distinct, chirping of a nest full of baby birds.

In the first line, the character is speaking personally about hearing the birds chirping. This sentence is written in first person. In the second, someone else is telling about the character hearing the birds. This sentence is written in third person.

With regard to third-person point of view, there are two subcategories: ***third-person limited*** and ***third-person omniscient***. In third-person limited, the narrator knows the thoughts of only one character. In third-person omniscient, the narrator knows the thoughts of more than one character, perhaps all of them. Consider the following examples:

> As Eleanor got onto the bus, she stared intently at the stranger. She knew that she had seen him before, but she could not remember where. She passed him slowly, still staring, and moved toward the back of the bus. The stranger simply returned the stare with a questioning expression.
>
> As Eleanor got onto the bus, she stared intently at the stranger. She knew that she had seen him before, but she could not remember where. She passed him slowly, still staring, and moved toward the back of the bus. The stranger simply returned the stare with a questioning expression, not wishing to reveal his recognition of her.

In the first example, the narrator knows what Eleanor is thinking but does not give any information about the thoughts of the stranger. The narrator's comments are limited to the thoughts of one character (third-person limited). The reader is thus left to determine what the stranger might be thinking. In the second example, however, the narrator reveals the thoughts of both Eleanor and the stranger, showing a more comprehensive knowledge of characters' thoughts (third-person omniscient).

- **Conflict** – The conflict is the struggle or difficulty in the story. That conflict and the subsequent solution create the intensity of the story. There are several possible types of conflict. A writer might use *man versus man*, which means that a human or humans are in conflict with other humans. There is also *man versus animal*, which pits a human against an animal, perhaps a wild bear or dog. Another form of conflict is *man versus nature*, which involves a conflict between a human and some aspect of the environment. If you can't get to school because there has been an ice storm, you are experiencing man-versus-nature conflict. If you are attempting to train a pet gerbil but it is not cooperating, you are experiencing man-versus-animal conflict. A fourth type of conflict is *man versus society*, which involves a human's struggle with societal issues, such as politics, stereotyping, or laws. It is important to remember that the conflict in a story does not have to involve hostility. If you are trying to help a friend to deal with a difficult situation, you are experiencing man-versus-man conflict that does not involve anger or fighting. Finally, there is the type of conflict that involves only one character: *man versus himself.* This occurs when a character is in conflict with his own conscience or feelings. If you are worrying about whether to go to college *A* or college *B*, you are experiencing man-versus-himself conflict. Often, a story can include a variety of conflict situations that mix together.

- **Suspense** – Certain elements keep the reader emotionally involved in a story. Your desire to know what is going to happen keeps you from losing interest. If you have ever heard anyone say, "I just couldn't put that book down," the reader is making reference to the suspense that keeps the interest level high. One great example of this occurs in Bram Stoker's novel *Dracula.* The story is told through a series of diaries. In chapter one, the diary of one character shares his experiences in Dracula's castle. At first, he is intrigued by the strange owner of the mansion, but after he finds Dracula in his coffin, he indicates that he believes he is in great danger. Just as the reader turns the page to find out whether the man will survive, the first chapter ends, and the second begins with the diaries of another character. The suspense is quite high at this point.

- **Climax** – The climax is the point of highest interest or greatest intensity in a story, the point at which the reader is the most emotionally involved. In *Goldilocks and the Three Bears*, the climax occurs at the point when the bears go upstairs and find Goldilocks sleeping. The reader knows at this point that the situation has come to a head; something is bound to happen, and the suspense keeps the reader involved. In *Cinderella,* the climax occurs when the Prince's servant arrives at the door to try the slipper on those in Cinderella's home and, because the evil step-sisters have locked Cinderella in her room, you don't know whether she will escape in time to try on the shoe and find her true love!

- **Resolution** – The resolution is the point at which the conflict is resolved or settled. This may not be a happy resolution; it simply means that the conflict is over. In *Goldilocks and the Three Bears*, the resolution occurs when the girl wakes up and runs from the house. In *Cinderella*, the resolution occurs when the Prince's servant tries the slipper on Cinderella's foot and the Prince finds the woman he loves.

- **Flashback** – A flashback is a reference in a story to some event that occurred previously. For example, if you were reading a story about a father named Jed Deskie and sometime during the story Jed remembers and shares an event that occurred during his teenage years, you would be seeing an example of flashback. This literary device is useful in writing because it allows the writer to help develop the characters by discussing or having them discuss the past events that shaped their lives and personalities.

- **Foreshadowing** – Foreshadowing involves the use of "hints" about events that may occur in a story. This literary device adds to your sense of suspense as you read, and it also encourages you to make predictions about the story. Suppose, for example, you are reading a story about a young girl who gets lost on a camping trip. At the end of one chapter, the text reads, "Marilyn wished she were safely back at camp; little did she know her journey was about to turn even more dangerous." The author has used foreshadowing to let you, the reader, know that she will not get back to camp anytime soon and, in fact, danger is on the way. You wonder what will happen, so you keep reading.

Chapter 6 Exercises—Literary Terms

Read the following untitled poem, and then use it to answer questions 1–3.

Please don't look at me with pity, or sadness in your eye.
The road will be even rougher to come.
I believe I have the strength to keep movin' on, and looking toward the Heavens.
See, I'm not alone,
I have the greatest force created always beside me, guiding me along my way.
It's not easy, I know.
Sometimes, it's harder to believe than not believe,
But I'm reminded every day that I'm loved.
When the sun shines upon my face,
Or when I hear the sweet melody of a bird.
I know, when I can go no further and I fall,
I shall be picked up and carried by someone who has such compassion for me.
Little ol' me. Who'd of thought?
So see, don't look at me with sadness. I may look rough on the outside,
But on the inside, I'm rejoicing.

—Jennifer Dodson

1. The speaker considers the sun and the melodies of birds to be symbolic of what?

A Her desire to rejoice
B The challenges of the world
C Those who view her as "rough"
D The presence of God

2. In which line can you detect a shift from a more formal tone to a less formal one?

A 4
B 8
C 13
D 15

3. What is ironic about this speaker?

A Others view her with pity, but she views her life as sad.
B She lives an easy life, but others see her as "rough."
C She lives a difficult life, but she has a positive outlook on life.
D She views others with pity, but she views herself as strong.

Read the following poem, and then use it to answer questions 4–9.

As I Sat There Watching the World Go By

As I sat there watching the world go by,
I saw a child eating ice cream, with delight in her eyes.
I wonder why this world has to be so cruel.
Why can't it go back to the times when kings, fairies, and elves ruled?
As I sat there watching the world go by,
I wished it could go back to its stage of tie dye.
Although I wasn't there,
I've heard about the peace, love, and long hair.
It was said that it was a wonderful time,
Back when you could buy moon pies for only a dime.
As I sat there watching the world go by,
I wondered if that little girl will cry,

Cry when she finds out there are no elves or monsters under her bed.
Cry when she finds out the world is ruled by money and greed,
Leaving homeless in need of more.
As I sat there watching the world go by,
I began to cry.

—Jennifer Dodson

4. The child in this poem is a symbol of—

A love
B innocence
C fear
D peace

5. Which of the following lines from the poem contains an example of allusion?

A 3
B 8
C 12
D 17

6. How does the connotation of the word *ruled* in line 14 contribute to the overall mood of the poem?

A It adds a feeling of helplessness.
B It creates a feeling of power.
C It adds a feeling of peace.
D It creates a feeling of love for mankind.

7. Which of the following ideas from the poem represents irony?

A The child is happy though she lives in a cruel world.
B The child is happy though she knows the world is cruel.
C The child is happy though the speaker is not.
D The child is happy though she knows the speaker is not.

8. The overall mood of the poem is one of—

A humility
B frustration
C bitterness
D indifference

9. The "times when kings, fairies, and elves ruled" from line 14 are symbolic of what?

A The English tradition of rule by a monarchy
B The period of childhood innocence
C The world found in fictional tales
D The difficult life of the speaker

Read the following excerpt from an essay, and then use it to answer 10–15.

"You can't catch me," five-year-old Megan screamed as she ran from her cousin. With all the determination a seven year old could muster, Stephen relentlessly chased after her. The beautiful, summer day filled the cousins with boundless energy. The two children had been playing together for over an hour in their grandma's large front yard. They had played the game of chase for that entire time. "I'm tired of this game," Stephen exhaled as he stopped to catch his breath.

"Me too!" Megan agreed emphatically. She almost always went along with whatever her cousin said. She was at an impressionable age. "Let's find something else to do," Stephen said. "I know! You run across the road and touch that oak tree, right there, and then I will too."

Stephen pointed a small finger at the tree he had mentioned. Considering that their grandma had given them specific instructions not to leave the yard for any reason, Stephen's idea was dreadfully mischievous.

"If you go first, then I will touch that tree," Megan countered. She was impressionable, but she wasn't about to let him trick her into getting into trouble by herself. She was suspicious because he had conned her into being the first one to disobey Grandma before. If she went first, he would probably fail to uphold his promise of actually crossing the road to touch the oak tree.

"Okay. How about we go together?" he suggested. Megan agreed, and they both flew across the road, touched the tree, and bolted back to Grandma's front yard.

"That wasn't much fun," Megan complained. The thrill of disobeying Grandma had lasted only a few seconds.

"You're right," Stephen conceded. "I have another great idea. Maybe we could go for a walk."

"Where?" Megan questioned eagerly.

"We could go look at the big bushes that Grandma has planted along the edge of the road," he said excitedly. Grandma loved flowers, so the children had a natural interest in the blooming bushes.

"Okay," Megan agreed. Indeed, she was a very agreeable child.

Stephen and Megan strolled leisurely toward the gorgeous, flowering bushes. They reached the first bush and paused to gaze in wonder at its beauty. The leaves were a healthy shade of green, and the large, white blossoms of the flowers were bunched together in perfect spheres. The children traveled from bush to bush, taking in the magnificent appearance of each individual plant. When they finished examining the last bush, thirty minutes had passed. Tired and ready for a long nap, Stephen and Megan turned around and slowly wandered back in the direction of Grandma's house. When they reached Grandma's driveway, they were alarmed to see Grandma standing in the front yard, arms crossed and feet planted.

10. This selection is told from which point of view?

A First-person limited
B First-person omniscient
C Third-person limited
D Third-person omniscient

11. The style of the selection can *best* be described as a(n)—

A tall tale
B fable
C autobiography
D narrative

12. Which type of conflict is *not* evidenced in the selection?

A Man versus man
B Man versus himself
C Man versus environment
D Man versus society

13. The line "The leaves were a healthy shade of green, and the large, white blossoms of the flowers were bunched together in perfect spheres" from the last paragraph contains what literary element?

A Oxymoron
B Imagery
C Simile
D Hyperbole

14. Which of the following is part of the setting for the selection?

A Grandma's front yard
B Grandma's back yard
C The line of bushes across the street
D Inside Grandma's house

15. What literary element is created by the last line of the selection?

A Flashback
B Foreshadowing
C Suspense
D Resolution

Read the following poem, and then use it to answer questions 16–18.

Ozymandias

I met a traveller from an antique land
Who said:—Two vast and trunkless legs of stone
Stand in the desert. Near them on the sand,
Half sunk, a shatter'd visage lies, whose frown
And wrinkled lip and sneer of cold command
Tell that its sculptor well those passions read
Which yet survive, stamp'd on these lifeless things,
The hand that mock'd them and the heart that fed;
And on the pedestal these words appear:
"My name is Ozymandias, king of kings:
Look on my works, ye Mighty, and despair!"
Nothing beside remains. Round the decay
Of that colossal wreck, boundless and bare,
The lone and level sands stretch far away.

—Percy Bysshe Shelley

16. Line 8, "The hand that mock'd them and the heart that fed;" provides an example of what literary device?

A Metaphor
B Imagery
C Personification
D Apostrophe

17. What is the overall theme of the poem?

A Respect cannot be created.
B Great works of sculpture never last.
C Great kings always rule by fear.
D The respect for kings is everlasting.

18. Lines 4 and 5, "Half sunk, a shatter'd visage lies, whose frown/ And wrinkled lip and sneer of cold command," provide an example of which literary element?

A Paradox
B Imagery
C Rhetorical question
D Allusion

Read the following poem, and then use it to answer questions 19–20.

Believe Me, If All Those Endearing Young Charms

Believe me, if all those endearing young charms,
Which I gaze on so fondly today,
Were to change by tomorrow, and fleet in my arms,
Like fairy-gifts fading away,
Thou wouldst still be adored, as this moment thou art,
Let thy loveliness fade as it will,
And around the dear ruin each wish of my heart
Would entwine itself verdantly still.

It is not while beauty and youth are thine own,
And thy cheeks unprofaned by a tear
That the fervor and faith of a soul can be known,
To which time will but make thee more dear;
No, the heart that has truly loved never forgets,
But as truly loves on to the close,
As the sunflower turns on her god, when he sets,
The same look which she turned when he rose.

—Thomas Moore

19. In line 4, "Like fairy-gifts fading away," which of the following literary devices is evident?

A Simile
B Metaphor
C Euphemism
D Jargon

20. Lines 7 and 8 create what literary device?

A Metaphor
B Allusion
C Personification
D Simile

Answers to Chapter 6 Exercises

1. **(D)** The speaker is reminded daily of love through the sun and melodies of birds; these were God's creations, so they are symbolic of His presence.

2. **(C)** Prior to this line, the speaker uses standard, almost formal language and seems to be quite self-confident; line 13 not only shifts to a more informal style, but it also shows the only lapse in self-confidence, almost as if the speaker feels too insignificant to be honored by God.

3. **(C)** The speaker implies that she lives a difficult life but views life positively because of God's love.

4. **(B)** The child represents the innocence that will allow one to eat ice cream and smile even though the surrounding world is cruel. Children, who may not have experienced any "evil," are easily made happy by simple pleasures, such as ice cream.

5. **(B)** This line makes a reference back to the seventies.

6. **(A)** The fact that the child will someday realize the world is ruled by greed indicates that there exists no possibility of changing the world.

7. **(A)** The child is content because she is not yet aware that cruelty surrounds her. Answer *C* is true—the child is happy and the speaker is not—but it is not ironic, and the child does not know of the speaker referred to in answer *D*.

8. **(B)** The speaker is frustrated by the fact that the child sits there innocently now but will someday face a cruel world. This knowledge causes the speaker to cry. There is no bitterness (severe hatred) indicated, nor is there indifference (lack of concern).

9. **(B)** The line about kings, fairies, and elves relates to the period when children are young and concerned only with fiction and make-believe, not the cruel realities of the world. The child's discovery that such a world—with fairies and elves—does not exist is symbolic of the transition into adulthood.

10. **(C)** The selection is narrated, and the personal thoughts of Megan are the only ones shared by the narrator. The characters themselves are not telling the story, so *first person* is not an option. Further, there are no subcategories of first-person point of view.

11. **(D)** This is simply a narrative.

12. **(C)** Man versus environment is not a style of conflict included in this selection. The children experience the environment, but it does not present a challenge to their actions. They do have conflict with one another, Megan wonders to herself whether she can trust Stephen (man versus himself), and the children also experience conflict with the rules of society represented by their grandmother.

13. **(B)** The beautiful description of the leaves and blossoms helps the writer to create a picture in the mind of the reader.

14. **(A)** Grandma's front yard is specifically mentioned. Her back yard is not, and the bushes are at the end of the front yard, not across the street. The entire selection takes place outdoors, so the *inside of the house* is not an option.

15. **(C)** Grandma is standing there, and the children have broken the rules. What will Grandma do? The reader wants to know. The final sentence contains no reference to the past, hints for the future, or the resolution of a conflict. In fact, conflict is probably just beginning.

16. **(C)** The hand and the heart are being given human qualities, but they are not human. There is no comparison, specific description, or direct address of an object.

17. **(A)** The king had the statue built so that his "power" would forever intimidate his subjects. Answers *B, C*, and *D* indicate themes that cannot be inferred from the information given in the poem. Some great works of sculpture may last, some kings may not rule by fear, and all kings are not given everlasting respect.

18. **(B)** The terms *frown, wrinkled lip*, and *sneer* all help the poet create a picture of the statue's face. The words are very descriptive. There is no paradox (seemingly contradictory statement), question (rhetorical), or reference to another well-known event, person, or place.

19. **(A)** A simile uses the term *like* or *as* to make a comparison. The fairy-gifts are being compared, through use of the word *like*, to the fading of charms.

20. **(C)** The *wish* of a heart cannot entwine itself around anything.

Chapter 7
Research

You have already studied how to write a solid essay. Writing about a topic you have researched involves the very same process. The difference relates to how you gather the information for the paper. For most essays and papers, you rely on your own knowledge to create the body. If you are asked to write about your hobbies, a vacation, or your greatest concern for America, you will write about your own ideas. Researching involves the search for ideas about a topic, usually a topic about which you know very little. Finding out what others say about a subject is a wonderful way to gain knowledge and construct a paper, but because you are dealing with ideas other than your own, you must pay careful attention to some special rules that apply. To practice the concepts involved in research, pretend that you have been given the following task: Write a paper about George Washington. (The SOL test would not give you such a task because you would need other resources to write such a paper; however, the test will require you to answer questions dealing with the process.)

7.1 STEP I: Choosing/Limiting the Topic

For the purpose of this chapter discussion, you are provided a topic. However, your teacher may sometimes ask you to choose your own topic for research. If this is the case, it will be important for you to remember one major point: try to choose a topic of interest to you. If you have a sincere interest in a subject, you will likely enjoy gathering and sorting through information. The research process is a time-consuming one, so if you are interested in all that you are reading, you will conduct a more thorough search and create a more solid paper. If you are asked to choose your own topic, think about your hobbies, interests, possible future careers, and other such areas of personal interest. If a topic is assigned to you, view it as a challenge to learn about a new area that you may find interesting. Also, if your topic is broad, you will have to limit or narrow it, and that also leaves you a wide spectrum of possible topics.

The topic you've been given for this chapter "assignment" is George Washington. This is a very broad topic because there are so many areas about this man's life that you can investigate. This is the time for brainstorming. You must limit the topic to avoid spending a lot of time reading information that may or may not be about the same aspects of his life. If you try to simply gather a lot of facts and put them into a paper, you will not end up with a cohesive and solid paper, but rather a fragmented one. Remember that your paper must have a thesis statement, one sentence in the introduction that states the main point of the whole paper, so you must know beforehand where you will focus your energy.

As you begin to brainstorm, suppose you come up with the following areas:

- Contributions to America
- Family life
- Education
- Presidency
- Different careers

These are five possible areas about George Washington that you could investigate. As you think about which one you'd like to pursue, remember to pick one that interests you and one on which you think information will be available. Sometimes it's possible to limit a topic so much that you have difficulty finding enough information. Of course, with the Internet available to you, you have a wealth of information at your fingertips that, years ago, might have been difficult to find.

Look at the subtopics again. It may be possible for you to include more than one of these, depending on the length of the paper, as long as you feel that you can adequately cover more than one topic and that those you cover relate and follow one another smoothly. For example, you might choose to discuss his education and how that led to his career in politics, or you might discuss the careers he held before and after his presidency, with his political positions included. Research is constantly evolving. You may start out looking for information on two topics but find that there is so much on one topic that you have to limit yourself to that one idea. Some students make the mistake of thinking that if they don't provide every bit of information possible, they haven't done an adequate job. However, just the opposite is true. Trying to stuff too much into a paper will just weaken it and frustrate the reader. If you are not sure what area you want to research within a broad topic, you may find it helpful to read about the subject. Do an Internet search, or check out a library book and simply read. As you do so, you may run across something that really peaks your interest, and your topic problem will be solved. Also, remember the audience for your paper: Who will be reading it? You want to be sure to select a topic that will provide information of interest for the intended audience.

7.2 STEP II: Asking Research Questions

For this research, suppose you have chosen the topic of George Washington's family life. Now that you have limited the topic, your job of searching for information will be much more focused because you will not have to spend time reading lots of literature on his political career and other aspects of his life. That is not to say, of course, that the information on those topics is unimportant; it simply does not relate to the focus of your paper. Now it is time for some more brainstorming in the form of research questions. These are investigative questions related to your topic that you hope to find through your study of the literature on Washington. Here are some possible research questions related to the family life of George Washington:

1. How and when did he meet his wife?
2. Is there information about their courtship?
3. What was his wife's background?
4. How long were they married?
5. Had either been married before?
6. Did she assist him in his career?
7. Did they get along well?
8. How many children did they have?
9. What were the names of the children?
10. What were the responsibilities of the children around the home?
11. Did all the children live to adulthood?
12. Were there grandchildren?
13. Did other relatives live with the Washingtons?
14. How did his wife die?
15. Did her death precede Washington's?
16. Are there interesting facts about the family of George Washington?

7.3 STEP III: Identifying Sources and Gathering Data

There are lots of sources of information available to you, but where you look is usually determined by your topic. For example, it probably won't help you to go to the magazine rack and start looking for information on George Washington's family in the current issues of *Time* and *Newsweek*. So, direct your search carefully. Here are some of the major sources of information for research:

Card catalog (online) – Most libraries have done away with the old card catalog drawers and now have their collected works online. However, the search process is the same; once you log on to the library database, you may search by title, author, or subject. Some online catalogs even narrow their listings down to key words and partial titles. Become familiar with your library and its format. To use the online catalog for your research on Washington, you could use a subject search and the name "George Washington." From this point, you may have to gather some books and search the table of contents for particular sections about his family.

Internet – The technology available to you today is wonderful, but it also presents you with a problem: Some of the information may not be valid. Anyone can post information to the World Wide Web, so you need to analyze the websites you visit to be sure they are reputable. Don't, for instance, base your paper on *Billy's Interesting Facts About Presidents* webpage. Look at sites that are provided by historical institutions, museums, or other reputable groups. One other difficulty with the Internet is that, because so much information is available, if you access a search engine and type in a general topic, such as "George Washington," you'll probably get 10,000 hits or more, and you do not have the time to scroll through all that looking for information specifically related to his family. Because the search engines are designed to look for specific information, a more limited search here would probably work quite well for you. If you try "George Washington's family," you might find quite a bit. You can also try different word combinations, such as "George Washington and his wife," "the children of George Washington," and "the family life of George Washington." You might also try using various search engines to gain access to a variety of information.

Reader's Guide to Periodical Literature – This is a guide to magazine articles written about various topics. It is a wonderful source that is available in bound volumes by year. If, for example, you look up the topic "George Washington" in the 1977 guide, it will identify every article written about that topic in hundreds of magazines for that year. It will also give you the information you would need to locate the article. Many libraries have their guides online, so, again, you must become familiar with your particular library.

Newspapers – Newspapers are a wonderful source. Again, many news agencies post their papers online and have archived information (that is, past articles) available for your review. Of course, for your particular topic, newspapers may not provide much help because of the time period, but you may find some articles written by present-day historians about Washington, so it never hurts to try.

Other sources of information – Videotapes, movies, audiotapes, and CD-ROMs are also valid sources of information. You may watch a documentary about Washington and find out a great deal about his life.

Microfilm and microfiche – These are methods of storing information. Because libraries have limited space, much of their information is stored on tiny sheets of special film that can be filed, hundreds of pages of information saved in a tiny amount of space. There are machines in the library that can help you read and copy the information.

Reference books – Reference books contain general information and are used for quick reference. They include such items as almanacs, encyclopedias, dictionaries, atlases, and biographical sketches.

As you begin collecting information related to your topic, continue to ask yourself if what you are finding is relevant. Is it directly related to your limited topic? Also, is the source credible and reliable? Is the information presented without bias? Depending on the topic you've chosen, you also need to consider the date of the materials you are locating. For example, if you are writing a paper on the new innovations in the use of lasers for surgery, you don't want to use articles from the 1970s because that information will be outdated.

7.4 STEP IV: Making Source Cards

Because you are using ideas and information found in books and articles written by people other than yourself, you need to provide a list of all these sources at the end of your paper. To keep up with the information you will need to complete this page, you should keep source cards, a collection of

3 × 5 index cards on which you list bibliographic information from each source. For books, the information you need consists of the author, title, city of publication, publishing company, and copyright year. For a magazine article, you need the author, article title, magazine title, date, and pages. The information on the source cards needs to be in the particular format required by your teacher and your textbook so that they will help you prepare the final page of your report. You should use a different card for each source so that you can number and order the cards alphabetically by the last name of the author. If your source has no author, you alphabetize by the first letter of the title. Below are sample source cards for a book and a magazine.

#1

Smithers, Elton. *George Washington, a Family Man.* New York: Fulton Publishing Co., 1967.

In the above sample, the items listed are the author, the title of the book (italicized), the city of publication, the publishing company, and the copyright year.

#2

Thompson, Jerome. "Famous Fathers." *Historical Archives* September 14, 1998: 56–65.

In the second sample, the items listed are the athor, the title of the article (quoted), the title of the magazine (italicized), the date, and the pages on which the article appears. Notice also that each card is numbered. If these were your cards, you would have, at this point, one book source (1) and one magazine source (2).

The source card information needed for other types of sources (videos, interviews, brochures, Internet sites) is available in the research section of your English textbook. As stated earlier, there are several formats (MLA, APA), so you do not have to feel as though you have to memorize the items needed. Your teacher will give you a great deal of direction, you can consult your textbook, and there are also online sources available for review. It is important, however, to know what is meant by the term *source card* and what general types of information will be included. You can probably guess that, if you are going to use a video for your paper, you will need the name of the video, the date produced, the production company, etc. For an interview, you will need the name of the interviewee, the date, and the type of interview (phone, personal, etc.). Below are some general samples for source card information in the MLA format, the format generally used by English textbooks in public schools in Virginia.

Book

Johnson, Nathaniel. *Living History*. Boston: Dell Publishers, 1990.

Magazine

Elliott, MaryAnn. "New Ways to Save Money." *Newsweek* Oct. 30, 2003: 43–47.

Interview

Dillon, Alex. Telephone Interview. 23 April, 1998.

CD-ROM

"The Wild West." *SMITHWELL Multimedia Encylopedia*. CD-ROM. New York: Software Inc., 1989.

Online source

Jackson, Earl. *A History of Art*. 1997. Online. Internet. Available http://www.arthistory.com

Once you have collected all of your sources and made your source cards, bind them with a rubber band or clip and put them in a safe place for later use.

7.5 Step V: Taking Notes

Now that you have collected many sources related to your limited topic, it is time for you to begin taking notes. One organized way to accomplish this task is through the use of note cards (3 × 5 index cards). Taking notes on cards is helpful because they allow you to sort and arrange the information you find. Notes taken on long sheets of paper are not as adaptable.

Every note card you create needs to include four elements:

- **A topic for the card** – If you label each card with an overall topic, you will find it easier to organize your cards in preparation for the outline. In other words, you categorize the cards according to the subtopics within the main topic you are researching. If you are researching treatments for cancer and you find an article about a new herbal remedy, you might label all of the note cards from that source "herbal remedy" or "natural treatments." If you have fifty to sixty notecards, you might have about seven or eight different card topics because you will most likely have more than one card per topic.

- **A source reference number** – If you are taking notes from the source that you labeled #1, then all note cards created from that source should carry that same number to remind yourself that you got the information on those cards from that source and not another. It is an organizational tool that helps keep your work in order.

- **The notes** – The rule of thumb for the note cards is to record only one idea per card. If you fill up the front and back of a note card, as you might a sheet of paper, then the cards will be little use to you in terms of organizing by keeping cards about similar topics together. Remember, therefore, to put only one main idea or point on each card. As you take your notes, remember these important points:

    1. Do not copy directly from any source. Read the information in the source, and then record the information on the card in your own words! This process will help you to avoid plagiarism and will help you write your paper in your own style and

vocabulary. You can either summarize a long passage into a brief text, or you can paraphrase a short piece of information by restating it in your own words.

2. Make sure the information on the cards is specific. If you are too general when you first create the cards, then you may have to go back to the sources to get more information later.

3. Use appropriate grammar, spelling, and format on the cards so that you will not have to recheck your sources later. Be sure that names are spelled correctly and titles are punctuated correctly.

4. If you do decide to use a direct quote—something that is stated so perfectly that you don't want to change it—be sure that you include quotation marks around it on your note card so that you will remember it was a direct quote.

- **A page number (if applicable)** – Always include the page number if one is available. You will need this later for in-text citations. If a page number is not available, you should put an alternate note in its place. For example, if you are on the Internet and a page number is not available, you can write "Internet" at the bottom of the card so that you will know, on later review, that you have not simply forgotten to record the page number.

Look at the sample note card below:

Home remedies	#3
Many people truly believe that the best way to treat a cold is by eating lots of chicken soup, especially the broth.	
Pg. 24	

The card topic, *home remedies*, is in the upper left-hand corner. The source reference, #3, is in the top right-hand corner. The notes are in the middle, and the page number is at the bottom.

7.6 Step VI: Outlining and Writing a Rough Draft

Now that you have collected all of your notes and organized them according to topic, you are ready to create an outline for the paper. Remember that you should choose a logical order for the information to be presented, and you should be sure that you have enough information to effectively support the thesis of the paper. Outlining was discussed in chapter 3, section 3.4. Refer back to this section for a review of outlining procedure and format.

Once you have completed the outline, you are ready to write the rough draft. The only difference between this rough draft and one for a nonresearch paper is the use of in-text citations. Remember that you must provide credit for the information you find. Of course, you will have the list of sources (Works Cited page) at the end of the paper, but that will not tell the reader where individual ideas and information originated. If you do not use citations, you may risk having others think that you are claiming the information as originally your own. Such an action, called *plagiarism*, is unethical and can bring you a great deal of trouble. An in-text citation is so named because it is a *citation* (direct reference to original source) that occurs *inside the text*. Look at the following example:

A lot of people still believe in treating colds with chicken soup (Smith 24).

The information in parentheses is the *in-text citation*. It makes reference to the author of the source where the information occurred and the page on which that specific idea can be found. When you write down information from one of your sources, you must include a citation to show where the information was found. A reader who wants to find the information in the original source can match the information in the in-text citation to the complete information on the Works Cited page.

When you directly quote information, you certainly must cite it. However, some students believe that direct quotes present the only situation that requires in-text citations. This is not true. You must cite any information that is not factual or considered "general knowledge." If you know that a particular piece of information can be easily found in several reference books, then you need not cite it. For example, biographical information about where a celebrity was born, raised, or educated would be general knowledge. Even though you might not actually know the information, you could easily find it in any source that lists biographical data of famous people. Most of your information will be paraphrased because the overuse of quotes takes away the conversational style and flow of a paper. If the information you paraphrase is factual or easily found in several sources, then you do not need an in-text citation. As a general rule of thumb, if you are not sure whether to cite information, then cite it. You are better off with too many citations than too few.

If an entire paragraph comes from the same source, you can include one citation at the end of the paragraph. If the paragraph is created from information found in more than one source, then the paragraph will require more than one citation. The specific requirements for unusual uses of in-text citations is covered in the research section of your textbook, but here are some general guidelines:

- Normally, an in-text citation calls for the author and page. However, if your source has no author, you use the title and then the page. If no page is available, you use only the author (or title).
- If you must use a title in the in-text citation becuase no author is listed, you punctuate it the same way in which it is punctuated on the Works Cited page.
- The citation should be considered part of the sentence and should, therefore, be included before the ending punctuation for the sentence or clause.
- Factual information that can be found in various sources does not need to be cited. If you are unsure whether to cite something or not, it is usually wise to go ahead and cite it.
- A direct quote, no matter what type of information it involves, requires an in-text citation.

Once you have completed the rough draft, you can proceed with the revising and proofreading steps discussed in section 3.6 on written expression. Finally, you can prepare the Works Cited page, so named because it is a listing of all of the works (sources) you cited in the paper. To complete this page, you simply use your source cards. They should be organized alphabetically by the author (or title if there is no author). Then, you need to put each entry into the proper format required by your classroom text. Although there are different formats for the entries on this page, there are some characteristics that will remain the same:

- Hanging indent – the second and all subsequent lines of each entry are indented, leaving the first line "hanging" to the left. This format allows the reader to easily scan the alphabetized entries.

- Titles for each entry follow the general rules for punctuation. They should be either quoted or italicized. If those titles are used in in-text citations because no author has been listed, they should be similarly punctuated.

Following is a sample Works Cited page using the sample formats provided in section 7.4:

Works Cited Page (Sample)

Dillon, Alex. Telephone Interview. 23 April, 1998.
Elliott, MaryAnn. "New Ways to Save Money." *Newsweek* Oct. 30, 2003: 43–47.
Jackson, Earl. *A History of Art.* 1997. Online. Internet. Available at http://www.arthistory.com
Johnson, Nathaniel. *Living History*. Boston: Dell Publishers, 1990.
"The Wild West." *SMITHWELL Multimedia Encylopedia.* CD-ROM. New York: Software Inc., 1989.

Chapter 7 Exercises—Research

1. **Theodore is planning to research the dangers of tanning beds. Which of the following sources would be *most* useful to him?**
   A An advertisement for a local company that sells the tanning beds
   B A brochure from a tanning bed parlor
   C Friends who have used tanning beds
   D A physicians' report on the effects of tanning beds

2. **Which of the following research questions will be *least* likely to help Theodore focus his research?**
   A How do tanning beds tan people's skin?
   B What is the average cost of a tanning bed?
   C Do individual tanning beds have to pass inspections?
   D What is the difference between ultraviolet rays emitted by tanning beds and those emitted by the sun?

Look at the following sample working source card prepared by Theodore, and then use it to answer question 3.

#5

Graham, Albert (M.D.). "Tanning Beds: A Dangerous Resting Place." *Newsweek* November 23, 1998: 45–53.

3. **From the card, we can infer all of the following *except*—**
   A Theodore has at least four other sources for his paper.
   B The source is probably reliable.
   C The source is a magazine article, not a book.
   D The source contains graphs and charts.

Look at the sample note card prepared by Theodore, and then use it to answer question 4.

Varieties of tanning beds #5

Even this type of tanning bed is not considered safe.

pg. 51

4. What error has Theodore made on this note card?
A His card topic is too vague.
B His notes are not long enough.
C His notes are not specific.
D He has forgotten to record the source reference.

Look at the following preliminary outline for Theodore's paper, and then use it to answer question 5.

I. Introduction
II. How tanning beds work
  A
  B
III. External effects
  A
  B
IV. Internal effects
  A
  B
V. Conclusions

5. Which of the following is *most* likely to be included in Theodore's paper?
A Varieties of tanning beds available for consumer use
B A review of the types of stores that carry tanning beds
C Statistics regarding the types of skin cancer that tanning beds can cause
D Theodore's personal experiences using tanning beds

6. Which of the following should *not* be a major consideration for Theodore as he collects information for his paper?
A The dates of the sources he will use
B The length of selections he is reading
C The authors of the information in the sources
D Unfamiliar medical terminology in the sources

7. Theodore's friend Cynthia has decided to write her research paper on the topic "sports." What will Cynthia need to do before she begins her project?
A Limit her very broad topic
B Broaden her very limited topic
C Select a topic that is more interesting
D Find out if there will be enough information on this topic

Read the following excerpt from a research report, and then use it to answer questions 8–15.

(1) Five handsome, charming, and talented young men from different parts of the United States, with passions for singing and dancing, come to Orlando, Florida, with the dream of stardom. **(2)** The group takes the name *N Sync, using the last letter of each of their first names to signify the perfect unity for their harmonies. **(3)** After being together for almost a year, the group releases an album in Europe and becomes a colossal hit. **(4)** An album is soon released in the United States, and it achieves worldwide success and fame. **(5)** This is the extraordinary story of *N Sync (Squires and *N Sync 5).

(6) *N Sync's origins can be traced back to the *Mickey Mouse Club.* **(7)** Joey Fatone was an extra on the show, and JC Chasez and Justin Timberlake starred on the show for nearly three years. **(8)** After the program was terminated, JC and Justin shared a vocal coach in Nashville while working on solo careers. **(9)** Fate soon brought JC and Justin back to Orlando where they met with Pittsburgh native Chris Kirkpatrick and Joey. **(10)** The newly formed quartet—JC,

Justin, Joey, and Chris—began working on an act built around a cappella. **(11)** Feeling as if something was missing from the group, they began their search for a bass. **(12)** Justin called his former vocal coach in Tennessee who gave him the name Lance Bass. **(13)** The group phoned Lance, and within a week, he arrived in Orlando to join *N Sync (Squires and *N Sync 24).

(14) *N Sync reached early success in Europe because "boy bands" were already popular there. **(15)** Unlike many other such bands at the time, however, *N Sync not only could dance but also had musical talents. **(16)** They released their first album, **N Sync*, in Europe with BMG records (*NSYNCstudio.com*). **(17)** The album was a hit, and it produced four hits for the guys. **(18)** They toured nonstop all over Europe, often seven days per week. **(19)** It amazed the guys that they couldn't go anywhere without a bodyguard in Europe, but they could still lead normal lives back in America (*NSYNCstudio.com*).

(20) After years of hard work, in 1988, *N Sync finally released their self-titled debut album in America, selling over ten million copies. **(21)** *N Sync was slow at becoming a hit back home in the United States, but this all changed by the fall, when they appeared on a Disney Channel special. **(22)** This appearance seemed to show the world the music and dance talents of the group. **(23)** To promote their album, *N Sync toured around the states on their first American tour. **(24)** In the fall of the same year, the group released a holiday CD, *Home for Christmas*, which features Christmas classics, such as "The Christmas Song," as well as original creations, such as "Under My Tree" (**NSYNC Official Website*).

WORKS CITED

**NSYNC Official Website*. Online. Internet. 13 Dec. 2002. Available www.nsync.com

NSYNCstudio.com. Online. Internet. 12 Dec. 2002. Available www.nsyncstudio.com

Squires, K.M. and *N Sync. **N Sync: The Official Book.* New York: Bantam Publishing Group, Inc., 1998.

8. The writer of this essay spelled the name of the band in several different ways. What is the *most* likely reason for this difference?

A The writer wanted to add variety to the essay.
B The sources used spelled the names differently.
C The reference format required the changes.
D The essay discusses more than one band with the same name.

9. The final number of source cards that the author used was

A 3
B 4
C 6
D 8

10. For what reason is the in-text citation in line 13 not italicized?

A It names a website.
B It is the title of a book.
C It names authors.
D It occurs at the end of the paragraph.

11. This paper consists mostly of—

A facts
B opinions
C theories
D autobiographical notes

12. Which of the following elements is *not* included in any of the entries on the Works Cited page?
A City of publication
B Author
C Website
D Volume number

13. What concern might the writer have with the book he is using as a source?
A It may not be as easy to read as the websites.
B It may not contain as much current information as is needed.
C It may not be as accurate as the websites.
D It may not spell the name of the band correctly.

14. What is the total number of in-text citations that occur in the selection?
A 4
B 5
C 6
D 8

15. Which of the following is *not* one of the main purposes for the author's use of in-text citations?
A To avoid plagiarism
B To give credit to individual sources for ideas used in the paper
C To show that the paper has been thoroughly researched
D To create plagiarism

Answers for Chapter 7 Exercises

1. **(D)** The physicians' report is the only one likely to have factual information on the topic. Advertisements and business brochures will focus only on positive information, and friends' information cannot be verified.
2. **(B)** Finding out the cost of a tanning bed will be of little assistance in preparing a paper on the potential dangers of tanning beds.
3. **(D)** There is no indication of whether or not the source contains charts and graphs. You can assume that Theodore has at least four other sources because this card is labeled #5. Also, the source is probably reliable because it has been written by a doctor. Finally, the fact that there are two titles, one quoted and one italicized, indicates an article in a larger work.
4. **(C)** Theodore's reference to "this type of bed" is vague. When he begins the paper, he may not remember the name. The card topic is clear because it relates to one specific section of the paper. The notes are supposed to consist of only one idea per card, and Theodore *has* indicated a source reference.
5. **(C)** The varieties of tanning beds and discussion of stores that carry them are not relevant to effects of tanning bed use. Also, personal experience/opinion of the writer is not included in a formal research paper.
6. **(B)** Theodore will not have to be generally concerned with length, but he will need to get current information (A) written by reliable authors (C), and he will need to define both for himself and the reader the meanings of unfamiliar terms (D).
7. **(A)** Cynthia's topic is much too broad. She could select any limited topic, from a player's biography to a discussion of sports medicine. She does not need to be concerned about availability of information until she determines the limited focus of her research.
8. **(B)** When you are using sources, you are not at liberty to change spellings, and no format (MLA, APA) requires spelling changes. Also, the essay is based on only one band.
9. **(A)** The writer has included only three reference citations in the paper, so there were three final cards used. There may have been more working source cards, but the final count was three.
10. **(C)** The other two citations both name titles of websites, but this citation names authors. The fact that a citation is at the end of a paragraph has nothing to do with whether or not parts of it are capitalized.
11. **(A)** The paper discusses factual information about the group's formation, tours, and album sales. Although it may contain transitional statements that appear to be opinions, it does not consist mostly of opinions or theories, which are sets of beliefs based on facts. Finally, answer D cannot be correct because this selection was not written by the members of the band.
12. **(D)** There are no volume numbers listed for any of the three sources.
13. **(B)** Because the book has a copyright date of 1998, it will not contain information on the activities of the band over the last five years. The other answer choices—ease of reading, accuracy, and spelling—are all points that can affect any source, not just a book.
14. **(B)**
15. **(D)** All of the other reasons given are important with regard to the use of in-text citations. You never want to create plagiarism.

PRACTICE TEST #1: EOC English: Writing (Multiple Choice Component)

1. Eddie is planning to write an essay about his reasons for playing golf. This essay will likely take what form?

A Persuasive
B Narrative
C Expository
D Descriptive

Here are two versions of Eddie's introductory paragraph. Read each, and then use them to answer questions 2–4.

Draft A:	**(1)** My favorite sport is golf. **(2)** I have been playing the game for about five years and I enjoy it more every day. **(3)** Golf is not an easy game to play, and it can be very difficult to do well.

Draft B:	**(1)** My favorite sport is golf. **(2)** I have been playing the game for about five years and I enjoy it more every day. **(3)** Golf is a very challenging game.

2. How has Eddie improved the final sentence in draft B?

A He added new details that were not mentioned in draft A.
B He took two similar thoughts and expressed them concisely.
C He changed the tense to match the rest of the paragraph.
D He did not improve the sentence.

3. How is sentence 2 in draft B correctly written?

A I have been playing the game for about five years, and I enjoy it more every day.
B I have been playing the game for about five years; and I enjoy it more every day.
C I have been playing the game for about five years and, I enjoy it more every day.
D As it is

4. Which of the following topics will most likely *not* fit into Eddie's essay?

A A discussion of the physical requirements of golf
B A discussion of the mental requirements of golf
C A discussion of the layout of a professional course
D A discussion of the amount of practice required

Bailey is planning to write a descriptive paper about her mother, and she has chosen to focus on physical qualities. Look at the web below, and then use it to answer questions 5–6.

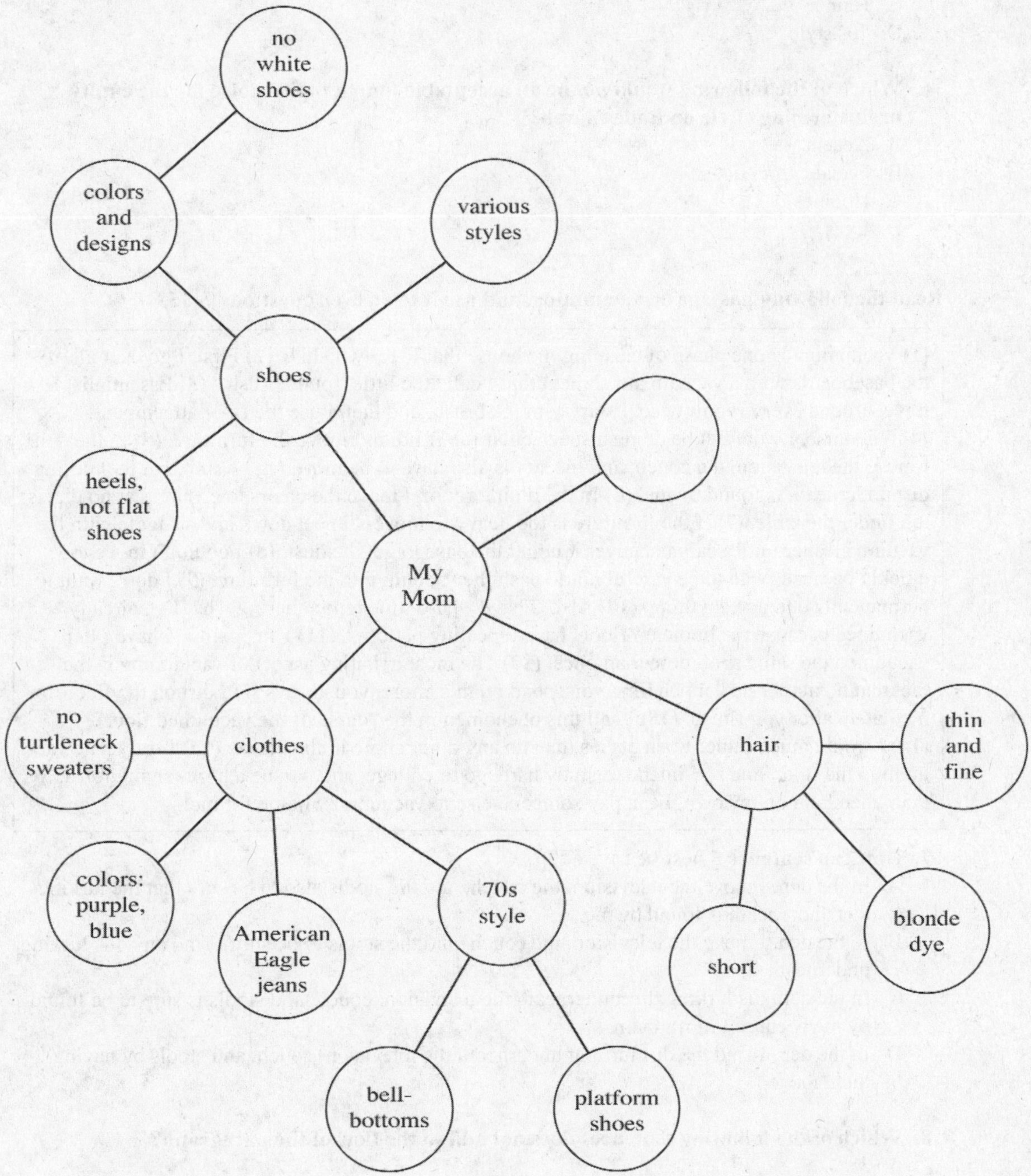

5. **Under which of her main categories does Bailey need additional specific categories?**
   A Shoes
   B Clothes
   C Hair
   D 70s style

6. **Which of the following would *not* be an acceptable fourth topic choice for the empty brainstorming circle on Bailey's web?**
   A Accent
   B Facial expressions
   C Hobbies
   D Eyes

Read the following passage on vacuuming, and use it to answer questions 7–15.

(1) Vacuuming is one phase of cleaning the house that I really dislike. **(2)** First, I go over all of the baseboards with a vacuum attachment that I call "the little, round brush." **(3)** Essentially, I travel around every room twice. I start with the brush, and then I use the floor attachment.
(4) Of course, I wouldn't be doing a spectacular job if I didn't move the furniture. **(5)** In the den, I move the television, the couch, and the stools also have to be moved to be sure that the lurking dirt underneath is found by me. **(6)** In the dining room, I move the chairs to ensure that no dirt is left under the table. **(7)** If the furniture is too heavy to move, I kneel down and struggle with the vacuum cleaner until I can maneuver it under the base to get the dust. **(8)** I couldn't move too quickly because I had to be careful not to bash the vacuum into the furniture. **(9)** I don't want to permanently damage anything. **(10)** Also, I have a hard time remembering what I've already vacuumed because the linoleum floors have repeating patterns. **(11)** I'm positive I have often vacuumed the same spot more than once. **(12)** The most irritating aspect of vacuuming is the fact that no matter how much time you spend on this chore, you always find dirt on the floor immediately after you finish. **(13)** I call this phenomenon the "curse of the vacuumed floor".
(14) I would much rather wash dishes than do any other chore in the house. **(15)** I truly hate vacuuming the floor, and so I intend to study hard, go to college, and pursue a high-paying job so that when I am on my own, I can pay someone else to vacuum my home for me!

7. **How can sentence 5 best be revised?**
   A In the den, I move the television, the couch, and the stools also to be sure that the lurking dirt underneath is found by me.
   B In the den, I move the television, the couch, and the stools to be sure I find any dirt lurking underneath.
   C In the den, the lurking dirt underneath the television, couch, and stools is sure to be found by me because I move them.
   D In the den, I find the dirt lurking underneath the television, couch, and stools by having them moved.

8. **Which of the following sentences does not add to the flow of the paragraph?**
   A 3
   B 7
   C 11
   D 14

9. **In sentence 13, how is <u>"curse of the vacuumed floor".</u> correctly written?**
   A "curse of the vacuumed floor."
   B 'curse of the vacuumed floor.'
   C "curse of the vacuumed floor,"
   D As it is

10. Which of the following sentences begins with a subordinate clause?

A 2
B 5
C 7
D 9

11. Which sentence contains a shift in the point of view?

A 11
B 12
C 13
D 14

12. In sentence 8, how is <u>too quickly because I had to be careful</u> correctly written?

A too quickly, because I had to be careful
B too quickly; because I had to be careful
C too quickly because, I had to be careful
D As it is

13. Which of the following errors occurs in sentence 8?

A Passive voice
B Tense shift
C Misplaced modifier
D Shift in point of view

14. In sentence 15, how is <u>college, and pursue a high-paying job so that when</u> correctly written?

A college, and pursue a high, paying job, so that when
B college, and pursue a high-paying job, so that when
C college and pursue a high paying job so that when
D As it is

15. Which of the following sentences uses a transitional expression?

A 1
B 2
C 8
D 11

Read the following essay about summer, and use it to answer questions 16–26.

(1) "I wish it were summer!" **(2)** That phrase is heard by parents throughout the fall and winter months as students yearn for the end of yet another school year and the freedom of a summer filled with fun. **(3)** However, once the season arrives, many students find themselves bored and frustrated because, suddenly, they have "nothing to do." **(4)** This need not be the case. **(5)** With a little investigation, students on summer vacation can find many activities to occupy their free time.

(6) One great summer activity for students is for them to participate in some of the summer programs that are offered by community centers. **(7)** The YMCA offers various sports leagues for children of all ages. **(8)** Community teams play against one another to compete for trophies and other awards. **(9)** This is a great activity because students from different schools may play on the same teams, forming friendships and bonds that otherwise may have been missed. **(10)** Also, participation on such teams allows students to exercise and stay in shape during the off-season for the sports they play at their own schools. **(11)** The cost involved in playing community sports is quite low because much of the equipment is borrowed from the organization sponsoring the sport. **(12)** Further, if transportation is a problem, parents of players can form carpools to take turns transporting students to and from practices and games.

(13) Another great summer activity for students involves volunteer work. **(14)** Giving of oneself to help others can be extremely rewarding for the volunteer and those who are assisted.

(15) There are various organizations and clubs that would welcome student assistance. **(16)** Groups such as the Salvation Army and the Red Cross can always use help sorting and organizing donated clothing and other items for distribution to those in need. **(17)** Nursing homes and hospitals would welcome volunteers who could visit the elderly, distribute books and magazines, or helping with crafts and musical programs. **(18)** Finally, students on break for summer could volunteer their time to help with tutoring programs for children attending summer school or for those learning English as a second language. **(19)** Simply taking time to read with a small child or helping a group of students with math would be a major benefit. **(20)** Also, it is important to remember that colleges view volunteer work as a major asset to students who apply to they're schools.

(21) Finally, students can spend their summer vacations working to make extra money. **(22)** For those who do not drive, neighborhoods provide a wonderful opportunity for summer work. **(23)** Perhaps students can mow lawns, clean garages, paint fences, or making small repairs. **(24)** Elderly neighbors who are not able to do a lot of physical work would probably be most grateful for the assistance. **(25)** Students could make money for summer spending as well as help those in the area. **(26)** For those who have transportation, perhaps a job at the local market or department store is the answer. **(27)** Most of these places accept applications on a daily basis, and many students find they thoroughly enjoy working when they don't have the responsibility of homework and long school days added to their schedules.

(28) Summer is an exciting time for students because they get a break from the tough academic endeavors of the past nine months. **(29)** However, the summer months don't have to be spent in boredom or wasted time. **(30)** There are exciting opportunities awaiting any student who simply takes a little time to investigate.

16. Which of the following sentences is the thesis statement?

A 2
B 3
C 4
D 5

17. Which of the following transitional expressions provides the most effective beginning for sentence 16?

A For example,
B However,
C And,
D In addition,

18. Which of the following is the most effective revision for sentence 20?

A Also, one must remember that colleges view volunteer work as a major asset to students who apply to their schools.
B Also, it is important to remember, that colleges view volunteer work as a major asset to students who apply to their schools.
C Also, it is important to remember that colleges view volunteer work as a major asset to students, who apply to their schools.
D Also, you must remember that colleges view volunteer work as a major asset to students who apply to their schools.

19. All of the following categories of support are offered *except*—

A free time in the summer can be spent helping others
B free time in the summer can be spent earning money
C free time in the summer can be spent learning a new hobby
D free time in the summer can be spent playing community sports

20. In sentence 27, how is <u>on a daily basis, and many students find</u> correctly written?

A on a daily basis; and many students find
B on a daily basis; and, many students find
C on a daily basis and, many students find
D As it is

21. Which of the following *best* captures the main idea of the essay?

A Summer can be extremely boring for students.
B Students can earn a great deal of money working during the summer.
C Summer can be spent in various constructive ways.
D Summer is a wonderful time of year for students.

22. Which of the following pairs of purposes for writing are *best* evidenced in this essay?

A Descriptive and narrative
B Narrative and expository
C Expository and persuasive
D Persuasive and descriptive

23. Which of the following sentences from the third paragraph is unrelated to the topic?

A 17
B 18
C 19
D 20

24. Which of the following is the best revision of sentence 6?

A One great summer activity for students is participation in community sports programs.
B One great summer activity for students is to participate in sports programs in their communities offered by community centers.
C One great activity for students in the summer is for them to go to community centers to participate in sports programs.
D One great summer activity for students is participation in sports programs offered by their community centers.

25. In sentence 20, how is <u>to students who apply to they're schools.</u> correctly written?

A to students who apply to there schools.
B to students who apply to their schools.
C to students who apply to his or her schools.
D As it is

26. In sentence 17, how is <u>would welcome volunteers who could visit the elderly, distribute books and magazines, or helping with crafts</u> correctly written?

A would welcome volunteers who could visit the elderly, distribute books and magazines, help with crafts
B would welcome volunteers who could visit the elderly, distributing books and magazines, or helping with crafts
C would welcome volunteers who could visit the elderly, distribute books and magazines, or help with crafts
D As it is

Read the following four thesis statements related to a paper about bees, and use them to answer questions 27–30.

1. The bee is one of the most beautiful members of the insect world.
2. Its work ethic and life of labor make the bee a fascinating insect.
3. My first experience with a bee is one I'll never forget.
4. Everyone should consider raising bees because it can be a fun and lucrative hobby.

27. Thesis statement 1 will most likely begin what type of essay?
A Persuasive
B Narrative
C Expository
D Descriptive

28. Thesis statement 2 will most likely begin what type of essay?
A Persuasive
B Narrative
C Expository
D Descriptive

29. Thesis statement 3 will most likely begin what type of essay?
A Persuasive
B Narrative
C Expository
D Descriptive

30. Thesis statement 4 will most likely begin what type of essay?
A Persuasive
B Narrative
C Expository
D Descriptive

Read the following two excerpts from a paper about computers, and then use them to answer questions 31–32.

Excerpt 1 **Computers can be used to find information. They can help one find information on various topics. The information can be found quickly. It is usually easy to find a lot of information on any topic.**

Excerpt 2 **Computers can be used to help one quickly, and easily find information on a variety of topics.**

31. How has the writer improved excerpt 2?
A By changing the information.
B By avoiding unnecessary repetition.
C By giving less information.
D By giving more details.

32. How is excerpt 2 correctly written?
A Computer's can be used to help one quickly, and easily find information on various topics.
B Computers can be used to help one quickly and easily find information on various topic's.
C Computers can be used to help one quickly and easily find information on various topics.
D As it is.

Read the following paragraph, and then use it to answer questions 33–35.

(1) If I could be any kind of animal, I would choose to be a dog because life as a canine would enable me to help others in many ways. **(2)** As a dog, I could help the disabled. **(3)** I could lead blind people safely across busy highways, and I could jump or run in circles around the deaf to warn them of danger. **(4)** I could even work for the police force by protecting law enforcement officials, capturing criminals, and sniffing out illegal drugs. **(5)** If I were trained as a rescue dog I could use my keen sense of smell to find people buried by an avalanche or a mudslide.
(6) Being able to help people would be extremely rewarding, and that is why, to me, life as a dog would be wonderful.

33. Which of the following is the *best* way to combine sentences 2 and 3?

A As a dog, I could help the disabled, I could lead blind people to safety and run in circles to warn the deaf of danger.

B As a dog, I could help the disabled by leading blind people to safety, and the deaf would be warned of danger by my running around in circles.

C As a dog, I could help the disabled by leading blind people to safety and running around in circles to warn the deaf of danger.

D As a dog, I could help the disabled; I could lead blind people to safety; I could run around in circles to warn the deaf of danger.

34. In sentence 5, how is <u>If I were trained as a rescue dog I could use</u> correctly written?

A If I were trained as a rescue dog; I could use

B If I were trained as a rescue dog: I could use

C If I were trained as a rescue dog, I could use

D As it is

35. In sentence 6, why are there commas around the phrase *to me*?

A It is a prepositional phrase.

B It is an appositive.

C It is a nonessential adjective clause.

D It is a parenthetical expression.

PRACTICE TEST #2: EOC English: Writing (Multiple Choice Component)

Regina has been asked to write a paragraph about why she loves owning a cat. Look at the two following rough drafts of her work, and use them to answer questions 1–5.

<u>DRAFT A</u>

(1) One of the reasons I love owning a cat is that I enjoy the companionship of my furry friend. **(2)** When I get home from school in the afternoons, Fluffy greets me by rubbing against my leg and meowing loudly. **(3)** She then jumps into my arms and I tell her all about my day while she sits quietly and listens. **(4)** I also love owning a cat because I am learning how to care properly for another living being. **(5)** I have to feed her every morning and evening. **(6)** I have to remember to fill her water dish. **(7)** I also have to take her to yearly veterinary appointments. **(8)** Finally, I love owning my cat because she is very entertaining. **(9)** She can jump from the couch to the chair in one, smooth leap, and she often appears out of hiding places that I never saw her enter! **(10)** It's also fascinating to watch her walk through a room without making even the slightest sound. **(11)** I once owned a snake that could slither around a checkerboard without moving the checkers. **(12)** I love owning a cat, and I wouldn't trade her for anything in the world.

DRAFT B

(1) I enjoy owning a cat for many different reasons. **(2)** First, I enjoy the companionship of my furry friend. **(3)** When I get home from school in the afternoons, Fluffy greets me by rubbing against my leg and meowing loudly. **(4)** She jumps into my arms, and I tell her all about my day while she sits quietly and listens. **(5)** I also love owning a cat because I am learning how to care properly for another living being. **(6)** I have to feed her every morning and evening, remember to fill her water dish, and take her to yearly veterinary appointments. **(7)** Finally, I love owning a cat because she is very entertaining. **(8)** She can jump from the couch to the chair in one, smooth leap, and she often appears out of hiding places that I never saw her enter! **(9)** It's also fascinating to watch her walk through a room without making even the slightest sound. **(10)** I love owning a cat, and I wouldn't trade her for anything in the world.

1. How has Regina changed sentence 1 in draft B?
A She has created a true topic sentence that does not yet begin discussing specific support.
B She has added a specific point of detail to make the sentence more interesting.
C She has added a transitional phrase.
D She has deleted the topic sentence.

2. What has Regina accomplished through the creation of sentence 6 in draft B?
A She has created a run-on sentence that adds interest to the paragraph.
B She has combined choppy sentences from draft A into one smooth sentence.
C She has added details not previously given in draft A.
D She has deleted information not pertaining to the topic of the paragraph.

3. Which sentence from draft A contains details that do not support the topic of the paragraph?
A 3
B 7
C 10
D 11

4. Which sentence from draft B does not contain a transitional phrase?
A 2
B 4
C 5
D 7

5. Sentence 12 in draft A can be correctly written in all of the following ways *except*—
A I love owning a cat, and I wouldn't trade her for anything in the world.
B I love owning a cat; I wouldn't trade her for anything in the world.
C I love owning a cat. I wouldn't trade her for anything in the world.
D I love owning a cat, I wouldn't trade her for anything in the world.

Read the following excerpt from a research paper about dreams, and use it to answer questions 6–8.

(1) What is a dream? **(2)** A *dream* is defined as a sequence of sensations, images, thought, etc. passing through a sleeping person's mind (Websters 442). **(3)** In other words, dreams are all the images, thoughts, and experiences one has ever had put into "scenes" while he is sleeping. **(4)** Some people believe dreams are messages from either themselves or from perhaps a higher power (Nelson). **(5)** As a result, people continue to be intrigued by the interpretation of dreams.

(6) One of the oldest recorded dreams is in Mesopotamian literature, and it involved a disaster about to occur (Lee 13). **(7)** The oldest dream book in the entire world, *Artimedorou's Oneiro-Critica*, contains Assyrian, Babylonian, and Egyptian dream-lore (Lee 13). **(8)** The Assyrians, Babylonians, and Sumerians had a god of dreams, An-Za-Oar, that held a court in an underworld, which was called the Great Land. **(9)** He kept helpers whose job was to pass on his divine instructions to sleepers (Lee 14). **(10)** There is an old Hittite prayer from the past. **(11)** Asking the help of higher powers in the following words: "Either let me see it in a dream or let it be discovered by divination, or let a divinely inspired priest or priestess find out by incubation of a dream whatever it is I demand of them" (Lee 13). **(12)** In the Old Testament of the Christian Bible, dreams were regularly associated with prophets from Israel (Nelson 115). **(13)** In the New Testament, God appeared to Joseph, the carpenter, in a dream after the announcement of the birth of Jesus Christ (115).

(14) There are four dream zones: the physical world where things physically happen; the emotional world, which involves energy, desire, and attraction; the mental world, which involves logic, beliefs, and inspiration; and the casual, or spiritual, world (Pierce 84).

Works Cited

Lee, Nerys. *Your Dreams and What They Mean.* New York: Bell Publishing, 1984.
Nelson, Thomas. *What Does the Bible Say About* . . . . Nashville, TN: 2001.
Pierce, Penny. *Dreams for Dummies.* New York: IDG Books Worldwide, 2001.

6. In sentence 7, how is world, *Artimedorou's Oneiro-Critica*, correctly written?
A world, "Artimedorou's Oneiro-Critica,"
B world, *Artimedorou's Oneiro-Critica*—
C world; "Artimedorou's Oneiro-Critica";
D As it is

7. In sentences 10 and 11, how is prayer from the past. Asking the help of higher powers correctly written?
A prayer from the past, asking the help of higher powers
B prayer from the past Asking the help of higher powers
C prayer from the past—asking the help of higher powers
D As it is

8. The author's purpose in shifting from the stated thesis about dream interpretation to the first body paragraph dealing with the history of dreams is—
A to establish a background of fascination with dreams
B to explain how the earliest dreams were interpreted
C to contrast historical dream interpretation with current thinking
D to introduce the origin of the book used to interpret dreams today

Jeremy is planning to write a paper about the differences between a novel and a movie based on the novel. Following is a preliminary outline of his planned categories of discussion. Use it to answer questions 9–11.

I. Introduction
   A. Name of book and movie versions
   B. Summary of the main storyline
   C. Thesis statement

II. Differences in setting
   A. Location of main character's home
   B. States visited on the summer journey
   C. Setting of the conflict surrounding the family reunion

III. Differences in characterization
   A. Introduction of step-sister, Marjory
   B. Casting of main character versus physical description in the novel
   C. Names and ages of the three young siblings

IV. Differences in events
  A. No storm in the novel
  B. Slightly different endings
  C. Appearance of Marjory

V. Conclusion

9. The main purpose of Jeremy's essay will be to—
A persuade
B entertain
C explain
D describe

10. Jeremy has planned to arrange his details in which type of order?
A Chronological
B Spatial
C Order of importance
D Reverse chronological

11. Jeremy has repeated information in which two paragraphs?
A I and II
B II and III
C III and IV
D II and IV

Read the following letter of adjustment written by an unsatisfied customer. Use it to answer questions 12–16.

May 4, 2004

Smithton Merchandise
5540 North Herring Road
Burbridge, NJ 22736

Dear Sirs:

(1) I recently made a purchase from your Spring 2004 catalog, and I am dissatisfied with the product. **(2)** I would either like the item replaced or for you to refund my money.

(3) I ordered item #88375647HHP, the green knit sweater, in size XL. **(4)** Consequently, I received item #88375647HHR, the blue knit sweater, in size XXL. **(5)** The price of each sweater is the same, $22.99 plus tax and shipping. **(6)** I paid for the original purchase with my VISA credit card, and the amount has already been charged to my credit account.

(7) I would still like to receive the green sweater. **(8)** Therefore, I am including in this package the blue sweater sent in error, along with a copy of the packing slip. **(9)** Please sent the item I originally ordered. **(10)** If that item is no longer available please credit my account for the full amount.

Yours Truly,

Nathaniel L. Rutledge
(554) 555-8221

12. In sentence 4, how is Consequently, I received item #88375647HHR, the blue knit sweater, correctly written?

A In addition, I received item #88375647HHR, the blue knit sweater,
B However, I received item #88375647HHR, the blue knit sweater,
C Therefore, I received item #88375647HHR, the blue knit sweater,
D As it is

13. Sentence 2 contains an error in—

A subject/verb agreement
B spelling
C parallel structure
D comma usage

14. How is sentence 9 correctly written?

A Please sending the item I originally ordered.
B Please having sent the item I originally ordered.
C Please send the item I originally ordered.
D As it is

15. In sentence 10, how is If that item is no longer available please credit correctly written?

A If that item is no longer available; please credit
B If that item is no longer available, please credit
C If that item is no longer available: please credit
D As it is

16. How is Yours Truly, correctly written?

A Yours truly
B Your truly,
C Yours Truly
D As it is

Read the following letter from Suzanne to her mother, and then use it to answer questions 17–22.

Dear Mama,

(1) I am having a wonderful time at camp so far. **(2)** Its beautiful here, and I have made many new friends.

(3) When we first arrived, we registered with the counselors and then moved our things into the cabins. **(4)** My roommates name is JoAnna, she is also from Vermont! **(5)** I thought that was neat! **(6)** After we checked in, we went to a big cabin with lots of tables, and we had an indoor picnic and got to meet the other campers. **(7)** I think I heard one counselor say there were seventy-five campers from ten different states. **(8)** After lunch, we went to the lake for safety instructions about fishing, boating, and swimming. **(9)** That night, we had a barbecue with chicken, hamburgers, hot dogs, chips, vegetables, and lots of deserts; Eating lots of food, the cook said we had big appetites!

(10) The next day, we went hiking, swimming, and canoeing. **(11)** I don't think I've ever been so tired at the end of the day. **(12)** JoAnna and me fell out of the canoe three times, but I didn't care because the water was cool. **(13)** I have also made friends with three really nice girls who's names is Tiffany, Megan, and Allison. **(14)** All of us spend the evenings talking around the campfires and eating roasted marshmallows.

(15) I will write more later when I have time. **(16)** I just wanted to let you know that I am having a great time. **(17)** Tell everyone at home hello for me!

Love,

Suzanne

ps. My Counselor who loves sweets asked if you would send some more of those cookies I brought with me?

17. In sentence 2, how is <u>Its beautiful here, and I have made many</u> correctly written?
A It's beautiful here and I have made many
B It's beautiful here, and I have made many
C Its beautiful here, and, I have made many
D As it is

18. In sentence 4, how is <u>My roommates name is JoAnna, she is also</u> correctly written?
A My roommates' name is JoAnna; she is also
B My roommate's name is JoAnna, she is also
C My roommate's name is JoAnna; she is also
D As it is

19. In sentence 9, how is <u>and lots of deserts; Eating lots of food, the cook said we had big appetites!</u> correctly written?
A and lots of desserts; the cook said we had big appetites because we ate lots of food!
B and lots of deserts; the cook said we had big appetites because we ate lots of food!
C and lots of desserts; eating lots of food, the cook said we had big appetites!
D As it is

20. In sentence 12, how is <u>I have also made friends with three really nice girls who's names is Tiffany,</u> correctly written?
A I have also made friends with three really nice girls who's names are Tiffany,
B I have also made friends with three really nice girls whose names are Tiffany,
C I have also made friends with three really nice girls whose names were Tiffany,
D As it is

21. At the end of the letter, how is <u>My Counselor who loves sweets asked if you would send some more of those cookies I brought with me?</u> correctly written?
A My counselor, who loves sweets, asked if you would send some more of those cookies I brought with me.
B My counselor, who loves sweets asked if you would send some more of those cookies I brought with me.
C My counselor, who loves sweets, asked if you would send some more of those cookies I brought with me?
D As it is

22. In sentence 12, how is <u>JoAnna and me fell out of the canoe</u> correctly written?
A Me and JoAnna fell out of the canoe
B JoAnna and I fell out of the canoe,
C JoAnna and I fell out of the canoe
D As it is

Edward, a high school senior, has been asked to judge some speeches written for a fourth-grade 4-H writing contest. One of the submissions he was asked to evaluate is provided below. Read it, and then use it to answer questions 23–28.

(1) As I am sitting in the classroom, I look at the clock, which says 2:39. **(2)** Suddenly, after a day full of work and fun, the clock strikes 2:40, and the bell rings. **(3)** "Bye" and "See you later" are phrases I hear all around me. **(4)** Some of my friends rush out to the buses that will take them safely home. **(5)** Others head to the parking lot outside the school to meet their parents or guardians. **(6)** I have a different alternative. **(7)** I attend the YMCA after-school program. **(8)** After gathering my books together, I set out on my long journey . . . downstairs to the cafeteria!

(9) As soon as I arrive at Aftercare, it's always a "hello" or "hey" to the teachers, who make sure everyone has arrived safely. **(10)** We have two teachers, who we call Miss Jenny and Mrs. Pam. **(11)** After calling the roll, we are ready to begin our day. **(12)** First, everyone splits into one of two groups: the homework group or the non-homework group. **(13)** The homework group, of course, does homework. **(14)** These students work on the right side of the cafeteria. **(15)** They are allowed to sit with friends, but they must work silently. **(16)** The YMCA provides pencils and paper, and Mrs. Pam and Miss Jenny are always willing to help any student who has a question. **(17)** The non-homework group heads for the toys provided by the program. **(18)** To be more specific about the toys, there is a dollhouse, blocks, puzzles, and board games, such as City Dogs and checkers. **(19)** My favorite is Topler, which involves balancing weights on an unsturdy diamond. **(20)** Because the after-school program includes children in kindergarten through sixth grade, there are games and toys to suit everyone. **(21)** So that all students have a chance to play the games they like, Mrs. Pam assigns students to certain "centers" and has students switch several times during the afternoon.

(22) After the homework group has did their homework, we all gather for a snack, which is something very healthy, yet very tasty. **(23)** We usually have combination snacks, such as apples and crackers or cinnamon sticks and peanut butter. **(24)** We also have juice or milk. **(25)** After the snack, Mrs. Pam reads us a book so that we can accumulate our accelerated reader points. **(26)** Then, we all head to the gym where we have basketballs, footballs, and our choice of regular or glow-in-the-dark dodge balls.

(27) Although Aftercare is always fun, some days are really special! **(28)** For example, every Friday we watch a movie, have a special snack, and get to buy a drink from the soda machine. **(29)** Holidays are fun, too, because we have parties, special crafts, and lots of food brought by the children and their parents. **(30)** Last Christmas, we made presents for family members and made handmade scarves for a charity drive. **(31)** While we worked, Miss Jenny served us "Christmas milk," which had been turned red with food coloring.

(32) As each school day draws to a close, the after-school students return to the cafeteria to wait for their parents or guardians. **(33)** My mom usually comes to get me, but my brother, who is in high school, is the one who comes inside to sign me out. **(34)** On the ride home I tell my Mom all about my day, and I begin to look forward to the next day at YMCA Aftercare.
(35) YMCA Aftercare is a great alternative for students!

23. In the last sentence of her first paragraph, the writer of the essay has—

A used a contrasting statement to create a conflict situation
B created a little humor to engage the reader
C used a transitional phrase to move to a new topic
D introduced a thesis statement

24. In sentence 10, how is <u>We have two teachers, who we call Miss Jenny and Mrs. Pam.</u> correctly written?

A We have two teachers who we call Miss Jenny and Mrs. Pam.
B We have two teachers, whom we call Miss Jenny and Mrs. Pam.
C We have two teachers whom we call Miss Jenny and Mrs. Pam
D As it is

25. Which error occurs in sentence 11?

A Dangling modifier
B Sentence fragment
C Incorrect verb tense
D Comma error

26. How is <u>After the homework group has did their homework,</u> in sentence 22 correctly written?

A After the homework group did their homework,
B After the homework group has done their homework,
C After the homework group have did their homework,
D As it is

27. What subtle shift occurs in line 35?

A The writer ends with a persuasive statement.
B The writer ends with a flashback.
C The writer makes a statement contradictory to the thesis.
D The writer changes to a negative tone.

28. How is <u>home I tell my Mom all about my day, and I begin</u> in line 34 correctly written?

A home I tell my Mom all about my day and I begin
B home I tell my mom all about my day, and I begin
C home I tell my mom all about my day and I begin
D As it is

Read the following personal narrative from a student who is describing her first experience jumping off the diving board, and then use it to answer questions 29–35.

(1) The first time that I ever jumped off of the diving board was a complete thrill, scare, and surprise for me! **(2)** On that beautiful June afternoon, I arrived at the pool, and as soon as I entered the door, I could see the diving board. **(3)** I just knew that today was the day I was going to attempt a jump. **(4)** I had been taking swimming lessons for several months and felt very comfortable in the water, but so far, I had been too afraid to approach the board. **(5)** Today, however, was going to be different. **(6)** I wanted to enjoy the pool to its fullest, and I knew it was time for me to "go for it." **(7)** With a confident mind and heart, I put on my sunscreen and walked what seemed ten miles over to the water's edge. **(8)** I entered the most shallow end of the pool so that I could gather my thoughts and courage. **(9)** While I was preparing myself, I felt a tap on my shoulder. **(10)** It was my older brother, Jay. **(11)** He was with my mother, and they asked me if I was ready. **(12)** "Yes," I said. "Let's go". **(13)** I then swam over to the deep end of the pool. **(14)** I climbed the ladder, got out of the pool, and turned toward the diving board. **(15)** As I approached it, there seemed to be a growing knot in my throat that kept getting bigger and bigger with each step I took. **(16)** My ears began to ring, and all other voices and sounds ceased as the ringing muffled them. **(17)** As I climbed the three steps to the top of the board, I wondered if I could actually go on! **(18)** Yes! I would not turn back this time. **(19)** Reaching the top of the board, I walked cautiously toward the end, and, surprisingly, the water seemed much farther away than I had anticipated. **(20)** Standing there, my head swirling, I heard a familiar sound pushing through the fear; it was my mom, shouting to me that everything would be fine! **(21)** It was my moment of truth. **(22)** I held my breath, took a running leap, and hit the cold clear water. **(23)** The next thing I knew, I was at the surface right next to my mom, who was hugging me and telling me how proud she was of me. **(24)** I was pretty proud of myself too. **(25)** Even though I was scared, I was glad I took the risk. **(26)** Since that day, I have spent many happy hours perfecting a variety of jumps off the board. **(27)** I can't imagine why I had ever been so frightened!

29. How is sentence 16 best revised?

A My ears began to ring, muffling all other voices and sounds.
B My ears began to ring, all other voices and sounds becoming muffled because of it.
C All the other voices and sounds ceased as my ears began to ring and muffle them.
D As it is

30. The writer achieves the suspense of the selection by—

A using short, choppy sentences
B including emotional details about her fear
C adding dialogue from other characters
D keeping the text very short

31. In sentence 22, how is <u>took a running leap, and hit the cold clear water</u> correctly written?

A took a running leap and hit the cold, clear water.
B took a running leap, and hit the cold, clear, water.
C took a running leap, and hit the cold, clear water.
D As it is

32. Which sentence uses informal, or slang, terminology?

A 4
B 6
C 14
D 15

33. How should sentence 12 be correctly written?

A "Yes," I said, "let's go."
B "Yes," I said, "let's go".
C "Yes, I said, let's go."
D As it is

34. For what reason is the comma used in sentence 9?

A Introductory participial phrase
B Introductory adverb clause
C Items in a series
D Parenthetical expression

35. How is sentence 11 correctly written?

A He was with my mother and they asked me if I was ready?
B He was with my mother, and they asked me if I was ready?
C He was with my mother and, they asked me if I was ready.
D As it is

Answers: PRACTICE TEST #1: EOC English: Writing

1. **(C)** Eddie will most likely be providing reasons to *explain* why he loves golf. He will most likely not be trying to persuade the audience, tell a story, or describe the physical characteristics of anything.
2. **(B)** Eddie did not add details; he simply combined similar ideas. Also, both drafts are in present tense, so he did not change tense.
3. **(A)** A comma is required in front of a conjunction that connects two complete thoughts. Answer *B* incorrectly uses a semicolon in front of a conjunction, and answer *C* shows the comma placed *after* the conjunction instead of before it.
4. **(C)** All of the other answers relate to his thesis statement about golf being difficult or challenging. The layout of a professional course is related generally to golf, but it is not related to the specific thesis statement in Eddie's introductory paragraph.
5. **(A)** Bailey needs to include more details about the various styles her mother likes. All the other categories contain many specific details.
6. **(C)** The "hobbies" category is not a physical feature. The others are.
7. **(B)** This revision is the most clear and concise of the four.
8. **(D)** The sentence about the dishes is unrelated to the flowing information about vacuuming.
9. **(A)** Periods always go inside closing quote marks. Single quote marks are used only for a quote within another quote, and a comma would not be acceptable because the sentence ends after the word *floor.*
10. **(C)** *If the furniture is too heavy to move* is an introductory adverb clause. Sentence 2 begins with an introductory adverb, sentence 5 begins with a prepositional phrase, and sentence 9 begins with the subject of the sentence.
11. **(B)** This sentence contains a shift to second person (you). The others are all in first person (I).
12. **(D)** There should be no comma or semicolon before the adverb clause, and there is no reason to follow the first word of the clause with a comma.
13. **(B)** The author has switched from present tense to past tense.
14. **(D)** Answer *A* incorrectly uses a comma in a compound adjective, answer *B* incorrectly places a comma in front of an adverb clause, and answer *C* has deleted the comma after *college,* punctuation that is necessary for the items in a series.
15. **(B)** Sentence 2 is the only one that begins with a transition. The other three begin with the subject.
16. **(D)** Sentence 5 is the last sentence of the introductory paragraph, the usual position for the thesis statement, and it also indicates the overall topic for the essay.
17. **(A)** Sentence 16 provides an example of the organizations and clubs mentioned in sentence 15. *However* indicates a contradictory statement; the terms *and* and *in addition* precede similar, equally important ideas.
18. **(A)** The spelling of *they're* should be changed to *their,* which is possessive. Answers *B* and *C* contain comma errors, and answer *D* contains a shift to second person point of view (you).
19. **(C)** Summer hobbies is the only category that is not mentioned in the selection.

20. **(D)** The comma before the conjunction is correctly placed. Semicolons are not used with coordinating conjunctions, and you would not place a comma after a conjunction that is connecting two complete thoughts.

21. **(C)** Although the other three answers do mention individual points that can be found in the essay, only answer *C* is general enough to be called the main idea.

22. **(C)** The essay explains how summer can be spent constructively, and as it does so, it seems to be gently suggesting that students try these ideas. It does not describe through sensory details or tell a story.

23. **(D)** All of the other sentences in the paragraph either introduce examples or provide support for examples.

24. **(A)** This sentence is the most concise and straightforward; the others contain repetition or wordiness.

25. **(B)** The word *they're* must be changed to the possessive form *their*. Answer *C* is incorrect because it uses singular pronouns (his/her) to refer to the plural noun *students*. That is an error in pronoun/antecedent agreement.

26. **(C)** The commas separate three items used as examples of how one could help in nursing homes or hospitals.

27. **(D)** The use of the term *beautiful* implies that the author will describe the physical aspects of the insect.

28. **(C)** Use of the terms *work ethic* and *life of labor* indicate an explanation and discussion of the lifestyle of the bee.

29. **(B)** The writer indicates that there is an unforgettable story to be told about an experience with a bee.

30. **(A)** The writer seems to be leading into a persuasive selection that will attempt to convince the reader to raise bees.

31. **(B)** The writer has not added details or changed the information. Further, the information has not been reduced; the repetition has simply been avoided.

32. **(C)** The terms *computers* and *topics* are both plural, not possessive. No apostrophes are required in excerpt 2.

33. **(C)** Answer *A* contains a run on, answer *B* contains a shift in voice (to passive), and answer *D* contains three choppy sentences connected with semicolons.

34. **(C)** The comma is required after the introductory adverb clause.

35. **(D)** The phrase is a prepositional phrase, but no rule requires commas for that reason alone. An appositive is a noun renaming a nearby noun, and an adjective clause contains a subject and a verb.

Answers: PRACTICE TEST #2: EOC English: Writing

1. **(A)** She has added a topic sentence that simply introduces the topic of the paragraph without going into detail. She does not need a transition yet because she is simply opening the paragraph.
2. **(B)** She took three choppy sentences and created one smooth sentence listing a series of items. She would not want to create a run-on sentence, and the information has been simply restated, not enhanced or changed.
3. **(D)** The information about the snake is interesting, but it is unrelated to the topic about cats.
4. **(B)** The other choices all contain transitional phrases: *First, also,* and *finally*
5. **(D)** All of the other choices are acceptable, but choice *D* creates a run-on sentence.
6. **(D)** It must be italicized because it is a book, and the commas are correctly placed.
7. **(A)** The comma is needed before the participial phrase. Choice *B* has a capitalization error, choice *C* incorrectly uses a dash, and the current form of the sentence contains a sentence fragment.
8. **(A)** The author wants to show that a fascination with dreams began long, long ago. He does not explain interpretation of early dreams, nor does he discuss how past interpretations compare with current thinking. Finally, the one book mentioned is not shown to be a book currently in use.
9. **(C)** Jeremy is going to explain the differences between the two forms of the story. He is not going to persuade the audience, tell a story, or use sensory details to describe.
10. **(C)** Jeremy will be explaining his differences in the order which he feels is most important. He is not using order over time (from current to past or from past to current), and spatial is reserved for the arrangement of objects in space.
11. **(C)** Jeremy will have to decide where he wants to introduce Marjory so that he will not repeat information.
12. **(B)** *However* is the best transition because the writer wants to show a contrast between what he wanted and what he got. *Consequently* and *therefore* are used to mean *as a result*, and *in addition* provides a similar example, not a contrasting one.
13. **(C)** The sentence should read, "I would either like the item replaced or my money refunded." The parallel structure would then be clear.
14. **(C)** The verb needs to be in the present tense, not the past or any of the other tense choices.
15. **(B)** Only a comma can follow the introductory adverb clause.
16. **(B)** Capitalize only the first word in a closing, and always follow it with a comma.
17. **(B)** You need the apostrophe in the contraction (it is), and you need only one comma in front of *and* because it connects two complete thoughts.
18. **(C)** You need the apostrophe before the *s* in *roommate's* because it is a singular possessive noun, and the semicolon is required between two complete thoughts.
19. **(A)** *Desserts* needs two *s*'s, and the misplaced modifier needs to be corrected. As the sentence is, it seems that the cook is the one who ate lots of food.

20. **(B)** The possessive form *whose* is correct, and the verb needs to be in the present plural form to agree with *names.*

21. **(A)** Commas are needed around the adjective clause *who loves sweets*, the *c* in *counselor* needs to be lowercase, and the end mark should be a period, not a question mark, because it is a statement and not a question.

22. **(C)** Because the pronoun forms part of the subject, the subjective form *I* should be used; also, no comma is needed because the phrase is not yet completed.

23. **(B)** In saying that she must take a long journey, *all the way* to the cafeteria, she introduces a little humor.

24. **(B)** The *who* should be changed to *whom* because it serves the object position in the adjective clause. There should also be a comma preceding the clause because it is nonessential.

25. **(A)** The ones calling the roll—the teachers—are not included in the sentence. They are being described, but they are not there!

26. **(B)** *Did* is past tense; *has done* is past participle, the required form.

27. **(A)** The essay explains all of the activities of YMCA Aftercare, but the writer ends by saying that it is a great alternative for everyone—perhaps a little persuasive comment to make the reader give it a try.

28. **(B)** *Mom* should not be capitalized because it is preceded by a possessive pronoun; also, the comma needs to remain in front of the conjunction because it connects two complete thoughts.

29. **(A)** This choice states the point in the clearest, most concise manner.

30. **(B)** She includes many details about how nervous and scared she feels; this creates the suspense that keeps the reader interested.

31. **(C)** The comma after *leap* needs to remain because there are items in a series. The comma between *cold* and *clear* is required because they are adjectives describing the same noun. There is no reason to follow *clear* with a comma.

32. **(B)** The phrase *go for it* is slang, and the fact that it appears in quotes helps make that point noticeable.

33. **(A)** The quotes only go around the actual stated material, and because the statement is one thought (introductory element and sentence), then the *l* in *let's* needs to be lowercase. Finally, the period always goes inside closing quote marks.

34. **(B)** "While I was preparing myself" is an adverb clause. It begins with a subordinate conjunction and contains a subject (I) and a verb (was preparing).

35. **(D)** The sentence does not ask a direct question, and the comma *precedes* a conjunction separating two complete thoughts.

PRACTICE TEST #1: EOC English: Writing (Direct Writing Component)

If you could spend the day with a famous American (past or present), whom would you choose? Why? What questions would you ask? What do you think you could learn from such an experience?

_____ Is the introduction clear and interesting?
_____ Is the thesis statement clear and focused?
_____ Does each body paragraph have a topic sentence related to the thesis?
_____ Does each body paragraph contain details to support the topic sentence?
_____ Are the details in the best order?
_____ Are there transitions to take the reader between ideas and paragraphs?
_____ Are the sentences varied in length and style?
_____ Does the conclusion leave the reader with an interesting point of closure?
_____ Has the work been checked for correct spelling?
_____ Has the work been checked for correct capitalization?
_____ Has the work been checked for correct usage and punctuation?

PRACTICE TEST #2: EOC English: Writing (Direct Writing Component)

In your opinion, what is the best movie of all time? Why? What are the characteristics that make it great?

_____ Is the introduction clear and interesting?

_____ Is the thesis statement clear and focused?

_____ Does each body paragraph have a topic sentence related to the thesis?

_____ Does each body paragraph contain details to support the topic sentence?

_____ Are the details in the best order?

_____ Are there transitions to take the reader between ideas and paragraphs?

_____ Are the sentences varied in length and style?

_____ Does the conclusion leave the reader with an interesting point of closure?

_____ Has the work been checked for correct spelling?

_____ Has the work been checked for correct capitalization?

_____ Has the work been checked for correct usage and punctuation?

PRACTICE TEST #1: EOC English: Reading/Literature and Research

Read the following introductory paragraph, and then use it to answer questions 1–5.

from THE MONEY (by Mary Pinch)

(1) The old lady waited. **(2)** She rocked, hummed, and waited. **(3)** She was ready for him. **(4)** She had always felt that one day the law would come. **(5)** She had not always been ready but had always felt that, eventually, her past would catch up with her. **(6)** She was waiting in the "telling room" where she told the local children the stories of the evils caused by the money and the children gasped and groaned, quite full of excitement. **(7)** The children had never seen money and could only imagine what it was and how it was used. **(8)** She had lived in the days of the money and had used money herself and told wondrous stories about how it looked and how it felt. **(9)** The old lady had so many stories about the days of money and how people killed to get it that they knew she was telling the truth. **(10)** She wasn't a "history book," telling a story with all the gory details left out; she really "knew stuff" as the kids put it, and told it as it really was and how it really happened. **(11)** She never just glossed over anything. **(12)** To the children, she was old as dust, but her memory was clear, and her voice was strong. **(13)** Sometimes, she even told her *own* story just as though it were the story of somebody else. **(14)** The year was 2075, and for forty years there had been no money, just the card. **(15)** She touched the small, plastic square hanging around her neck, and rocked and waited.

1. This selection was written for what purpose?
A To explain (expository)
B To entertain (narrative)
C To describe (descriptive)
D To persuade (persuasive)

2. Which of the following statements about point of view is true.
A The excerpt is written in first-person point of view.
B The excerpt is written in third-person limited point of view.
C The excerpt is written in third-person omniscient point of view.
D The excerpt is written in third-person, but whether it is limited or omniscient cannot yet be determined.

3. Based on the excerpt, you can infer that the selection is written in what style?
A Stream of consciousness
B Science fiction
C Fable
D Autobiography

4. In what year had the use of money stopped?
A 2075
B 3015
C 2035
D None of the above

5. What literary term is used in the following excerpt from line 12: "To the children, she was old as dust . . ."?
A Allusion
B Euphemism
C Simile
D Apostrophe

Read the following excerpt from Patrick Henry's famous "Speech to the Virginia Convention," in which he attempts to persuade the members that the colonists should fight for independence from British rule. Then, use it to answer questions 6–12.

from **"Speech to the Virginia Convention"**

(1) I have but one lamp by which my feet are guided, and that is the lamp of experience. **(2)** I know of no way of judging of the future but by the past. **(3)** And judging by the past, I wish to know what there has been in the conduct of the British ministry for the last ten years to justify those hopes with which gentlemen have been pleased to solace themselves and the House. **(4)** Is it that insidious smile with which our petition has been lately received? **(5)** Trust it not, sir; it will prove a snare to your feet. **(6)** Suffer not yourselves to be betrayed with a kiss. **(7)** Ask yourselves how this gracious reception of our petition comports with those warlike preparations which cover our waters and darken our land. **(8)** Are fleets and armies necessary to a work of love and reconciliation? **(9)** Have we shown ourselves so unwilling to be reconciled that force must be called in to win back our love? **(10)** Let us not deceive ourselves, sir. **(11)** These are the implements of war and subjugation; the last arguments to which kings resort. **(12)** I ask gentlemen, sir, what means this martial array, if its purpose be not to force us to submission? **(13)** Can gentlemen assign any other possible motive for it? **(14)** Has Great Britain any enemy, in this quarter of the world, to call for all this accumulation of navies and armies? **(15)** No, sir, she has none. **(16)** They are meant for us: they can be meant for no other. **(17)** They are sent over to bind and rivet upon us those chains which the British ministry have been so long forging. **(18)** And what have we to oppose to them? **(19)** Shall we try argument? **(20)** Sir, we have been trying that for the last ten years. **(21)** Have we anything new to offer upon the subject? **(22)** Nothing. We have held the subject up in every light of which it is capable; but it has been all in vain. **(23)** Shall we resort to entreaty and humble supplication? **(24)** What terms shall we find which have not been already exhausted? **(25)** Let us not, I beseech you, sir, deceive ourselves. **(26)** Sir, we have done everything that could be done to avert the storm which is now coming on. **(27)** We have petitioned; we have remonstrated; we have supplicated; we have prostrated ourselves before the throne, and have implored its interposition to arrest the tyrannical hands of the ministry and Parliament. **(28)** Our petitions have been slighted; our remonstrances have produced additional violence and insult; our supplications have been disregarded; and we have been spurned, with contempt, from the foot of the throne! **(29)** In vain, after these things, may we indulge the fond hope of peace and reconciliation. **(30)** There is no longer any room for hope. **(31)** If we wish to be free—if we mean to preserve inviolate those inestimable privileges for which we have been so long contending—if we mean not basely to abandon the noble struggle in which we have been so long engaged, and which we have pledged ourselves never to abandon until the glorious object of our contest shall be obtained—we must fight! **(32)** I repeat it, sir, we must fight! **(33)** An appeal to arms and to the God of hosts is all that is left us!

6. The term *storm* in line 26 is being used as a metaphor for which of the following?

A The British government
B The colonists
C The peak of the conflict between the British and the colonists
D The concern about the placement of British soldiers in the colonies

7. What is the overall mood of the selection?

A Light and witty
B Confident and forceful
C Vain and self-serving
D Timid and cautious

8. Which of the following arguments does Patrick Henry *not* use to support his opinion that the colonists have no choice but to wage war on Britain?

A The government of the colonies has been arguing with the British government over policies for the last ten years, but nothing has changed.
B The government of the colonies has made all possible suggestions for a peaceful resolution to the conflict between themselves and Britain.
C The British soldiers being placed in the colonies will soon be so great in number that they will be able to enforce the unfair rules of the British government.
D The government of Britain has been unfair to the colonists by imposing taxes and other regulations.

9. According to Patrick Henry, why is it ironic that the British government is sending soldiers to the colonies?

A Because Britain has enemies in that section of the country
B Because the British government has acted as if they are interested in listening to the colonists' viewpoints and reaching a peaceful agreement
C Because Britain intends to enforce the rules it has set forth for the colonies
D Because according to Patrick Henry, the British soldiers are only there to intimidate and frighten the colonists into doing what the British government has required

10. The term *forging* in line 17 means—

A dissolving
B creating
C fearing
D whispering

11. Which of the following elements does Patrick Henry use to help create an emotional attachment with the members of the Convention?

A Loaded terms, such as *tyrannical hands*, *glorious object*, and *insidious smile*
B Clear, logical arguments about how the government of the colonies has already attempted to work with the British government
C Short, choppy sentences that make each point concisely
D Exclamation points at the ends of most of the sentences

12. Which of the following is used as a symbol to represent knowledge?

A Kiss
B Chains
C Lamp
D Snare

Read the following selection, and then use it to answer questions 13–15.

(1) In a world filled with variety and choices, people are faced with important decisions on a daily basis. **(2)** Teens, especially, are challenged to make good choices in the wake of fads, peer pressure, and potentially unhealthy habits. **(3)** One specific area of concern relates to food.
(4) Today, more than ever, teens eat a lot of "junk food" and turn from more healthy items, such as fruits and vegetables. **(5)** One reason for this choice could be that junk food is widely available. **(6)** Vending machines are loaded with snacks having little or no nutritional value.
(7) Some teens seem to consider soda, chips, and a candy bar a balanced meal. **(8)** When they snack on these foods, however, they decrease their appetite for more healthy selections.
(9) Fruits and vegetables have many of the minerals and vitamins necessary for a growing body. **(10)** For example, fruits contain large amounts of vitamin C, a nutrient that is needed to keep one's immune system working efficiently. **(11)** Vegetables, such as carrots, provide the body with nutrients that help keep one's eyes in good physical condition. **(12)** Many teens, especially girls, don't get enough calcium in their diets. **(13)** Although this deficiency doesn't usually cause problems during the teenage years, it may later in life. **(14)** One such potential result of

decreased calcium is osteoporosis, a condition in which the bones become brittle and are easily fractured. **(15)** Many teens also do not drink enough water. **(16)** Much of the human body consists of water, which needs to be replenished each day because of the amount lost during the day. **(17)** Water loss can be especially dangerous during extended periods of exercise or very hot weather. **(18)** Though today's teens live in a fast-paced world full of fast-food choices, they should consider the consequences and possible long-term effects of poor eating habits.

13. What is the main idea of the selection?

A Fruits and vegetables are healthier than soda and chips.
B Vitamin C is the body's most important nutrient.
C Teens need to observe more healthy eating habits.
D Girls need more nutrients than boys do.

14. The meaning of the word *potential* in line 14 is—

A possible
B positive
C female
D mental

15. Which of the following ideas is *not* covered in the selection?

A Failure to consume foods with enough nutrients can affect one's physical health.
B Girls are more likely than boys to have a calcium deficiency.
C Water is not a major source of nutrients for teenagers.
D Most vending-machine snacks contain few nutrients.

Read the following poem, and use it to answer questions 16–20.

The Night Has a Thousand Eyes

The night has a thousand eyes,
And the day but one;
Yet the light of the bright world dies
With the dying sun.

The mind has a thousand eyes,
And the heart but one:
Yet the light of a whole life dies
When love is done.

—Francis William Bourdillon

16. The poem is based on the use of what term?

A Allusion
B Personification
C Simile
D Oxymoron

17. What is the main idea of the poem?

A The world is much brighter than the night.
B An individual item can have as much power as a group of items.
C Light can be compared to love.
D Love never lasts.

18. The "thousand eyes" is a metaphor for—

A hearts
B keys
C stars
D lives

19. What word in the poem is used to symbolize power?

A Light
B Heart
C Love
D Life

20. What is the rhyme scheme of the poem?

A abab abab
B abab cdcd
C abab baba
D abba abba

Read the following poem, and use it to answer questions 21–25.

Holy Sonnet 10

Death, be not proud, though some have called thee
Mighty and dreadful, for thou art not so;
For those, whom thou think'st thou dost overthrow,
Die not, poor death, nor yet canst thou kill me.
From rest and sleep, which but thy picture[s] be,
Much pleasure, then from thee much more must flow,
And soonest our best men with thee do go,
Rest of their bones, and soul's delivery.
Thou'rt slave to fate, chance, kings, and desperate men,
And dost with poison, war, and sickness dwell,
And poppy or charms can make us sleep as well,
And better than thy stroke; why swell'st thou then?
One short sleep past, we wake eternally,
And Death shall be no more; Death, thou shalt die.

—John Donne

21. The use of apostrophe in the poem has what effect?

A Creates the image of the speaker actually talking to another person, making death seem more real
B Identifies the speaker
C Forces the poet to reconstruct the poem, using third person point of view
D Creates a negative atmosphere

22. The last line of the poem contains an example of what literary device?

A Simile
B Paradox
C Idiom
D Allusion

23. What is the main idea of this poem?
- A Death is a form of sleep, during which one looks like a picture.
- B All humans must die, whether they are rich or poor.
- C Death should not be feared because it represents a short sleep before entry into the afterlife.
- D Death is extremely powerful and should be feared by all humans.

24. What is the tone of the poem?
- A Fearful
- B Confident
- C Humble
- D Humorous

25. What is meant by line 9, "Thou'rt slave to fate, chance, kings, and desperate men,"?
- A Fate, chance, kings, and desperate men are the only ones who fear death.
- B Death can actually be compared to a slave under the control of a king.
- C Death cannot act alone without the situations in life that cause people to die.
- D Humans are really the slaves of death, who can kill at any time.

Read the following poem about Virginia, and then use it to answer questions 26–28.

Virginia is the
State we have learned
To love. This state is home to many
Things, like the dove. It was home to many
Presidents too. George Washington and Thomas Jefferson
Both lived in Virginia. Monticello was Jefferson's home. The
State bird, the Cardinal, likes to roam. The state tree is the
Flowering Dogwood in old Virginia, my home. The beach to the east is where the waves
Crash, making foam. To Virginia's east are the Appalachian Mountains. Richmond is the capital.
The other name for Virginia, Old Dominion, is my home, sweet home. This great state got its name
From Queen Elizabeth of England. Martinsville is a small town in Virginia. It's small, but it is known for
Its racetrack, the Martinsville Speedway. Laurel Park, the coolest school, is located in my sweet home, Virginia.

—Lynn Robertson,
Martinsville, VA

26. From the poem about Virginia, you can infer all of the following *except*—
- A The writer loves her home.
- B The writer knows many facts about Virginia.
- C The writer has traveled outside the state of Virginia.
- D The writer is proud of Virginia's background.

27. This selection is what type of poem?
- A Narrative
- B Elegy
- C Concrete
- D Haiku

28. If this poem were written in traditional stanzas rather than in the shape of a state, it would be considered what type of poem?
- A Narrative
- B Lyric
- C Ballad
- D Ode

Read the following introduction to Joseph's paper, and then use it to answer questions 29–32.

(1) Try to imagine that you must take all of your daily breaths through a straw (National Institutes of Health). **(2)** You would likely find that task very stressful; however, there are many people in the United States who must endure just such a challenge. **(3)** The simple act of breathing, one many take for granted, becomes quite difficult for those who suffer from asthma attacks. **(4)** During an attack, the lining of one's airways becomes swollen and releases a thick mucus, which causes the muscles around the airways to become narrower. **(5)** Something as simple as a smell, exercise, cigarette smoke, or change in temperature can trigger such an attack. **(6)** Luckily, there are many medicines available to help prevent and treat this chronic lung disease that affects millions of Americans each day (National Institutes of Health).

29. According to the thesis statement of the research paper, the body could include all of the following ideas *except*—

A the use of inhalants to help asthma patients during an attack
B a discussion of different allergy medicines to control sinus activity
C an analysis of the areas in restaurants that can help asthma patients avoid smoke and other smells
D a discussion of the reaction of the internal organs to particular chemicals designed to treat asthma

30. How is sentence 3, The simple act of breathing, one many take for granted, becomes quite difficult for those who suffer attacks of asthma., best revised?

A The simple act of breathing, which is a simple act that many take for granted, becomes quite difficult for those who suffer asthma attacks.
B The simple act of breathing becomes difficult for those who suffer asthma attacks even though others take it for granted.
C The simple act of breathing, which many take for granted, becomes quite difficult for those who suffer asthma attacks.
D Those who suffer asthma attacks cannot take the simple act of breathing for granted because breathing becomes quite difficult for them.

31. Which of the following sources would be *least* helpful to Joseph in his search for information about asthma?

A Hospital website outlining asthma symptoms and treatments
B Interviews with two adults diagnosed with asthma
C Novel about a young girl growing up with asthma
D Entry in a medical encyclopedia

32. Joseph plans to discuss symptoms, treatments, and causes of asthma. What would be the most logical order in which to develop details?

A Treatments, symptoms, and causes
B Treatments, causes, and symptoms
C Causes, symptoms, and treatments
D Causes, treatments, and symptoms

Look at the following example of one of Joseph's source cards, and then use it to answer questions 33–34.

> #4
>
> Smithers, Jonathan. Innovations in the Treatment of Asthma. Chicago, West Publishing Co., 2002.

33. An error occurs in which of the following source card elements?

A Title
B Author
C Source reference number
D Publishing company

34. This source is *most* likely which type?

A Magazine article
B Book
C Internet site
D Newspaper article

Look at the following example of one of Joseph's note cards, and then use it to answer question 35.

> Bronchodilators #2
>
> Theophylline, another bronchodilator, also opens the airways by relaxing muscles around them.
>
> pg. 56

35. From reading the note card, you can infer all of the following *except*—

A Joseph has at least two sources.
B Joseph will discuss at least two types of bronchodilators in his paper.
C This information comes from a book.
D Joseph understands the format for note cards.

PRACTICE TEST #2: EOC English: Reading/Literature and Research

Read the following student essay about a television show, and then use it to answer questions 1–7.

Imagine trying to survive in an isolated, unfamiliar location with sixteen strangers for thirty-nine days. On top of that, imagine having to cook, build a shelter, and look for food. If one were a contestant on the reality show *Survivor*, he would have to participate in all of these activities to win the title of Sole Survivor. This reality show is my favorite television program for many reasons.

One characteristic I love about the show is that it is filmed in a different location every season. Watching Survivor for the past six seasons, I saw many landscapes. For each season, a new, exotic location was chosen. The first six seasons were shot in Pulau Tiger, the Australian Outback, Africa, Thailand, Marquesas, and the Amazon. I loved the scenic views. The first season at Pulau Tiger showed the beautiful scenery of the Malaysian jungle. While watching season two, which was filmed in Australia, I saw a famous landmark, Ayers Rock. Watching the African season, I saw the endless, grassy plains. The season in Marquesas enabled me to see Tahiti's beautiful, tree-covered environment. Watching the Thailand season, I was amazed by the trees and plants. I especially enjoyed the season in the Amazon, during which I saw the beautiful canopies of the jungle surrounding the river. Learning about the cultures in each new location also provided me with great enjoyment. During the season in Africa, two of the contestants won a trip to visit a village to see what day-to-day life was like in the villages and to view the safari personally. I got to see the natives dance in their festival costumes. Seeing the role of the lions and gazelles in villagers' lives made me understand more of the problems the animals cause. A few times during every season, Jeff Prost, the host, told legends unique to the settings. During the Australian Outback season, he told the story, according to the Aborigines, about how Ayers Rock originated. The different locations also allowed me to see the wildlife around the globe. The season in the Amazon enabled me to catch glimpses of many species of monkeys; the array of birds I saw was also amazing. During the Australian season, crocodiles sometimes lay on the shore beside the sunbathing contestants. I also got to see many kangaroos, for they hopped around the campsites.

Another reason *Survivor* is my favorite show is because of the contestants. I enjoyed hearing about each contestant's background. Every season brought a diverse group of people from all over the United States and very different walks of life. Rocket science, bartending, used car sales, and athletics were just a few of the fields in which contestants worked. Another reason I liked the contestants was that the people were not actors, so I was able to relate to them. By the second week or so of the game, the contestants really began missing their families. Likewise, when I'm away from my loved ones, I miss them very much. Furthermore, every person also brought a unique strategy to the game, just as people tend to do in life. For example, when I have to work with a group, I approach whatever the assignment may be differently depending on the personalities of those with whom I'm working. Also, the show had people similar to those that I encounter in my life. Some people on the show worked hard and completed the chores necessary to survive. On the other hand, there were others that lay in the hammock and didn't help hunt or cook but wanted to eat when suppertime came.

Lastly, I enjoy *Survivor* because the show is entertaining. Every show had both immunity and reward challenges. The contestants had to participate in often "gross" activities. They had to do everything from trying to eat the most insects in a given amount of time to standing on a pole in the ocean till everyone else gave up and swam to shore. Another entertaining aspect of the show was the Tribal Council. At the end of the show, the contestants had to vote for a member to be removed from the tribe. The person getting the most votes had to leave. I was often surprised about who got voted off the show. I realize that everything that happened influenced the votes, yet I only saw a small portion of what really occurred during the week. I was also amused by participants' choices of their luxury items. Contestants on the show were allowed to bring one item that was not necessary for survival. I enjoyed seeing what each person brought and what his reason for the choice was. Contestants brought items such as a Bible, a razor, a Texas flag, a journal, and a hackey sack.

Survivor is my favorite show because of the contestants, the entertainment, and the new locations. I love to be able to watch a show and learn yet be entertained at the same time. *Survivor* does this for me, and that is part of the reason it is my favorite television show.

1. Which of the following details least contributes to the exotic description of the show's settings?

A "... during which I saw the beautiful canopies of the jungle surrounding the river."
B "... crocodiles sometimes lay on the shore beside the sunbathing contestants."
C "Watching *Survivor* for the past six seasons, I saw many landscapes."
D "I got to see the natives dance in their festival costumes."

2. This selection is *best* described as—

A a dramatic monologue
B a narrative
C an expository essay
D a biographical account

3. Which of the following was not one of the settings for the show *Survivor*?

A Malaysia
B Tahiti
C Africa
D Ecuador

4. The author's purpose for using the opening two sentences is most likely to—

A establish a connection between the reader and the topic to be discussed
B state the thesis for the essay
C provide an element of satire
D create a transition between the details used to support the thesis

5. Which of the following is *not* one of the reasons for which the author enjoys watching *Survivor*?

A She enjoys learning about faraway lands and cultures.
B She is intrigued by the climactic Tribal Councils each week.
C She is often away from her own family.
D She reflects on the similarities between the show and her own life.

6. This essay is written in—

A first-person point of view
B first-person omniscient point of view
C third-person limited point of view
D third-person omniscient point of view

7. Which of the following statements from the essay indicates the author's insight about the nature of this particular reality show?

A "Every season brought a diverse group of people from all over the United States and very different walks of life."
B "Some people on the show worked hard and completed the chores necessary to survive."
C "I realize that everything that happened influenced the votes, yet I only saw a small portion of what really occurred during the week."
D "I love to be able to watch a show and learn yet be entertained at the same time."

Read the following descriptive essay, and use it to answer questions 8–12.

(1) I remember when I was about six years old and in the first grade, each afternoon when school let out, I would run down the hall to see my grandma, who taught the fourth grade. As she straightened her desk and got ready to leave, I would take a seat in one of the desks. Sitting there made me feel much older because my room had only small tables and chairs. I loved her room. It was always decorated according to the season of the year or current holiday. My favorite was the annual Easter egg tree. The children would each color a hollow egg and then place it on the bare branches of a little stick tree that was used each year. Those eggs just seemed to bring that little tree alive with color and personality.

(2) When Grandma was finally ready to leave, we would walk, hand in hand, next door to my great-grandma and great-granddaddy's house. They had both passed away, but my two aunts still lived there. It was a beautiful old two-story house with a screened-in porch running along the whole left side. Three brick steps led up to the yard level, and a stone walkway led to the front door. To the right of this walkway was the tallest and most overwhelming white dogwood tree that I have ever seen. In the springtime, there grew around its trunk what seemed to me a thousand bright yellow daffodils, black-eyed susans, daisies, and multicolored, velvet pansies. Around the rest of the house grew a wide variety of bushes, trees, and wildflowers. The steps up to the front door were made of stone that looked quite old and worn. To the right of the door was a huge, glass window with a large pane divided into little squares. The inside of the window held a large, wooden sill that became my favorite place of retreat during winter. On the other side of the squeaky screen door stood a huge, carved oak door with a beautiful, clear glass doorknob. It had always seemed strange to me then that even though the knob was just within my reach, I had never been strong enough to get the heavy door open by myself. Grandma opened the door and stepped aside to let me enter first. Once inside, I always greeted everyone with great enthusiasm as though I had not seen them in years!

(3) The first little room beyond the front door was where I spent most of my time. It was sort of a dining room and parlor combined. All of the furniture had an antique look, the pieces placed around the room in such a way so as to leave just enough space for walking. It was very comfortable and felt so cozy. Whenever I entered this room, I would almost always find my Aunt Dora sitting in her green chair next to the window and either knitting or sleeping. Her snoring always made me laugh! Uncle Buddy could almost always be found sitting in the old wicker rocking chair by the kitchen door. He was old, had a big pot belly, and seemed to fill—even overfill—the whole chair. Sometimes, he would sit me on his lap and tell me stories or just talk to me. Every Christmas, he gave me a silver dollar, which Daddy said to save but which I always spent. Uncle Buddy actually lived in a house up the Old Mill Road, yet he was always there, sitting and visiting in that rocking chair, smoking his pipe when I came home from school.

(4) In the kitchen, I would always find Aunt Sarah, Dora's sister. She was the oldest in the family and did most of the cooking. I always looked forward to her delicious homemade cookies, cake, or pie after school. Sometimes, she would mix up a batch of taffy and let me help her pull it until it turned from a clear, caramel color to an almost milky white. One thing that I will always remember about her is that she never scolded. No matter what went wrong, especially with me in the kitchen helping, she never lost her temper. I loved the way she called me "sugar pie." Her endearing nickname made me feel very special.

(5) Sometimes, Grandma let me go into the living room, but only if she accompanied me. A dark red, velvet couch, a matching chair, another chair covered in silk, a lamp decorated with a picture of my cousin, and a rolltop desk are the objects I most remember from that room. Adjoining the living room was the music room, which held a piano, some bookshelves, a small fireplace, two armchairs, and a beautiful china cabinet. Ironically, the cabinet did not attract me because of its store of delicate plates and bowls, for it held none. Instead, every shelf was filled with dolls that had belonged to my grandmother and my aunts since their childhoods. Most of them were china dolls with such lifelike faces and expressions that I found it hard to believe they were not real. Occasionally, the cabinet was unlocked, and I was allowed to examine the dolls more closely. My favorite was a china doll named Celia. She had fine brown hair, blue eyes, and a lovely blue gingham dress with a white frock tied over it. I was allowed to hold Celia only if I was sitting down, so I would rock her, and we would have long conversations, usually about school or the mean little boy next door.

(6) At other times in the music room, I would plunk away on the piano, always knowing that at the end, my aunt would clap and tell me that it was "just fine!" Once, she taught me to play "Chopsticks," and I thought I would burst with pride when Daddy came to pick me up and I got to play it for him.

(7) I vividly remember the times my sister (who was two years younger than I) and I would spend the night at my grandmother's house. After dinner, we would draw or play with the never-ending supply of toys. There was no television in the house, but we never really noticed; there was always something to keep us busy. When bedtime came, Aunt Sarah would lock up the house while Aunt Dora took us upstairs. Sometimes, I would linger behind and slide down the smooth, wooden banister, even though I knew that Aunt Dora would yell down from the top stair, "Suzanne! How many times must I tell you not to do that? You could fall and break something!" Aunt Sarah would just look at me, wink, and say, "You won't do it again, will you sugar pie?"

(8) Once everyone was in her nightgown with face washed, teeth brushed, and prayers said, we would all snuggle into our beds. Both of my aunts slept in the same room. My sister slept with Aunt Dora in her brass bed, and I slept with Aunt Sarah in the bed with the huge, hand-carved headboard. That bed had been a present for her sixteenth birthday. My sister and I were each given a small flashlight to keep under our pillows in case we needed to see our way to the bathroom in the middle of the night. We all said our goodnights, amid a lot of talking, laughing, and playing with the flashlights until Aunt Dora would say, "First one to sleep, whistle!" Of course, this brought on a barrage of whistling and snoring! Eventually, we all fell asleep, the only sounds an occasional chime on the nearby church clock or a train passing over the nearby bridge.

(9) That old house that I so dearly loved and remember with such fondness was torn down by the school about thirty-five years ago to provide more building space. The only evidence that remains is the stately and enduring dogwood tree. That the house is gone forever saddens me, but its memories will never die; they will remain forever alive in my heart.

—Suzanne Pebworth Sweatt

8. Which of the following concepts is *not* described in the story?

A Characteristics of the members of the writer's extended family
B Descriptions of the house and its contents
C Humorous memories
D Biographical comments about the previous owners of the home

9. What does the author imply from the following sentence found in paragraph 2: "It had always seemed strange to me then that even though the knob was just within my reach, I had never been strong enough to get the heavy door open by myself."

A As an adult, she realizes that children have unique ways of looking at common situations.
B She now realizes that the adults purposely had the door handle at a level that would keep the child from opening the door by herself.
C She does not understand why she could never open the door by herself.
D There was never actually a glass doorknob on the heavy oak door.

10. What is the *most* likely reason that the speaker was only allowed to hold Celia while she was sitting down?

A Her grandma was afraid the doll would be taken to another room.
B Her grandma was afraid the doll would get broken.
C Her grandma did not like to share the doll.
D Her grandma wanted to take a picture of the child with the doll.

11. What is the overall tone of the essay?
A Reflective
B Exciting
C Depressing
D Judgmental

12. What literary device is evident in the last line of paragraph 9: "... its memories will never die; they will remain forever alive in my heart."
A Onomatopoeia
B Hyperbole
C Personification
D Metaphor

Read the following warranty, and use it to answer questions 13–17.

Warranty Information

Customers in the U.S. and Canada Only

One-Year Limited Warranty for Electronic Product

This Texas Instruments ("TI") electronic product warranty extends only to the original purchaser and user of the product.

Warranty Duration. This TI electronic product is warranted to the original purchaser for a period of one (1) year from the original purchase date.

Warranty Coverage. This TI electronic product is warranted against defective materials and construction. THIS WARRANTY IS VOID IF THE PRODUCT HAS BEEN DAMAGED BY ACCIDENT OR UNREASONABLE USE, NEGLECT, IMPROPER SERVICE, OR OTHER CAUSES NOT ARISING OUT OF DEFECTS IN MATERIALS OR CONSTRUCTION.

Warranty Disclaimers. ANY IMPLIED WARRANTIES ARISING OUT OF THIS SALE, INCLUDING BUT NOT LIMITED TO THE IMPLIED WARRANTIES OF MERCHANTABILITY AND FITNESS FOR A PARTICULAR PURPOSE, ARE LIMITED IN DURATION TO THE ABOVE ONE-YEAR PERIOD. TEXAS INSTRUMENTS SHALL NOT BE LIABLE FOR LOSS OF USE OF THE PRODUCT OR OTHER INCIDENTAL OR CONSEQUENTIAL COSTS, EXPENSES, OR DAMAGES INCURRED BY THE CONSUMER OR ANY OTHER USER.

Some states/provinces do not allow the exclusion or limitation of implied warranties or consequential damages, so the above limitations or exclusions may not apply to you.

Legal Remedies. This warranty gives you specific legal rights, and you may also have other rights that vary from state to state or province to province.

Warranty Performance. During the above one (1) year warranty period, your defective product will be either repaired or replaced with a reconditioned model of an equivalent quality (at TI's option) when the product is returned, postage prepaid, to Texas Instruments Service Facility. The warranty of the repaired or replacement unit will continue for the warranty of the original unit or six (6) months, whichever is longer. Other than the postage requirement, no charge will be made for such repair and/or replacement. TI strongly recommends that you insure the product for value prior to mailing.

Software. Software is licensed, not sold. TI and its licensors do not warrant that the software will be free from errors or meet your specific requirements. All software is provided "AS IS."

Copyright. The software and any documentation supplied with this product are protected by copyright.

13. This warranty applies to which of the following?

A Anyone who buys the calculator and has a signed receipt
B Only the first two owners of the calculator
C Only the first owner of the calculator
D Anyone who owns the calculator within the first year after the original purchase

14. The warranty will cover the product in which of the following situations?

A If the product is damaged in an accident
B If the product is misused
C If the product is lost
D If the product has defective materials

15. The warranty on this product lasts for—

A one year
B two years
C five years
D a lifetime

16. Which of the following might the company do if you return the product under the terms of the warranty?

A Cancel the warranty
B Replace the defective model with a new product
C Repair the defective model
D Issue a refund of the purchase price

17. If the product were repaired and you had three months left on the original warranty, which of the following would be true?

A You would be issued a new one-year warranty.
B Your warranty would continue for three months.
C Your warranty would continue for six months.
D Your warranty would continue for nine months.

Read the following poem and use it to answer questions 18–22.

Life Is a Dance

Life is a dance
It begins at conception
And ends when God calls us home.
Parts we waltz,
While others must be taken two steps at a time,
Lest we forget to tango.
God has blessed us with a new day:
Dance
Twirl
Live every day as if it's the last step.
One day, God will pick you up off your feet.
You'll glide to the Heavens above, and
There, you'll dance for eternity.

—Lynn Robertson

18. This poem can best be characterized as a(n)—

A sonnet
B analogy
C metered poem
D ode

19. The poet uses the term *twirl* in line 9 to represent—
- A a suggestion to face life with excitement
- B a warning against taking life too lightly
- C the concept of growing old gracefully
- D the confusion of a very busy lifestyle

20. The focus of the poem shifts from the concept of life to the concept of death in line—
- A 6
- B 8
- C 11
- D 12

21. The overall mood of this poem is—
- A comforting
- B troubling
- C demanding
- D exciting

22. The theme of this poem is best captured by which of the following statements?
- A Life is too short to be taken very seriously.
- B Life can be compared to different types of dances.
- C Life should be lived to its fullest, for we don't know when it will end.
- D Life may be difficult at times, but we can dance our way to eternity.

Read the following poem, and use it to answer questions 23–25.

My Heart and I

I.

ENOUGH! We're tired, my heart and I.
We sit beside the headstone thus,
And wish that name were carved for us.
The moss reprints more tenderly
The hard types of the mason's knife,
As heaven's sweet life renews earth's life
With which we're tired, my heart and I.

II.

You see we're tired, my heart and I.
We dealt with books, we trusted men,
And in our own blood drenched the pen,
As if such colours could not fly.
We walked too straight for fortune's end,
We loved too true to keep a friend;
At last we're tired, my heart and I.

III.

How tired we feel, my heart and I!
We seem of no use in the world;
Our fancies hang grey and uncurled
About men's eyes indifferently;
Our voice which thrilled you so, will let
You sleep; our tears are only wet;
What do we here, my heart and I?

IV.

So tired, so tired, my heart and I!
It was not thus in that old time
When Ralph sat with me 'neath the lime
To watch the sunset from the sky.
'Dear love, you're looking tired,' he said;
I, smiling at him, shook my head:
'Tis now we're tired, my heart and I.

V.

So tired, so tired, my heart and I!
Though now none takes me on his arm
To fold me close and kiss me warm
Till each quick breath end in a sigh
Of happy languor. Now, alone,
We lean upon this graveyard stone,
Uncheered, unkissed, my heart and I.

VI.

Tired out we are, my heart and I.
Suppose the world brought diadems
To tempt us, crusted with loose gems
Of powers and pleasures? Let it try.
We scarcely care to look at even
A pretty child, or God's blue heaven,
We feel so tired, my heart and I.

VII.

Yet who complains? My heart and I?
In this abundant earth no doubt
Is little room for things worn out:
Disdain them, break them, throw them by
And if before the days grew rough
We *once* were loved, used, —well enough,
I think, we've fared, my heart and I.

—Elizabeth Barrett Browning

23. Which stanza involves a shift in tone?

A III
B V
C VI
D VII

24. What does the speaker accomplish through the use of the repetitive phrase, "my heart and I"?

A She emphasizes the connection between humans and their feelings.
B She relates the many broken relationships she has endured.
C She establishes the fact that her love is now dead.
D She reminds the reader of the fragile nature of the human heart.

25. This poem takes place in—

A the speaker's home
B a church
C a graveyard
D a seashore

Read the following poem, and then use it to answer questions 26–28.

The Wood-pile

Out walking in the frozen swamp one grey day
I paused and said, "I will turn back from here.
No, I will go on farther—and we shall see."
The hard snow held me, save where now and then
One foot went down. The view was all in lines
Straight up and down of tall slim trees
Too much alike to mark or name a place by
So as to say for certain I was here
Or somewhere else: I was just far from home.
A small bird flew before me. He was careful
To put a tree between us when he lighted,
And say no word to tell me who he was
Who was so foolish as to think what *he* thought.
He thought that I was after him for a feather—
The white one in his tail; like one who takes
Everything said as personal to himself.
One flight out sideways would have undeceived him.
And then there was a pile of wood for which
I forgot him and let his little fear
Carry him off the way I might have gone,
Without so much as wishing him good-night.
He went behind it to make his last stand.
It was a cord of maple, cut and split
And piled—and measured, four by four by eight.
And not another like it could I see.
No runner tracks in this year's snow looped near it.
And it was older sure than this year's cutting,
Or even last year's or the year's before.
The wood was grey and the bark warping off it
And the pile somewhat sunken. Clematis
Had wound strings round and round it like a bundle.
What held it though on one side was a tree
Still growing, and on one a stake and prop,
These latter about to fall. I thought that only
Someone who lived in turning to fresh tasks
Could so forget his handiwork on which
He spent himself, the labour of his axe,
And leave it there far from a useful fireplace
To warm the frozen swamp as best it could
With the slow smokeless burning of decay.

—Robert Frost

26. What type of conflict is evidenced in lines 2 and 3?

A Man versus animal
B Man versus himself
C Man versus society
D Man versus man

27. Which of the following is *not* an indication that the pile of wood has lain there untouched for a long time?

A The wood was discolored
B The bark was coming off the logs
C An old axe was leaning against the pile
D There were no tracks to indicate someone arriving or leaving the area

28. Clematis, mentioned in line 30, is most likely a—

A person
B bird
C plant
D swamp

Read the following document, and then use it to answer questions 29–31.

"The Bill of Rights"
Amendments 1–10 of the *Constitution*

The Conventions of a number of the States, having at the time of adopting the Constitution, expressed a desire, in order to prevent misconstruction or abuse of its powers, that further declaratory and restrictive clauses should be added: And as extending the ground of public confidence in the Government, will best ensure the beneficent ends of its institution:

Resolved by the Senate and House of Representatives of the United States of America, in Congress assembled, two thirds of both Houses concurring, that the following Articles be proposed to the Legislatures of the several States, as amendments to the Constitution of the United States, all or any of which Articles, when ratified by three fourths of the said Legislatures, to be valid to all intents and purposes, as part of the said Constitution; viz.

Amendment I

Congress shall make no law respecting an establishment of religion, or prohibiting the free exercise thereof; or abridging the freedom of speech, or of the press, or the right of the people peaceably to assemble, and to petition the Government for a redress of grievances.

Amendment II

A well regulated Militia, being necessary to the security of a free State, the right of the people to keep and bear Arms, shall not be infringed.

Amendment III

No Soldier shall, in time of peace be quartered in any house, without the consent of the Owner, nor in time of war, but in a manner to be prescribed by law.

Amendment IV

The right of the people to be secure in their persons, houses, papers, and effects, against unreasonable searches and seizures, shall not be violated, and no Warrants shall issue, but upon probable cause, supported by Oath or affirmation, and particularly describing the place to be searched, and the persons or things to be seized.

Amendment V

No person shall be held to answer for a capital, or otherwise infamous crime, unless on a presentment or indictment of a Grand Jury, except in cases arising in the land or naval forces, or in the Militia, when in actual service in time of War or public danger; nor shall any person be subject for the same offence to be twice put in jeopardy of life or limb, nor shall be compelled in any criminal case to be a witness against himself, nor be deprived of life, liberty, or property, without due process of law; nor shall private property be taken for public use without just compensation.

Amendment VI

In all criminal prosecutions, the accused shall enjoy the right to a speedy and public trial, by an impartial jury of the State and district wherein the crime shall have been committed; which district shall have been previously ascertained by law, and to be informed of the nature and cause of the accusation; to be confronted with the witnesses against him; to have compulsory process for obtaining witnesses in his favor, and to have the assistance of counsel for his defense.

Amendment VII

In Suits at common law, where the value in controversy shall exceed twenty dollars, the right of trial by jury shall be preserved, and no fact tried by a jury shall be otherwise re-examined in any Court of the United States, than according to the rules of the common law.

Amendment VIII

Excessive bail shall not be required, nor excessive fines imposed, nor cruel and unusual punishments inflicted.

Amendment IX

The enumeration in the Constitution of certain rights shall not be construed to deny or disparage others retained by the people.

Amendment X

The powers not delegated to the United States by the Constitution, nor prohibited by it to the States, are reserved to the States respectively, or to the people.

29. The term *amendments* can *best* be defined as—

A exceptions
B additions
C corrections
D conclusions

30. The word *infringed* in Amendment II means—

A allowed
B deleted
C prevented
D created

31. Which of the following amendments to the Constitution addresses one's right to have an attorney?

A Amendment V
B Amendment VI
C Amendment VII
D Amendment VIII

Read the following research report, and then use it to answer questions 32-38.

(1) The profession of midwifery was mentioned first in the Bible (*History of Midwifery*). The word midwife has different meanings in different cultures. In Old English, midwife means "with woman," which just implies a woman's support, and in French, it means "wise woman" (Saunders). Midwifery seems to have been started as a woman's community-based network for helping and healing, but the practice evolved from a male-dominated priesthood to a male-controlled medicine before the women gained more control of the practice (Feldhusen). The education of midwives has changed from no formal education, where the knowledge was gained from being an apprentice, to schools specifically for training nurse-midwives. The history of midwifery has changed a great deal over the years.

(2) Midwifery seems to be one of the oldest professions. References are made to female midwives in the Old Testament; when Rachel was in labor, a midwife told her not to fear, for she would soon have another son. Midwives were seen by colonial people and some historians as being knowledgeable and respected members of society (Giraldo). Since women have been giving birth, they have wanted support from others. Historians have found mention of midwifery in ancient Egyptian records, papyri, and in ancient Hindu records. The history of midwifery was started at an unknown time when some women became designated as the wise women to help others with childbirth. The jobs of the first midwives were to be caretakers and healers. Also, they used herbs and potions for healing, acting as early pharmacists. The midwives not only tried to help alleviate pregnant women's pain, but they also came up with potions that helped other sick people in the community as well. These remedies, consequently, made them respected and <u>revered</u>. In some instances, their abilities produced awe and fear as well. Many times throughout history, people who could bring fertility or heal a person were thought to be witches since most people could not perform such acts (Sullivan). The midwives' understanding of science, no matter how basic, was a mystery to the average person. Most people assumed that the midwives' power had to come from a supernatural source, such as the devil. Because of this belief, many midwives were killed during the witch-burning frenzy (Sullivan). The respect of midwifery as a profession took many centuries to develop.

(3) The education of midwives has varied greatly. The first midwives lacked much formal education; their only training came from what they heard others say and from their own birthing experiences. Hippocrates was the first person to educate midwives formally. Midwives passed their knowledge and skills down through generations by apprenticeships (*History of Midwifery*). In the early sixteenth century, one of the first schools for midwives was opened in the Hotel-Dieu, Paris. In the United States, Philadelphia chartered the first medical school in 1765. While Dr. William Shippen began the first formal training for midwives with courses in anatomy and midwifery, a short course for midwives led by Dr. Valentine Seaman began in 1799 in New York. In 1840, many medical schools and colleges added midwifery to their curriculum, and the Royal College of Physicians and Surgeons awarded diplomas in midwifery. Nightingale Ward King's College Hospital began to train nurses in midwifery in 1862 (Feldhusen). In the early 1900's, women did not have access to the growing knowledge and changing world of health care.

(4) Around 1925, the first five nurse-midwifery schools were started. The graduates were able to provide care to women who, through geography, poverty, language, culture, or race, were unable to receive birthing care at established hospitals (*History of Midwifery*). The American College of Nurse Midwives, ACNM, was formed in 1955 to train nurse-midwives, and the Children's Bureau started to fund some of the nurse-midwifery education programs. In 1967, the Teachers of Nursing Act allowed qualified teachers and registered nurses to register for a pilot midwifery-training course. By 1970, national certification in nurse-midwife educational programs began. In 1975, the Central Midwives Board, on behalf of the government, controlled the training and practice of midwifery. Also, in 1975, midwifery training was offered at one hundred and sixteen schools. Division of Nursing in the United States of America in 1976 provided more funding for nurse-midwifery education programs (Feldhusen). In 1989, Project 2000 implemented a new career structure for nurses and midwives, concentrating on nursing practice, manpower, education, leadership, and management.

(5) Over the years, the requirements to be a midwife have varied. The Greeks and Romans were the first to create qualifications for midwifery practice (*History of Midwifery*). In ancient

Greece, midwives were required by law to have given birth themselves. By the seventeenth century, English bishops wanted to prevent witchcraft in births. To do this, the bishops tried to make sure that midwives were loyal to the decrees of the church and state regarding births, so midwives were required to receive an Episcopal license before practicing midwifery. Bishops believed that the licensing prevented the practice of witchcraft by the midwives when assisting in the birth of a child. In 1720, Maubay, a teacher, required his midwifery students to be thin, considerate, grave, patient, pleasant, and obedient. In the eighteenth century, midwifery became a respectable job for men. As recently as 1960, nurse-midwives could practice legally only in three jurisdictions in the United States: the states of New Mexico and Kentucky, and the city of New York. Licensing standards for the practice of midwifery vary from state to state in the United States of America. Even today, one is not required to take an exam to begin a practice. As a result of the input from numerous practitioners and midwifery educators, no clear definition of "midwife," let alone the scope of her responsibilities, exists (Feldhusen).

(6) Midwives have held many different beliefs and practices throughout history. Prior to the fifth century, childbirth was entrusted to the informal care of a female relative or neighbor who had given birth herself (*One Chapter*). No changes in the practices of midwifery occurred between the Dark Ages and the Middle Ages (Saunders). The earliest settling midwives in the United States of America were not only expected to care for childbearing women, but they also provided basic health care for other members of the community (*History of Midwifery*). The practices of the ancient Greeks were for the expectant mother to squat on a birth stool with female relatives or friends around her and the midwife to squat with her hands ready to catch the newborn baby. The birthing custom of the Sioux Indians, on the contrary, was for the woman to give birth standing up, facing her husband, and for the midwife to catch the baby from behind (*A History . . . in Pictures*). During colonial times, the English society did not consider midwives to be part of the medical profession at all, for they only saw the midwives as people performing a special social function. As more immigrants came to the United States of America, they brought their birthing practices with them to the new country. These women were often called "Granny Midwives," and the new midwives added to the knowledge and skills of the midwives already practicing and providing care to the women throughout the United States of America (*History of Midwifery*). In the sixteenth century, two brothers invented and began to use the forceps in the birthing process. In the 1970s, midwives began using new birthing rituals of birth education and replaced drugs with relief of pain through breathing exercises.

(7) Over the years, the use of a midwife has fluctuated. References are made to female midwives in the Old Testament as being knowledgeable and respected members of society. According to an article in the *Nursing Times*, the shift from female to male midwives began in the latter part of the sixteenth century after the invention of the obstetric forceps (Giraldo). In the early nineteen hundreds, a debate was raging over whether or not the practice of midwifery should be totally stopped, for only a few supported the education and regulation of midwifery (*History of Midwifery*). The rising middle classes of the nineteenth century began to prefer obstetric care to that of a midwife while the poor could only afford a midwife (Feldhusen). From the nineteen twenties to the nineteen thirties, the opposition to midwives kept growing. Despite this, congress passed the Sheppard-Towner Act. This act, with the help of the Children's Bureau, focused on using money to improve the care of mothers and infants in the United States by improving the care providers. Also, the act provided public health nurses to teach and supervise the "amateur" midwives. In addition, in the nineteen thirties, Mary Breckinridge came to the United States of America from England with a group of formally trained nurse-midwives. Their original purpose was to provide health care to women in the remote areas of Kentucky (*History of Midwifery*). Midwives attended fifty percent of all births in 1930, but by 1935, midwives were only at twelve and a half percept of all births. Doctors, rather than midwives, became more common at births because of medical practitioners' promise of speedy and less painful births. The new and improved drugs relieved women from the problems and dangers of childbirth that had previously been viewed as normal (Giraldo). Due to increased dependence on doctors for obstetrical care by the 1940s and 1950s, most midwives in America served needy women in cities and remote rural areas for a wide range of needs, excluding childbirth. Only twenty-seven percent actually helped with births. The majority of midwives at the time were maternity educators who supervised the maternity departments in hospitals, consulted on state boards of health, and had various other jobs working with women (*History of Midwifery*). Because of the advancements in the medical profession, the number of males entering the field of child birthing increased (Giraldo). In 1972, ninety-two percent of births happened in hospitals with doctors instead of at home with midwives. Midwives were present at fewer than one percent of United States births by the middle of the 1970s. The "baby boomers" population began to have babies of their own. With a shortage of obstetricians, the demand for birth attendants grew high. In addition, the women's movement and feminism took hold, and with them came an increase in demand for nurse-midwives. Today, ten percent of the births in the United States have midwives present (*History of Midwifery*). Some states have as high as twenty percent of births performed by midwives (Sullivan). The average child born anywhere in the world arrives with the assistance of a midwife, yet practicing midwifery is still illegal in many parts of the United States of America.

(8) Hospitals have played an important part in the history of midwifery. In an attempt to keep mother and infant deaths down, childbirths are occurring more often in hospitals than in homes, but even with this preventive measure, deaths and illnesses during childbirth continue to be high (*History of Midwifery*). The Pennsylvania Hospital was the first permanent general hospital built to provide care for the sick in the United States of America. Many of the hospitals even until the 1900s would not allow midwives to assist with childbirth, and if they were allowed, a physician had to be present. The public's perception of midwifery and natural childbirth modified over the years, and by 1971, the Birth Center of Santa Cruz opened its doors. The National Association of Childbearing Centers was established in the United States of America in 1983.

(9) Today, almost all hospitals have a maternity ward and provide health care to babies even before they are born. The knowledge available, the facilities, the requirements, the practices, and the beliefs for midwives have changed much over time. Colleges' nurse-midwives have become well trained for their jobs. Though many unnecessary requirements and obstacles existed for midwives in the past, today's midwives, with their proper training, are able to help pregnant women have healthier and safer births.

Works Cited

A History of Midwifery in Pictures. Online. Internet. 18 November 2003. Available www.geocities.com/Wellesley/Atrium/5148/history/html

Feldhusen, Adrian. *The History of Midwifery and Childbirth in America: A Time Line*. 2000. Online. Internet. 18 November 2003. Available http://www.midwiferytoday.com/articles/timeline.asp

Giraldo, Michalle. *History of Midwifery*. 1997. Online. Internet. 14 November 2003. Available www.duke.edu/~mg7/history.htm

History of Midwifery. Online. Internet. 16 November 2003. Available mnmidwife.org/History.html

One Chapter in the History of Midwifery. Online. Internet. 17 November 2003. Available www.lisarosscenter.org

Saunders, Suzi. *Midwifery Links Pregnancy and Childbirth*. Online. Internet. 18 November 2003. Available www.midwifery.com/midwifery/

Sullivan, Nancy. *A Short History of Midwifery*. Online. Internet. 16 November 2003. Available www.midwifeinfo.com/history.php

32. In paragraph 2, the word *revered* means—

A ridiculed
B feared
C admired
D loved

33. Midwifery became a respectable profession for men during what years?
A 1600s
B 1700s
C 1800s
D 1900s

34. Some early midwives were feared because—
A people did not understand their knowledge of science
B midwives did not attend church services
C midwives were often friends with those believed to know witchcraft
D doctors did not support them

35. Which of the following areas of the topic of midwifery is *not* covered in the research text?
A The education of midwives over time
B Legislation regarding midwifery
C Customs and beliefs related to midwifery over time
D A biographical sketch of one well-known midwife

36. Some of the in-text citations consist of titles whereas others consist of names because—
A the citations that name titles are used more than once each
B not every reference contains an author
C using the same in-text citation format creates redundancy
D authors are not used for in-text citations for websites

37. In paragraph 8, the word *modified* means—
A decreased
B changed
C originated
D ceased

38. In general, how has the author organized the details of this paper?
A Chronologically within separate paragraph topics
B Chronologically from beginning to end
C Spatially within separate paragraph topics
D Through order of importance

Answers: PRACTICE TEST #1: EOC English: Reading/Literature and Research

1. **(B)** The story is written to entertain. Its main focus is not to explain, describe, or persuade. Though these elements may be present in the story, they do not constitute the main purpose.
2. **(C)** You know that the selection is written in third person because the story is not being told by a character. Now, you must determine whether the narrator is knowledgeable about the mind of only one character or more than one. The narrator knows what is in the old woman's mind, and the narrator also comments that the children believe the woman to be as "old as dust." They would not have made that comment to the woman, so the narrator must know some of their thoughts. Therefore, the answer is third-person omniscient.
3. **(B)** Because the story takes place in the year 2075 and there is no longer the use of money, you can assume it will involve elements of science fiction.
4. **(C)** The use of money stopped forty years before the current year of 2075.
5. **(C)** Because the comparison between the woman and "dust" uses the word *as*, the correct answer is simile.
6. **(C)** Because of all the conflict between the two countries and the fact that Britain is placing soldiers in the colonies, Patrick Henry believes that the whole situation has reached its climax.
7. **(B)** Patrick Henry is not being witty, vain, or timid. He is forcefully sharing his opinions with the members of the Convention. You can tell this by the use of strong language, exclamatory statements, and logical arguments.
8. **(D)** Of course, this statement is true, but it does not provide support for Patrick Henry's argument that war is the *only* choice left to them.
9. **(B)** According to Patrick Henry, members of the British government have acted as if they wish to cooperate and negotiate with the colonists, but if that were so, why would they place British soldiers in the colonies? None of the other answers for this section are ironic; they are simply either true or false.
10. **(B)** The British government has been creating symbolic chains with which to "enslave" the colonists, according to Patrick Henry.
11. **(A)** Patrick Henry's use of such emotional phrases helps create a strong attachment. Logical arguments would not evoke emotion, and there is no abundance of short, choppy sentences. Finally, although the use of exclamation marks does indicate strong emotion, you must remember that this was delivered as a speech, so the emotion would have been in Henry's voice, not in his punctuation.
12. **(C)** Patrick Henry says that the lamp of experience guides his feet, so that lamp represents his knowledge of the correct path for his life.
13. **(C)** In general, the theme is that teens need to view foods in a different way. Answer *A* is true, but it is not the main idea. Answers *B* and *D* cannot be inferred from the selection.
14. **(A)** The previous line introduces the idea of problems occurring later in current teens' lives; then, sentence 14 suggests one such problem is osteoporosis, so this is a possible result.

15. **(C)** The fact that water may or may not be a major source of nutrients is not discussed; the selection only states that the water in the body needs to be replenished.

16. **(B)** The poem uses many examples of human characteristics being attributed to nonhumans. There are no references to other well-known people or places, no similes, and no oxymorons (two-word phrases consisting of terms with opposite meanings).

17. **(B)** The poem indicates that although the night has a thousand eyes and the day only has one, the world ceases to be lit when the sun "dies" (sets); the poem goes on to say that although the mind has a thousand eyes and the heart only one, the light of one's life "dies" when love is over. You can infer from these comparisons that a small number can hold as much, or more, power than a large group. The other answers contain statements that may relate in some way to the wording of the poem, but they do not express the main idea shared by the poet.

18. **(C)** The stars are the lights that brighten the night; the sun is the only "eye" of the daytime.

19. **(A)** The light of both the world and the life "die" when their one light (sun, heart) dies.

20. **(A)** Lines 1, 3, 5, and 7 rhyme, so all are labeled "a." Lines 2, 4, 6, and 8 all rhyme, so all are labeled "b."

21. **(A)** The fact that the speaker is actually "talking" to death provides the feeling of a conflict between two humans rather than between a human and a nonhuman concept. You can almost envision the speaker pointing his finger at death, scolding him for being so arrogant.

22. **(B)** A paradox is a statement that may seem contradictory but actually expresses a truth. The line indicates that death will be gone, that death will "die." Death will never be gone because it is a fact of nature, and death cannot "die" because it is a concept, not a human. However, if you reflect on the rest of the poem, you may come to the same conclusion as the speaker, that "death" is actually a transition to the afterlife. Therefore, if you do not fear death, then the concept of death does actually "die" in your life.

23. **(C)** The explanation is the same as that for the previous question.

24. **(B)** The speaker, who is representative of the tone of the writer, seems quite confident. The words are forceful and clear.

25. **(C)** The speaker is talking directly to death, so the "Thou" in line 9 is addressing death. If death is a "slave" to those concepts mentioned, then death must be, to a degree, ruled by them. The speaker is making the point that death is ruled by the ways of the world and the circumstances under which humans "cease to exist." You would not say, "Death killed the man." You would more likely say, "An accident killed the man." So, technically, "death" did not kill and does not get the credit. The poet is attempting to show that death's power is not great.

26. **(C)** The writer makes no statement indicating that she has traveled outside of Virginia.

27. **(C)** Concrete poems are written in shapes that represent their topics or themes.

28. **(B)** If this poem were written in stanzas, it would be a poem sharing the poet's thoughts and feelings about Virginia. It would not be a story (A), a ballad, which tells a story in a metered rhythm (C), or an ode, a poem of praise (D). The poet is talking about the great characteristics of Virginia, but an ode is rather more formal and contains great phrases of praise and glory for the topic. This poem is more informal and conversational.

29. **(C)** This is the only answer that does not deal with medicines, the focus of the thesis statement.

30. **(C)** This is the most clear and concise choice. The others include repetition or wordiness.

31. **(C)** A novel, by definition, is fiction, so it would not provide factual evidence for Joseph's paper.

32. **(C)** Logically, the causes affect the body; then the person notices symptoms and seeks treatment. This naturally occurring order would provide the best organizational basis for details.

33. **(A)** The title should be italicized because it is a book. If you do not italicize it on the source card, you may forget to italicize it on the Works Cited page.

34. **(B)** If it were a magazine, there would be two titles (article and magazine) and no publisher; if it were an Internet site, there would be a website listed; and if it were a newspaper article, there would be two titles (article and paper).

35. **(C)** Just this information does not provide the type of source. The source reference (#2) indicates that this information comes from the second of at least two sources. You know that Joseph will discuss more than one type of bronchodilator because the notes make reference to "another type of bronchodilator." You also see the format is correct, so he knows how to write a card.

Answers: PRACTICE TEST #2: EOC English: Reading/Literature and Research

1. **(C)** This is the only choice that does not include at least one sensory detail. It simply says that the author saw the different landscapes.
2. **(C)** This essay explains why the author loves the television show. It does not tell a story or biographical account, and a dramatic monologue is a poetic form.
3. **(D)** Ecuador was not mentioned as one of the locations for the show.
4. **(A)** By asking the reader to imagine the scene, the author creates a connection. The thesis has not been stated, the author does not use satire to ridicule the topic, and the details have not yet been provided.
5. **(C)** She does say that she, like the contestants, misses her family when they are not together, but she does not say that she is *often* away from them.
6. **(A)** The author is giving her personal opinion, using the pronoun *I,* so it is in first person. There is no such thing as first-person omniscient.
7. **(C)** Through this statement, the author indicates that she knows that many things probably happen away from the cameras that affect the contestants' decisions about who to vote for in Tribal Council. She is implying the tendency of television to show only selected sections.
8. **(D)** There is no discussion about who might have owned the home previous to the author's grandmother.
9. **(A)** Looking at the situation now, realizing that the door was simply too heavy for her to open, she remembers that she thought it strange that she could reach the knob, yet she couldn't open the door. She is looking at childhood feelings and memories through the eyes of an adult.
10. **(B)** Because the dolls were kept in a locked cabinet and had been loved by the grandmother and her sisters since their childhoods, they were probably very special to them. The author most likely had to sit down so that she would not walk around and possibly drop and break the doll.
11. **(A)** The speaker is reflecting upon the memories of her childhood. She is not depressed or judgmental, and although some elements show aspects of excitement on the part of the speaker as a child, the tone of the overall work is reflective.
12. **(C)** The speaker says that the memories will "live forever," and since memories are not human, they cannot be given that particular human characteristic. There are no "sound" words, no comparisons, and no conscious exaggerations.
13. **(C)** The warranty indicates in the opening sentence that it covers only the original purchaser and user of the product.
14. **(D)** The product will be covered only if the original materials used to create it were defective. The product is not warranted against accidental damage, misuse, or loss.
15. **(A)** The warranty duration is one year.
16. **(C)** The warranty says nothing about canceling the warranty or issuing a refund. It does mention possibly replacing the product, but only with a reconditioned model, not a new one.

17. **(C)** You would have three months left on the original—and the warranty says you would have continued warranty coverage for the time left—or six months, whichever is longer. So, you would have six months.

18. **(B)** This poem makes a comparison between life and a dance. Because it continues throughout the length of a poem and provides several points of comparison, it is an analogy. It cannot be a sonnet because it is not fourteen lines in length. It is not metered because it has no regulated pattern of rhyme or rhythm. It is also not a serious poem of praise.

19. **(A)** Twirling is more active than, say, waltzing, and just after the direction to "Twirl" comes the comment that one must live every day as if it were his last.

20. **(C)** In this line, the speaker says that after dancing for a long time through many new days, God will pick you up, and you will glide to the Heavens. This line represents the transition from life on Earth to eternal life in Heaven.

21. **(A)** The mood is one of comfort. The poet describes the connection between life and dancing, and he goes on to describe God lifting us gently to Heaven at the end of life where we will go on dancing forever. The poem is not troubling or demanding. Though a couple of lines indicate that we should face life with excitement (Twirl), the overall mood is not one of excitement.

22. **(C)** The message is that life is like a dance; though sometimes we must "dance" slowly and at other times the pace may increase, we should face it with joy and a positive attitude. The poet is not advising the reader to take life lightly or seriously. He does say that at times life must be taken more slowly, but he still indicates that we should face it with the knowledge that each day could be the last.

23. **(D)** In all of the previous stanzas, the speaker indicates that she is tired, frustrated, and even depressed. However, in the last stanza, she indicates that she feels blessed to have, at least, been loved at all. That is a somewhat more positive tone.

24. **(A)** She wants to emphasize that what she has endured has involved two "people": herself and her heart. She speaks almost as if they are partners. The other statements may relate to inferences that can be made about what the speaker has experienced, but the fact that she and her heart have suffered together creates a bond between humans and feelings.

25. **(C)** The first stanza indicates that the speaker and her heart are sitting beside a headstone.

26. **(B)** The speaker first indicates that he will turn back, and then he says that he will go on and "see." He is struggling a little between his desire to turn back and his curiosity about what he may find if he goes on.

27. **(C)** All of the other comments are included in the speaker's discussion about the possible age of the wood pile; he mentions an axe in line 37, but he is commenting only about the irony that someone cut the wood with his axe and then left it.

28. **(C)** Because the speaker has discussed the apparent age of the wood, the fact that it is discolored, sunken, and warped, you get the image of a pile left for some time in the forest. "Clematis" had wound strings around it, like a bundle. That is most likely a plant that has grown up through the logs, winding strands of leaves around the timbers. The "strings" here are not likely to have been placed there by the woodcutter because "strings" could not hold heavy lumber.

29. **(B)** The introductory statement indicates that further clauses should be added, so you can conclude that these are additions, not exceptions or corrections. Further, the term *conclusions* implies information *resulting* from what has already been determined, so that answer also does not apply.

30. **(C)** This selection is entitled "The Bill of *Rights,*" so you may conclude that these are rights given to the people of the United States. Amendment II deals with the rights of the American people to bear arms, or weapons, and the fact that the *right* shall not be *infringed* indicates that the right shall not be taken away, or *prevented.*

31. **(B)** Amendment VI states that the accused shall have the "assistance of counsel for his defense." Several of the other Amendments make reference to trials and juries, but only Amendment VI addresses one's right to counsel.

32. **(C)** The sentence indicates that, because of their remedies, the midwives were *respected and revered*, so you can assume this word is synonymous with *respected*, and the appropriate choice will be *admired*.

33. **(B)** The text (paragraph 5) indicates that midwifery became a respectable profession for men in the eighteenth century, which would be the 1700s.

34. **(A)** Some people did not understand how women could seem to know so much about science, so they were assumed to have some association with the devil. This is the only one of the four answers that is suggested by the text.

35. **(D)** There are no biographical sketches of particular midwives in this text.

36. **(B)** Not every reference contains an author, and when an author is not given, the in-text citation format requires the use of a title.

37. **(B)** The conclusion to this sentence states that as a result of these modified ideas, the Birth Center of Santa Cruz opened its doors. The previous sentences indicates that midwifery was still not fully accepted, so we know that a *change* in attitude took place.

38. **(A)** The author uses chronological details to support each of the separate paragraph topics.

Glossary of Terms

Adjective – a word that describes a noun or pronoun

Adjective clause – a group of words that begins with a relative pronoun, follows a noun, and acts as an adjective describing that noun

Adverb – a word that describes a verb, adjective, or another adverb by telling how, why, when, or in what way or to what extent something exists or is done

Adverb clause – a group of words that begins with a subordinating conjunction, a word that, in itself, carries meaning. That conjunction is followed by a subject, verb, etc., and the entire clause functions as an adverb does, telling how, when, or under what conditions something is done

Allegory – a story in which the characters, events, and even the setting serve both a literal and a symbolic purpose

Alliteration – the repetition of consonant sounds at the beginnings of three or more words in lines of poetry placed closely together

Allusion – a literary device whereby one work of literature includes a reference to another well-known work of literature, event, person, or place

Analogy – a comparison (like a simile or metaphor) between two things; however, an analogy is usually presented as a situation rather than simply as a phrase

Anecdote – a short, usually funny account of an event in someone's life

Antagonist – the character (or characters) in a story who opposes the main character

Aphorism – a short, wise saying that expresses a truth of some sort

Apostrophe – a literary device in which the speaker directly addresses an inanimate object, concept, or absent person

Appositive – a noun that renames a nearby noun (usually directly before it)

Approximate rhyme – a rhyme that is close but not exact

Aside – a secret told on stage during a play

Assonance – the repetition of similar vowel sounds

Autobiography – the story of a person's life written by that person

Ballad – a narrative poem that is meant to be sung

Biography – the story of a person's life written by someone else

Brainstorm – the earliest writing stage in which the writer thinks freely about the subject and writes down all of the topic possibilities

Characters – the people, animals, etc. that perform the action of the plot

Citation – an element used to document ideas and give credit to the original source

Climax – the point of highest interest in a story

Comparisons – the three possible forms of adjectives and adverbs: positive (the base form of the word), comparative (used in a comparison between two), and superlative (used in a comparison involving three or more)

Conclusion – the last sentence of a paragraph or the last paragraph of an essay; it closes the topic in a smooth and interesting way

Concrete poem – a poem written in the shape of some object, person, place, or idea

Conflict – the struggle or difficulty in a story

Conjunction – a word that joins words, phrases, or sentences

Connotation – the feeling associated with a particular word

Consonance – repetition of a final consonant sound on accented syllables

Contraction – a combination of two words in which one of the words uses an apostrophe to replace omitted letters

Coordinating conjunction – one of seven conjunctions that are used to join words, phrases, or sentences: and, but, or, nor, for, so, yet

Couplet – two consecutive rhyming lines of poetry

Dangling modifier – a descriptive word or phrase that causes confusion because the referent is missing; a modifier that is attempting to describe something or someone that is missing

Denotation – the actual dictionary definition of a word

Description – a style of writing that attempts to use descriptive terms to create a picture in the mind of the reader

Direct address – a situation in which the writer speaks directly to a person or character

Direct quotation – someone's exact spoken words

Double negative – an error that occurs when a sentence contains two negatives within the same thought

Dramatic irony – when the audience knows something that the characters don't know

Dramatic monologue – a poem in which one speaker talks to one or more silent listeners

Dramatic poem – a poem in which the situation, setting, characters, and actions are revealed through the dialogue of two or more characters

Elegy – a sad poem about death

(Elizabethan) sonnet – a sonnet form made famous by William Shakespeare, a famous English playwright and poet

End rhyme – a pattern formed by rhyming words at the ends of two or more lines

Epic poem – a long, narrative poem that tells the adventures of a hero and sometimes contains graphic or gory language

Euphemism – a "delicate" term or phrase that is substituted for one that could be considered offensive or harsh

Exposition – writing that explains or informs

Fable – a story that usually has animals as characters and usually teaches a lesson or moral

Fantasy – a story that could not happen

Fiction – information that is false

Figurative language – a general term that includes language that is not meant to be taken literally

First-person point of view – a point of view in which one character is telling the story

Flashback – a reference in a story to some event that occurred previously

Foot – a general term for a combination of lightly and heavily accented syllables

Foreshadowing – the use of "hints" about events that may occur in a story

Fragment – an incomplete thought punctuated as a complete thought

Free verse – poetry without regular rhyme or rhythm

Haiku – a poem of Japanese origin that uses syllable patterns to form the poetic lines

Hyperbole – an intentional exaggeration used for emphasis

Iamb – a foot that consists of two syllables: one light accent followed by one heavy accent

Iambic pentameter – a line of metered poetry that contains five iambs

Idiom – an expression that has an overall meaning that is very different from the literal meaning of each of its words

Imagery – the use of words that create "pictures" in the mind of the reader

Indefinite pronoun – a pronoun that refers to a general individual or group rather than a specific group or person

Independent clause – a formal word for *complete thought* or a clause that can stand alone as a sentence

Interjection – a word or phrase that expresses emotion (light or heavy) and is usually at the beginning of the sentence

Internal rhyme – a pattern of rhyme that occurs within the same line of poetry

In-text citation – a citation that occurs within the natural flow of the research paper

Introduction – the opening paragraph of an essay

Irony – the difference between appearance and reality

Irregular verbs – those that do not form their past and past participle forms by adding –d or –ed

Jargon – highly technical terms or terms associated only with particular sports, careers, or hobbies

Legend – a blend of fact and fiction

Linking verb – a verb that connects the subject with a word that identifies or describes it

Lyric poetry – poetry that shares the thoughts and feelings of the speaker about a particular subject

Metaphor – a comparison made without using the words *like* or *as*

Metered poetry – poetry that has structured patterns of rhyme and rhythm

Microfilm and Microfiche – methods of storing information

Misplaced modifier – a descriptive word or phrase that causes confusion because its referent is not clear; a modifier that is attempting to describe someone or something, but is out of place and, therefore, causes confusion

Modernism – a period during the early twentieth century during which writers began to take bold, new approaches to writing literature and poetry

Mood/atmosphere – the overall feeling of the selection

Myth – an anonymous story that usually attempts to explain the belief or ritual of a particular culture

Narration – writing that tells a story

Narrative poem – a poem that tells a story

Naturalism – an extension of realism; it suggested that humans were shaped and influenced by their environments, over which they have no control

Nominative pronoun case – the form used when the pronoun serves as the subject in a sentence or clause

Nonfiction – information that is true

Note cards – a collection of 3 × 5 index cards used to record notes taken from sources used for research

Noun – a word that names a person, place, thing, or idea

Novel – a long work of fiction

Objective pronoun case – the form used when the pronoun serves as the object in the sentence or clause

Ode – a dignified lyric poem written about a serious subject

Onomatopoeia – the use of words that imitate their meaning

Outline – the stage of the writing process in which the writer organizes the ideas recorded during brainstorming

Oxymoron – a two-word phrase in which the two words are opposites, but they work together to form one meaning without confusing the reader

Parable – a short story in which a simple situation from life can teach a valuable lesson or moral

Paradox – a seemingly contradictory statement that actually expresses a truth

Parallel construction – the use of words or phrases that are in coordinate form

Paraphrase – to restate a sentence in one's own words

Parenthetical expression – a word or phrase that does not deal directly with the topic at hand but, rather, is inserted into the flow of thought and adds a sort of pause for thought or reflection

Parody – a funny interpretation of a serious work

Participle – an "action adjective"; a word that shows action but does not function as the verb in a given sentence

Past participle – the verb form that is used after one of three helping verbs: *have*, *has*, or *had*

Personification – writing that attributes human characteristics to nonhumans

Persuasion – writing that attempts to sway the reader's opinion or convince the reader to take a particular action

Petrarchan (Italian) sonnet – a sonnet named after the Italian poet Petrarch, who lived during the fourteenth century

Plagiarism – the act of presenting others' words and ideas as one's own

Plot – the events that occur in a story

Plural – a word expressing connection to more than one item

Point of view – the viewpoint from whom a story is being told

Possessive – a word that shows ownership

Prefix – a group of letters, with its own meaning, that is added to the front of a word to change its meaning

Preposition – a word used to form a ***prepositional phrase,*** which consists of a preposition and a noun or pronoun and shows a relationship between items in a sentence

Prompt – a suggested topic for writing

Pronoun – a word that takes the place of a person, place, thing, or idea

Pronoun/antecedent agreement – an agreement in number between a pronoun and the word which it replaces

Proofread – the stage of the writing process in which the author checks the text for grammatical, usage, and spelling errors

Protagonist – the main character in a story

Purpose of the writing task – the reason for writing: narrate, inform/explain, describe, or persuade

Quatrain – a four-line poem or a four-line stanza (individual unit) in a poem

Rationalism – a belief that the world's problems could be better solved through reason rather than through emotion, intuition, faith, or tradition

Reader's Guide to Periodical Literature – a guide to magazine articles written about various topics

Realism – a nineteenth-century literary movement suggesting that life should be portrayed as exactly as possible without idealizing it or making it sound better than it actually was

Reference books – books that contain general information and are used for quick reference

Regionalism – writings set in specific geographic locations

Regular verbs – verbs that form their past and past participles by adding –d or –ed to the base, or present, form

Relative pronoun – one of five words that introduces an adjective clause: who, whom, whose, which, that

Renaissance – time during the nineteenth century that involved an explosion of American literary production

Research questions – investigative questions related to a topic to be researched

Resolution – the point at which the conflict in a story is resolved or settled

Revise – the stage of the writing process in which the author checks the text for structural and organizational errors

Rhetorical question – a question to which you do not actually expect an answer

Rhyme scheme – the pattern of rhyme in a poem

Romanticism – a reaction against the logical ideas of rationalism

Root – a group of letters, with its own meaning, to which prefixes and suffixes are added to form new words

Rough draft – the first draft of the actual written paper, complete with introduction, body, and conclusion

Run-on sentence – an error that occurs when one connects two sentences either without any punctuation at all (*fused sentence*) or with simply a comma (*comma splice*)

Satire – writing that pokes fun at people, politics, society, or life in general to show weaknesses and, possibly, bring about change

Scansion – the analysis of a poem to determine its meter

Science fiction – a story that usually takes place far into the future or in space

Setting – indicates where and when the action in a story takes place

Short story – a short work of fiction

Simile – a comparison between two things made by using the words "like" or "as"

Singular – a word expressing connection to only one item

Soliloquy – a long speech given by a character who is alone on stage, pouring out his or her feelings

Sonnet – a lyric poem that is fourteen lines in length

Source cards – a collection of 3 × 5 index cards used to record bibliographic information from sources used in research

Standard unit of credit – a credit earned through completion of instructional hours of a course and receipt of a passing grade

Stream of consciousness – a technique that attempts to imitate the natural flow of thoughts in a character's mind

Subject/verb agreement – an agreement in number between a subject and its verb

Subordinating conjunction – one of a group of words that attaches itself to a complete sentence and subordinates it as a method of joining sentences

Summarize – to pull the main points from a long text

Suspense – the element that keeps the reader emotionally involved in a story

Symbol – a noun that has a literal meaning but also stands for some greater meaning

Tall tale – a very funny, very exaggerated story that is not at all believable

Tense – the element of a verb that expresses when the action or state of being (associated with linking verbs) takes place

Theme – the main idea or the main point of a work of literature

Thesis statement – the sentence in a selection that expresses the main idea of the entire selection

Third-person point of view (limited) – a point of view in which a narrator who knows the thoughts of only one character is telling the story

Third-person point of view (omniscient) – a point of view in which a narrator who knows the thoughts of more than one character is telling the story

Tone – the author's attitude toward the topic

Topic sentence – the sentence (usually first) in a paragraph that sets the topic for the paragraph

Transcendentalism – a nineteenth-century movement that suggested individuals could obtain "truth" by moving, figuratively, past the physical world and reflecting on spiritual and sensory experiences

Understatement – a phrase that states less than is true to emphasize a point

Verb – a word that expresses action or links the subject to the rest of the sentence

Verified unit of credit – a credit earned through receipt of a passing grade in both the course and on its related Standards of Learning test

Works Cited page – a formal listing of all sources cited in a research paper

Index

BARRON'S COLLEGE GUIDES

AMERICA'S #1 RESOURCE FOR EDUCATION PLANNING

PROFILES OF AMERICAN COLLEGES, 26th Edition, w/CD-ROM
Compiled and Edited by the College Division of Barron's Educational Series, Inc. Today's number one college guide comes with computer software to help with forms and applications. Book includes profiles plus Barron's INDEX OF COLLEGE MAJORS! Vital information on majors, admissions, tuition, and more.
$26.95, Can. $38.95, (0-7641-7575-0)

COMPACT GUIDE TO COLLEGES, 14th Edition
A concise, fact-filled volume that presents all the essential facts about 400 of America's best-known, most popular schools. Admissions requirements, student body, faculty, campus environment, academic programs, and so much more are highlighted.
$9.95, Can. $14.50, (0-7641-2311-4)

BARRON'S BEST BUYS IN COLLEGE EDUCATION, 8th Edition
Solorzano
Here are detailed descriptions—with tuitions and fees listed—of 300 of the finest colleges and universities in America judged on a value-for-your-dollar basis.
$18.95, Can. $27.50, (0-7641-2310-6)

BARRON'S GUIDE TO THE MOST COMPETITIVE COLLEGES, 3rd Edition
Barron's latest and most innovative college guide describes and examines America's top 50 schools. What makes this guide unique is its special "insider" information about each school including commentaries on faculty, and more.
$16.95, Can. $24.50, (0-7641-2299-1)

PROFILES OF AMERICAN COLLEGES: THE NORTHEAST, 16th Edition
Comprehensive data specifically for students interested in schools in Connecticut, Delaware, D.C., Maine, Maryland, Massachusetts, New Hampshire, New Jersey, New York, Pennsylvania, Rhode Island, or Vermont.
$16.95, Can. $24.50, (0-7641-2312-2)

THE ALL-IN-ONE COLLEGE GUIDE
Marty Nemko, Ph.D.
This book tells even the most serious college-bound student and family everything they need to know to choose, get into, find the money for, and make the most of college.
$10.95, Can. $15.95, (0-7641-2298-3)

BARRON'S HEAD START TO COLLEGE PLANNING
Susan C. Chiarolanzio, M.A.
Here's the book to help parents plan for their child's academic success. It explains the many kinds of college options available for students having different interests and aptitudes.
$11.95, Can. $17.50, (0-7641-2697-0)

Prices subject to change without notice. Books may be purchased at your bookstore, or by mail from Barron's. Enclose check or money order for total amount plus 18% for postage and handling (minimum charge of $5.95). New York State, Michigan, and California residents add sales tax to total. All books are paperback editions.

Visit us at www.barronseduc.com

BARRON'S

BARRON'S EDUCATIONAL SERIES, INC.
250 Wireless Blvd., Hauppauge, NY 11788
In Canada: Georgetown Book Warehouse
34 Armstrong Ave., Georgetown, Ont. L7G 4R9
$ = U.S. Dollars Can.$ = Canadian Dollars

(#8) R7/04